WITHDRAWN

TED HUGHES AS SHEPHERD OF BEING

Ted Hughes as Shepherd of Being

CRAIG ROBINSON

St. Martin's Press   New York

First published in the United States of America in 1989

Printed in the People's Republic of China

ISBN 0–312–03202–1

Library of Congress Cataloging-in-Publication Data
Robinson, Craig, 1954–
    Ted Hughes as shepherd of being / Craig Robinson.
        p.   cm.
    Bibliography: p.
    Includes index.
    ISBN 0–312–03202–1 : $35.00 (est.)
    1. Hughes, Ted, 1930–   —Criticism and interpretation.
    I. Title.
PR6058.U37Z85   1989
821'.914—dc20
                                        89–32802
                                        CIP

To my family

To my family

Contents

Acknowledgements

My greatest debts are to those mentioned in my dedication, but I also owe special thanks for their generous help and guidance over many years to Keith Sagar and to Richard Dutton; and to the following: Frances Arnold, J. B. Beer, Adrian Cunningham, the late John Fisher, Terry Gifford, Igor Hájek, Derek Hyatt, Graham Eyre, the B. W. Lloyd Charitable Trust, Roy Matthews, Gerard O'Daly, Dušan Puvačić, Neil Roberts, Valery Rose, Felicity Rosslyn, Annie Schofield, A. C. H. Smith, and the staffs of the BBC Written Archives Centre at Caversham Park, Reading, the National Sound Archives in London and the University Library at Lancaster.

The author and publishers would like to thank the following who have kindly given permission for the use of copyright material:

Faber and Faber Ltd and Olwyn Hughes Literary Agency, for the extracts from poems by Ted Hughes included in *Moortown*: 'Prometheus on his Crag', 'Seven Dungeon Songs', 'Adam and the Sacred Nine', and 'The Skylark came'; for extracts from poems included in *Crow*: 'Crow's Account of the Battle', 'Criminal Ballad', 'Truth Kills Everybody', 'Snake Hymn', and 'Littleblood'; for extracts from poems included in *Gaudete*: 'Prologue', 'Mrs Holroyd', 'I hear your congregations . . .', 'Having first given away . . .', 'The Sea Grieves . . .', 'What will you make of half a man . . .', 'I watched a wise beetle', 'What steel was it the river poured', and 'Every day the world gets simply'; for extracts from poems included in *The Hawk in the Rain*: 'Egg-Head' and 'The Conversation of the Reverend Skinner'; for the extract from 'November' in *Lupercal*; and for the poems 'Stations', 'Mountains' and 'Full Moon and Little Frieda' from *Wodwo*.

Faber and Faber Ltd and Viking Penguin Inc., for the extracts from *Cave Birds: An Alchemical Cave Drama*, by Ted Hughes, © 1978 by Ted Hughes.

Olwyn Hughes Literary Agency, for permission to quote uncollected extracts from Ted Hughes' writings: from the first version of the 'Myth and Education' essay, Sagar and Tabor C240, 'Children's Literature in Education'; from the review of *Emily Dickinson's Poetry* by Charles R. Anderson, published in the *Listener*, 70:394, 12 September 1963, Sagar and Tabor C145; from the review of *Vagrancy* by Philip O'Connor in *New Statesman*, 66:293, Sagar and Tabor C144; from 'Dogs: a Scherzo'; from the essay 'A Reply to My Critics', *Books and Issues*, 1, nos 3–4 (1981); from the *Crow* record-sleeve, Sagar and Tabor H9/F8; from the second interview with Ekbert Faas, *Ted Hughes: The Unaccommodated Universe*, p. 214; from the introductory comments to a number of pieces in *Cave Birds* broadcast on Radio 3, 23 June 1975; from poem 44, *Orts* (Rainbow Press); from the story 'The Head', published in *Saturday Night Reader* (London, 1979) edited by Emma Tennant, pp. 81–99; from *Writers, Critics and Children* (p. 92) the second version of the 'Myth and Education' essay, Sagar and Tabor B78; and from the Foreword to 'Children as Writers', Sagar and Tabor B74.

Laurence Pollinger Ltd and Alfred A. Knopf, Inc./Random House, Inc., for the extracts from John Crowe Ransom's 'Persistent Explorer' in *Selected Poems, Third Edition Revised and Enlarged*, copyright 1927 by Alfred A. Knopf, Inc. and renewed 1955 by John Crowe Ransom.

A Note on the Texts Used

The following list gives details of the editions of Hughes' works cited in the text. The place of publication is in all cases London. Unless otherwise stated, the publisher is Faber and Faber, and the text chosen is the first English trade edition.

Beauty and the Beast, in *The Coming of the Kings* (1970).
Cave Birds: An Alchemical Cave Drama (1978).
Cave Birds, broadcast, BBC Radio 3, 23 June 1975.
A Choice of Emily Dickinson's Verse (1968).
A Choice of Shakespeare's Verse (1971).
Crow: From the Life and Songs of the Crow (1970).
Difficulties of a Bridegroom (unpublished; broadcast, BBC Third Programme, 21 January 1963).
Dogs: A Scherzo (unpublished; broadcast, BBC Third Programme, 12 February 1964).
Eat Crow (Rainbow Press, limited edition, 1971).
Flowers and Insects, Some Birds and a Pair of Spiders (1986).
Gaudete (1977).
The Hawk in the Rain (1957).
The Iron Man (1968).
Lupercal (1960).
Moortown (1979).
Orghast (unpublished; performed 1971).
Poetry in the Making (1967).
Remains of Elmet (1979).
River (1983).
Season Songs (1976).
Selected Poems 1957–1981 (1982).
Seneca's Oedipus (1969).
Wodwo (1967).

Introduction:
Hughes and Heidegger

This book attempts to trace the main stages, so far as they are
reflected in the chronology of his trade editions, of Ted Hughes'
pursuit of a redefinition of human maturity in our time. It looks at
his criticisms of some of the available, orthodox models of thinking,
feeling and action, at his sense of what they ignore or exclude,
and at the progression of artistic strategies Hughes has developed
to describe and engender the creative conjunction of excluder and
excluded. The progression is as interesting as the thought itself,
and all references are therefore to the first English trade edition of
Hughes' works (see p. ix); the book is divided into four parts
corresponding to phases in Hughes' development. Quotation has
been kept to a necessary minimum.*

The approach varies. *Gaudete, Cave Birds* and *Moortown* form the
core of an achievement as substantial as that of any English-
born poet since Wordsworth, and the chapters treating these are
relatively full. Those dealing with prior volumes are preliminary,
highlighting themes and images which are to be caught up and
modified in the denser, richer structures of the works of the later
1970s. The closing chapter examines some of what Hughes has
written outside and after the core achievement, in its light.

Hughes has been severally placed in literary history: in opposition
to the Movement, in relation to the new importance of the North
and the provinces in cultural life since the Second World War, on
one side or other in the feud between Modernism and traditional-
ism; but perhaps the most profitable placing is in relation to the
Romantic, and especially Blakean, struggle for liberation from the
excesses of Enlightenment rationalism. To place him in this context
is to see him not as a throwback to a finished era, nor yet as simply
another exemplar of an eternal struggle between two universal
tendencies, Classicising and Romantic, but as a figure who might

* Quotations from works not by Hughes are taken from the editions specified in
the Bibliography. Page references given following or otherwise in association with
such quotations relate to the same editions.

1

require us to rewrite our account of poetry in the last two and a half centuries, so that developments which we now regard as subsequent and unrelated may eventually be seen as the masks, refractions and offshoots of the forces which came to focus around the turn of the eighteenth century.

In the early 1960s Hughes earned from his detractors a reputation, such as Lawrence (who is one of the most deep-seated influences on him) had earlier borne, for proposing the resignation of the reasonable parts of the mind in favour of an unbridled licence for the instincts. Though Hughes' view has, as we shall see, changed in some respects over the years, he has never been a straightforward anti-rationalist, but has stood against the tyranny of a diminished reason over the psyche, always seeking an augmentation, harmonising and attunement of its faculties. The battle is not for or against reason, but, as the *Moortown* poem 'Tiger-Psalm' shows, over what the word reason shall be taken to include. Here and there in the early works (later ones reflect a much more complex view) there is an espousal of a relatively simple vitalism which prefers the physically durable to the cerebrally over-complicated. Even in these cases it should be clear, however, that Hughes sought some human equivalent of what he admired in the animal world, an acutely sensitive attunement to the environment such as he felt had been lost in the evasions, complacencies and proud posturings of the human society around him. The gap he seeks to bridge is that between an otter, alert from tip to tail, and the human disposition so succinctly evoked in the image from the *Hawk in the Rain* poem 'October Dawn' of 'A glass half full of wine left out/To the dark heaven all night'. His attack on what he calls 'the psychological stupidity, the ineptitude, of the rigidly rationalist outlook' goes hand-in-hand with his sense of the blunting of sensitivity it has produced in excluding other aspects of us from participation in a fuller being. Hughes' characteristic movement is from closure to openness, from the rigid to the flexible, from the merely human to the fully human.

In this he is like Jung, whose writings are frequently concerned with a pattern of development which proceeds by means of the death of a dry, rigid, one-sided and closed ego and an irrigation by the contents of the unconscious in a process of imaginative amplification, until the psyche bears the fruit of a new, balanced and flexible self. Jung, whose influence on post-war artists (including major presences such as Tippett, Heaney and Redgrove) is insufficiently recognised, has been important to Hughes too. He has appealed to composers and writers partly because, though himself a scientist, he held in high esteem the artistic imagination and its health-bringing capabilities.

This esteem was shared by a second thinker I want to call upon in giving a sense of the position Hughes wins through to, a man who has been, amongst many other roles, one of the fathers of the vision of the ecological movement which feeds Hughes' latest works. I know of no evidence that Hughes is familiar with the writings of Martin Heidegger, and there are certainly many areas in which there is no consonance between the two men, most notably politics. Nevertheless, the commentator wanting not only to explicate Hughes' meanings, but also to suggest their implications and their unity lacks a suitable vocabulary – a lack itself a measure of the task Hughes has undertaken, and one which Jung alone cannot make good. The sense of the role of the poet, the confrontation with death, the critique of science and technology, the deprecation of television, the attack on the Socratic heritage, the recurrence of a goddess who is triple in a new sense (having natural, religious and human aspects), the respect for Heraclitus and for myth – how can the unity and cogency of this body of thought, interesting for its relevance more than its novelty, be suggested? Heidegger, provided there is clarity at the outset as to the limits of kinship, may help. Nevertheless, even in his later works, Heidegger employs his own densely technical terminology, so that the very strictness and completeness of thought which recommends him over say, a Roszak, makes him difficult to quote piecemeal, and I have had to reserve most of the briefest of discussions of him for this Introduction.

Heidegger's high valuation of the poet is part of his sense of the importance of thought and of language. Language, for him as for Hughes, is not the closed circuit of mutually interrelated arbitrary signs of the linguistician – it is an ever-closing, but openable path to Being, the reality of what is. The closing is the fall from true and original (that is, poetic) language into the cliché-ridden, merely assertive or representational language of ideas and the idle chatter of the They, the crowd (all of us most of the time) who have turned our backs on the call of Being; in *Poetry, Language, Thought* he says, 'everyday language is a forgotten and therefore used-up poem, from which there hardly resounds a call any more' (p. 11). Heidegger is himself a great burrower back into the roots of words to recover their lost connections with Being. Hughes, likewise, reconnects words with their roots, sometimes simply reinvesting clichés with new feeling and conviction, sometimes taking an abstract word back to its physical basis (as he does with the word 'abstract' itself in 'A Disaster' in *Crow*), and, more often, as we shall see, through his music. He also makes much use of the power of metaphor, which, in saying A is B, makes vital reconnections and argues for world unity by generating a sense of sameness within difference.

For Heidegger,

> Language is the precinct (*templum*), that is, the house of Being. . . . It is because language is the house of Being, that we reach what is by constantly going through this house. . . . All beings . . ., each in its own way, are *qua* beings in the precinct of language. This is why the return from the realm of objects and their representation into the innermost region of the heart's space can be accomplished, if anywhere, *only in this precinct.*
>
> (*Poetry, Language, Thought*, p. 132)

It is the poet who is given this task and in discharging it he fulfils man's most important task: to achieve his essence, which is, as *The Question Concerning Technology* has it, 'to be the one who waits, the one who attends upon the coming to presence of Being in that in thinking he guards it. Only when man, as the shepherd of Being, attends upon the truth of Being can he expect an arrival of a destining . . .' (p. 42), a finding of true purpose. For Heidegger, the real poet is exceedingly rare; for Hughes, he is the better part of each of us.

Being is Heidegger's most important and elusive notion, and, though he strenuously defended it against assimilation with other notions, especially those of biology and psychology, it has note-worthy similarities to the goddess of Hughes' later works, but is wider. Hughes' goddess is coextensive with life, the inanimate is bereft of her; Heidegger's Being encompasses whatever is, animate and inanimate. The divine is important to Heidegger, but not the feminine, though he does call our attention to a goddess in Parmenides. (The pre-Socratics are significant, for Heidegger, for evincing a true openness to Being lost in post-Socratic thought; Hughes discovers something like this other, non-Classical Greece in Seneca's *Oedipus*, and offers a parallel valuation of the pre-

Socratics in 'Myth and Education'.) This goddess, Aletheia, is Truth, which is the unconcealedness of Being. Being is present only in beings, but is not the same as any one or any group of them; when we apprehend a being we therefore do and do not apprehend Being, which remains hidden even in its unconcealedness. Hughes says of his goddess, who is present only in her creatures, but not the same as any one or any group of them, 'She reveals herself, and is veiled' (*Gaudete*, p. 185).

The path along which Being grows nearer is partly that of feeling and emotion, especially *Angst* (Heidegger's word) or pain (Hughes'), which breaks the characteristic tranquillised (Heidegger's word) or numb (Hughes', in *Gaudete*) mood of our usual divorce from Being. By feeling or emotion is meant not, or not just, our fleeting changes of temper, but the spectrum of deep persistent moods or dispositions each of which accompanies and underpins an understanding of the world. The persistent base mood which underpins the narrowly rational understanding is only one of many possibilities, but it has become dominant amongst us, buttressed as it is by systems of logic which claim probative force precisely by avoiding the questioning of their existential assumptions. As we move through Hughes' career we shall meet a broad spectrum of moods and understandings, for like all but the most cerebral of poets, Hughes is concerned in part with relicensing feelings as part of a thinking which gives renewed and broadened access to reality, feelings (and intuitions) which have been banned by the unwritten codes which dictate successful behaviour in the modern technological world. Heidegger observes,

> Occasionally we still have the feeling that violence has long been done to the thingly element of things and that thought has played a part in this violence, for which reason people disavow thought instead of taking pains to make it more thoughtful. But . . . what is the use of a feeling, however certain, if thought alone has the right to speak here? Perhaps however what we call feeling or mood, here and in similar instances, is more reasonable – that is more intelligently perceptive – because more open to Being than all the reason which, having meanwhile become *ratio*, was misinterpreted as being rational.
>
> (*Poetry, Language, Thought*, pp. 24–5)

In calling on Heidegger to help define and place Hughes' creative attack on a debased reason, I want to be seen as making a gesture complementary to Leonard Scigaj's exploration (in *The Poetry of Ted Hughes: Form and Imagination*) of Oriental influences on Hughes. Both ways of looking at him serve to emphasise that Hughes' enduring concern has been to augment ordinary modern Western consciousness. The path of thought-with-feeling which runs through the poet's precinct of language towards Being, runs also via the unsettling confrontation with one's own death. It is this which calls us from inauthenticity to authenticity, from exile from Being to its nearness. The pattern of development which Heidegger traces at the beginning of Division II of *Being and Time* has points of contact with Jungian paradigm, with its ego-death, and needs to be set alongside *Cave Birds*, the chief amongst many works of Hughes' which make this same confrontation central.

The connection between the attack on a narrow rationalism and the process of ego-death is made clear in Heidegger. The endlessly remade confrontation with death establishes the primacy of Being over ideas and theory, and reminds the individual that he is a Being-in-the-world, with responsibilities to that world, and not a separate unshatterable atom cut off by a defensive wall of opinion. When this comes about in the individual it is a reversal of the general trend of our era, with its fall from unity of man-and-world into the Socratic–Cartesian dualism of subject and object, man-set-over-against-world:

> Objectifying, in representing, in setting before, delivers up the object to the *ego cogito*. In that delivering up, the *ego* proves to be that which underlies its own activity . . . i.e., proves to be the *subiectum*. The subject is subject for itself. The essence of consciousness is self-consciousness. . . . Man . . . rises up in the subjectivity of his essence. Man enters into insurrection. The world changes into object. In this revolutionary objectifying of everything that is, the earth, that which first of all must be put at the disposal of representing and setting forth, moves into the midst of human positing and analysing. The earth itself can show itself only as the object of assault, an assault that, in human willing, establishes itself as unconditional objectification. Nature appears everywhere . . . as the object of technology.
>
> (*The Question Concerning Technology*, p. 100)

Heidegger characterises this kind of rationalism as 'Enframing'.

Using it and used by it, man exiles himself from world (and thus also from himself, since he is a Being-in-the-world) and becomes the self-aware subject (as much so whether alone or in a collective made up of other self-aware subjects) who has reduced the world to a picture, a representation in ideas. It is through our devotion to ideas that the world dwindles to a technologically exploitable resource and to what Heidegger calls the 'standing-reserve':

> As soon as what is unconcealed no longer concerns man even as object, but does so, rather, exclusively as standing-reserve, and man in the midst of objectlessness is nothing but the orderer of the standing-reserve, then he comes to the very brink of a precipitous fall; that is, he comes to the point where he himself will have to be taken as standing-reserve. Meanwhile man, precisely as the one so threatened, exalts himself to the posture of lord of the earth. In this way the impression comes to prevail that everything man encounters exists only insofar as it is his construct. This illusion gives rise in turn to one final delusion: It seems as though man everywhere and always encounters only himself. . . . *In truth, however, precisely nowhere does man today any longer encounter himself, i.e., his essence.*
>
> (*The Question Concerning Technology*, pp. 26–7)

Man has stepped out of the world (leaving himself behind) so that he can turn back and look at it like a framed picture. In his talk on 'Myth and Education' (*Children's Literature in Education*, 1, March 1970, p. 55), Hughes tells a story of a photographer who continued to take pictures whilst a tiger killed a woman, and takes him as the quintessence of the kind of rationalism we have been examining:

> he was to all practical purposes a monster – at that moment it was a completely unhuman activity, clicking a camera. What he showed was a complete detachment from all that human life inside him, that was undergoing what the girl was undergoing in pure fellow feeling, natural compassion, automatic imitation. He showed in other words complete absence of soul, feeling and imagination, complete absence of any natural or sensible quality. He was in the condition, in fact, of a neurotic who was so benumbed that he no longer suffers even his own distress. And this is what we hear around us, in psychoanalytical literature, in writing about the arts and so on more and more. A scientifically

biased education has produced a chronically sick society . . . we have now just such a state of apathy – detached, impersonal passivity – towards our inner life, as we have towards the mountainous outer world of facts and actions.

Hughes' photographer, dead to inner and outer dimensions because he is the product of a culture which has separated the two, is an example of Heidegger's Enframing rationalism. The use of binoculars, telescope and camera in *Gaudete* may be placed in the same interpretative context. Heidegger's term helps also with the various barriers in the early poetry (the cages separating man from beast, and the water surface which separates man from fish). The Hughesian attack on the excessively rational mind, on scientific–technological thinking and Cartesian dualism, on earth rape, and on psychological closure – all these are aspects of a single and united body of thought.

Both Heidegger and Hughes are incorrigibly optimistic, and in two senses: first, in their belief that error is the source of salvation, and that Nothing is a positive; and, second, in the nature of their key terms. Because Being is the ultimate foundation, the deepest layer of reality, it encompasses and underpins even all deviations from itself and can never be defeated by rational–technological thinking. In Hughes parallels abound: in the second of the 'Seven Dungeon Songs' in the murderous male figure seen as a deviant part of the all-encompassing female; in the goddess of *River* who 'will wash herself of all deaths'; and in the unkillable female presence in 'The Head' who walks, arms outstretched, towards the hunter's firing rifle.

This optimism is reflected in a view of cultural history which expresses itself, for Hughes, partly in the master time-scale of *Remains of Elmet*, partly in the hope of a reversal of the seventeenth-century dissociation of sensibility and descent towards the wasteland which *Cave Birds* seeks to encourage; and in Heidegger in the notion of the Turn, a grand reversal of our long drift from Being, initiated now in the attempt at making a new era propitious for the return of the god. Perhaps the art work must always have this optimism: Blake's 'A Little Girl Lost', with its appeal to 'Children of the Future Age', exemplified Heidegger's 'truth . . . thrown toward the coming preservers' – its indictment of contemporary error is made in the sure hope that things were not and will not always be thus. Hughes, who has often enough been portrayed as a dark pessimist, shares this faith.

Heidegger has a further use for the reader of Hughes – in his delineation of the components of the disposition needed to undo and replace the confident, assertive manner of the excessively rational. Heidegger speaks of reticence, of the courage of submission, of a willingness to have one's thoughts overturned again and again, of reverence before Being (and the relationship of this to creativity), of a kindness which allows what is a lodging in the heart's space, and above all of questioning, as the piety of thought, the mode by which thinking becomes thanking, our way of repaying the world for existing. Each of these finds many echoes in Hughes. Perhaps the most important is the last, since a number of the major works move towards the question as the mode of mature thought.

I mentioned earlier two of the ways in which Hughes has chosen to use his language to open us to Being. A deeper way is his music, which is so varied that many shifts might be picked out for comment as we move between works and between phases. A recurrent drive is towards simplification and a line which reveals the deepest music already latent in words, instead of adding a poetical melody to their surface. His aim is partly what he identifies in Emily Dickinson's 'slow, small metre': 'a device for bringing each syllable into close-up and liberating its resonances'. Of John Crowe Ransom he has said 'every word in the line is physically connected to the way it's being spoken. There is a solid total range of sensation within the pitch of every word.' This quality is very noticeable in Hughes' readings of his own verse, and it prompts the remark that in liberating the deepest resonances in a syllable Hughes is not taking it back from meaning into the realm of pure sound, but from abstract, disembodied meaning to its roots in visceral and gestural meaning. His favouring of heavy stresses, monosyllables that make us pause, and large vowel sounds, stems from a desire that each word bear its full weight of world. His loosening and simplification of syntax, and his use of line breaks and punctuation, working as they do to give a nominal or an adjectival phrase or a verb more room, show Hughes inviting us to take to heart each element of a scene or action in turn. Through the forming of the poem's sounds in the reader's mind and body, the therapeutic power of the verbal music has its righting effect. The closing lines of 'Nightjar' from *Flowers and Insects* provide a small example of each of these qualities of Hughes' music:

> Stars spark
> From the rasp of its cry.
>
> Till the moon-eater, cooling,
> Yawns dawn
> And sleeps bark.

But we begin some way from the style of this recent piece.

Part I

1

The Hawk in the Rain, 'The Burning of the Brothel' and *Lupercal*

I

'Egg-Head' seems to begin with a catalogue of occasions which have produced naked confrontations with the power of nature:

> A leaf's otherness,
> The whaled monstered sea-bottom, eagled peaks
> And stars that hang over hurtling endlessness,
>   With manslaughtering shocks
>
> Are let in on his sense:
> So many a one has dared to be struck dead
> Peeping through his fingers at the world's ends,
>   Or at an ant's head.

But these opening confrontations are not genuine, being rather the pretences of the Egg-Head himself, who runs no real risk of annihilation in making them. The abstract language used in listing the various portions of eternity tells us as much: 'otherness' and 'endlessness' are a critic's words, not those of one who has really undergone exposure. And 'shocks / Are let in on his sense' suggests not surrender and openness to the uncanny and alien, but a careful regulation of what enters the mind, and a proud defence of the intellect's supremacy (all dealings are kept safely visual). 'Dared' suggests the self-regarding and further increases our sense of an unwarranted pride at work here – a pride which is one of the chief targets of *The Hawk in the Rain*. And it turns out anyway to be only a show of daring, a pride which masks cowardly 'peeping' (a frequent pejorative in this volume). The pretence of openness is actually a sophisticated cloak for the 'militant pride' of the intellect itself.

13

The poem goes on to offer an alternative to these false postures. Better 'are the freebooting crass/Veterans of survival and those champions/Forgetfulness, madness'. The real requirement is participation, not the Egg-Head's timid withdrawal behind a barricade of ideas. Hughes is here inviting us to jettison what separates man from the animals. 'Forgetfulness, madness' promote success in the war of life because they bring the ability to go on fighting no matter how many failures and defeats lie in the past (of which memory would remind us) and no matter what the odds against success (which sanity would call to mind); they recommend themselves precisely because they lack what the logical and prudential evaluation of experience offers. This is a simplistic vitalism manifestly at odds with any picture of the human make-up which might account for how poems get written and held valuable, and it has no place in Hughes' important works of later decades.

The poem is more central in what it says about the Egg-Head. All the devices of intellectualism for gathering and dealing with information and creating theories, presenting themselves as and easily mistaken for openness to life, are revealed as closure against it:

> Brain in deft opacities,
> Walled in translucencies, shuts out the world's knocking
> With a welcome

The intellectual is closed to the vital energies, to reality, to change, and has set up in their stead an artificial substitute; but, since nature is the only source of energy, this must be a futile self-consuming; Hughes speaks of it as feeding 'on the yolk's dark and hush of a helplessness', thus pointing up its immaturity. What, we must ask, after the yolk has all been consumed? Either of the possibilities would mean an end to the Egg-Head as such.

The self-defeating closure of rationalism masquerades as something else; 'Fragility' and 'helplessness' present themselves as 'a staturing "I am"' and as 'the upthrust affirmative head of a man', thus calling to mind the crucial gesture of standing upright which separated man from the other higher primates, making him, in his own estimation, pinnacle of evolution, and setting him on a path divergent from the rest of nature. This same gesture is to appear in radically different light in 'Prometheus on his Crag' and 'Adam and the Sacred Nine'. Here it offers us the Egg-Head blindly proud and complacent in his self-image, apart and aloof. The close of the poem is devoted to revealing the emptiness of his pride, and to establishing the real inequality of the forces on either side of the dualism the intellect calls into being. What the Egg-Head spurns is the whole earth (to him just 'muck'); what he sets against 'the whelm of the sun' is nothing more than 'his eye's flea-red / Fly-catching fervency'. The disproportions involved make his stance not merely impossible but ludicrous.

In 'The Man Seeking Experience Enquires his Way of a Drop of Water' the object of attack is again the rigidly rationalist. This poem too begins with a catalogue. The man lists all that the droplet has seen since the beginning of creation: it has survived the whole of evolution and every aspect of life and death. In addition to this superhuman length and breadth of experience, it possesses the capacity for objectivity, since it is without heart, head and nerves – without, that is, all the faculties that go to create what is for him a regrettable human subjectivity, prejudice and incompleteness of vision. When he addresses it, his self-important magniloquence tells its own story. His concern with 'a plain lesson' already suggests closure and the search for a safe verbal substitute for reality; he even undertakes to deliver the lesson for the droplet, thus making his closure complete. He is another Egg-Head and his listening is not a sign of kinship with the elements but a mask for the opposite. His treating of the droplet as a single and enduring entity capable of objective wisdom is foundationless; the man has projected onto the droplet his own desire to remain inviolate. The end of the poem undercuts his grand pose:

> This droplet was clear simple water still.
> It no more responded than the hour-old child
>
> Does to finger-toy or coy baby-talk. . . .

The droplet's silence is its own and the man's vacancy of wisdom. In merely being, it becomes a gesture of contempt for him, a revelation of all his magniloquence as no more than 'coy baby-talk'. Again we have the charge of immaturity raised.

In its first days the baby who 'lies long, long and frowningly / Unconscious under the shock of its own quick' joins the battle for life on much the same terms as 'those cham-pions / Forgetfulness, madness', since it has neither experience to remember, nor standards of sanity to which to refer; life comes to it willy-nilly and it does not seek after experience nor indulge in a pretence of openness. In fighting for survival and growth, the baby is, it may be inevitably, asserting itself as a separate individual. Its first cry is that of nascent ego:

> that first alone-in-creation cry
> When into the mesh of sense, out of the dark,
> Blundered the world-shouldering monstrous 'I'.

This recalls Lawrence's 'Baby Tortoise': 'your bright, dark little eye . . . your indomitable will and pride of the first life / Looking round / And slowly pitching itself against . . . The vast inanimate'. Lawrence's words 'will and pride' and 'against' do what in Hughes' poem is done by 'I': they emphasise the element of ego in every life. Hughes returns to this problem in *Crow* and in *Cave Birds*, which faces its protagonist (and the reader) with discovering whether his crime has been merely being alive or some rationalist error in the use of life. Both are present here.

'The Man Seeking Experience' probably owes something to John Crowe Ransom's 'Persistent Explorer'. The beginning comes closest:

> The noise of water teased his literal ear
> Which heard the distant drumming, and so scored:
> 'Water is falling – it fell – therefore it roared.
> Yet something else is there: is it cheer or fear?'
>
> He strode much faster, till on the dizzy brink
> His eye confirmed with vision what he'd heard:
> 'A simple physical water.' Again he demurred:
> 'More than a roaring flashing water, I think.'
>
> But listen as he might, look fast or slow,
> It was common water, millions of tons of it
> Gouging its gorge deeper, and every bit
> Was water, the insipid chemical H_2O.

Like Hughes' man, Ransom's explorer feels the waterfall ought to tell him something, that it has a lesson. So he approaches closer in the hope of learning whether it means 'cheer' or 'fear'. He too finds no answer, only H_2O. We hear the speaking voice of the explorer, as we heard the man's, but the clues it provides to his mentality are fewer and less definite: 'it fell – therefore it roared' perhaps make us think him an heir of Descartes, but he is not the object of unalleviated satire, and the water's failure to respond is not the clinching humorous snub of Hughes' poem. In the remaining eight stanzas of development, the explorer begins to get a vague but powerful apprehension of divinity in and from the waterfall. Perhaps because the religious dimension is alien to his 'literal ear', this mutates into something more psychological, releasing or preparing to release forces he normally keeps safely locked in his unconscious. He feels threatened and decides, like a rationalist, to retaliate by repressing these forces:

And if the smoke and rattle of water drew

From the deep thickets of his mind the train,
The fierce fauns and the timid tenants there
That burst their bonds and rushed upon the air,
Why, he must turn and beat them down again.

The poem closes with the explorer saving his ego by going away from the waterfall and its menace and deciding to explore elsewhere; but his very desire to go on exploring suggests the unsatisfactory nature of his refusal of the contents of his deep mind.

Hughes speaks of Ransom as an influence mainly stylistic and musical, but a comparison of their thought is also informative. There is a shared concern with a series of fundamental dualisms: life *versus* death, nature *versus* culture, reason *versus* instinct. In Ransom these are less obvious, though no less important, than in Hughes, but Ransom is much less decided about which element of the opposition will enjoy the weight of his support. He is concerned to hint gently at their joint presence under the surface of situations, and his poems remain richly ambiguous, subtle and unresolved. He makes his capital out of an irony which was a crucial force in the phase of literary studies to which he belonged. It aims to guarantee the absence of sentimentality and to strengthen the truth of a poem by giving it more than one foundation. A whole critical vocabulary was developed to identify the literary effects and satisfactions associated with such ironising. Hughes has never been a devotee of this kind of irony, and his own work must be taken as an implicit judgement that, if we are to view poetry in a more than literary perspective, as potentially a force for health in the whole community, such ironising has not served its turn. An attempt to regenerate a pre-dissociation centrality, it fritters off into a refined and exclusive intellectual game, becomes a mask of uncommitment. Hughes, by contrast with Ransom, is always keen to locate the side on which energy and vitality stand; in the poems just examined it is impossible to doubt his decision against the Egg-Heads. This may indeed limit the poem's effectiveness: the reader is perhaps granted too sure an interpretative foothold, with the result that he will always see the Egg-Head as someone other than himself. The complex narrative-dramatic procedures of the sequences we shall examine in Part III work to unsettle and disorient the reader, thus implicating him more thoroughly in their processes.

The ego-bound and excessive rationalism of the Egg-Head is only one aspect of the modern mind involved in our estrangement from nature and the sources of energy; there is also the failure of the religious sensibility in a Christianity whose ascetic strain, dominance by the masculine ethos, militancy, and postponement of hope to the after-life have often become, in the churches, a world-denying outlook which goes hand-in-hand with, and helped create, rationalism itself. These are themes much developed in Hughes; one of the first poems to touch on them is 'The Conversion of the Reverend Skinner', which broaches the matter within the context of the volume's concern with relations between the sexes. The usual convert is, perhaps, a reformed reprobate, a dissolute sinner who has seen the light and turned to God. Skinner's conversion goes the other way. As vicar, he starts out as the representative of a high-minded puritanical Christianity which condemns sexual licence. When he happens on a prostitute (what is he doing in this part of town?), he reproves her, but, far from bowing to the vicar's superior moral and social position, the girl answers back by slapping his cheek and telling him it is precisely his moral code which has created her kind in outlawing sex and making it dirty and secret. The Church's cursing has made her black; labelling sex evil it has made it so. And thus the puritanical repressiveness at the root of this is itself, and in another and truer sense, evil: the Church which has blackened her is black too. Announcing her own preference in relation to these two 'evils' of repression and immorality, she leaves with her latest client.

The shock of her response turns the vicar's 'tongue right over', inverting his moral position and bringing about the first stage in his conversion. It is an early example in Hughes of an enantiodromia, the term Jung borrows from Heraclitus for the psychological mechanism by which a too rigid and one-sided conscious outlook is suddenly, after the build-up of forces in the unconscious which embody all those aspects of life previously ignored, converted into its opposite; Hughes' own term is 'occult cross-over', and, in defining it in his Note to *A Choice of Shakespeare's Verse* (p. 192), he speaks of 'the mysterious chemical change that converts the resisting high-minded puritan to the being of murder and madness'. Skinner commits no murder, but the rest of the formulation fits him well. The first phase of his enantiodromia is a swing from extreme digust at sex to extreme self-disgust, from the high moral tone of the opening line to a self-mortifying adoption of the depths of the gutter:

> But he lay there stretched full length in the gutter.
> He swore to live on dog-licks for ten years.
> 'My pride has been the rotten heart of the matter.'
> His eyes dwelt with the quick ankles of whores.
> To mortify pride he hailed each one:
> 'This is the ditch to pitch abortions in.'

Self-disgust now deepens into disgust at everything. Life itself becomes horrible and irredeemable:

> He stared up at the dark and he cursed that;
> 'As if my own heart were not bad enough,
> But heaven itself must blacken with the rot!'

We may think of this as the kind of madness Hughes mentions in his Note, but in another sense it is only an intensification of the vicar's initial disposition, and merely a prelude to his true conversion, for which a second shock is necessary. After the girl's response to his first moral outburst comes that of heaven itself to his last: it presents him with a vision of the white of the moon (and the white and red of an injured woman's flesh), both in stark contrast with the blackness to which he has reduced everything. It is a startling reminder to Skinner that he must now step beyond the concern with self still lurking behind his disgust at everything and consider instead his victim, the universal feminine, which has been so deeply hurt and starved by all that is implicit in his puritanical code. The sight of 'the thin moon staggering through the rough / Wiping her wound' brings true conversion: Skinner ceases to curse and leaves behind the terminology of sin, which, whether directed outward or inward, has always carried within it a refusal of the created universe; he makes his first positive gesture, implying acceptance of the world, including those aspects he once condemned:

> And he rose wild
> And sought and blest only what was defiled.

We may be reminded of late Yeats, but the poem broaches themes and patterns centrally Hughesian, running from here into *Gaudete*, assuming greater importance on each revisiting. It serves, too, to introduce us (as some of the love poems in *The Hawk in the Rain* do not) to what is to become the important symbolic relationship between the sexes in Hughes' later works: an essential feminine devalued by masculine attitudes.

A longer, uncollected poem, 'The Burning of the Brothel', published much later, in 1966, uses these same materials. The Reverend Bladderwrack, despite fulminating regularly against the sins of the flesh, finds his congregation unresponsive and dwindling, the brothel doing better business than the church. Disconsolate, he starts to drink. Finding himself outside the brothel, he staggers in, determined to administer correction and clean out the cesspit. Watching him enter, the whores do not notice his intentions – all they see is his immense power and virility; even as he begins to address them as 'My lost sheep', they are feeling him over, more like hungry wolves. They toss him round and stomp on him, like Bacchantes about to tear a Pentheus apart, but he clings on until one of the whores claims him for her own use. Believing it will force her into submission, punish her for her sins and claim her as a bride of Christ, the supercharged Bladderwrack mounts her. He has, unawares, suffered the enantiodromia, invasion by the excluded. His plan backfires: Katie, and more so Bella, the next to be 'punished' in this fashion, actually enjoy the Reverend's 'awful stroke'; those whores he frightens into running out dash straight into the arms of the waiting populace – the whole town is given over to a sexual licence previously confined to the brothel; and Bladderwrack in trying to claim souls for God has turned himself into a 'rose horned . . . Lucifer'. But there is worse.

Such is the friction the Reverend generates in his spree that the brothel catches fire. Bladderwrack is so absorbed in his task that he continues with it as the place is consumed. Many whores escape to bring pleasure and companionship to men here and in other places in the future. But Bladderwrack dies in the conflagration. God, it seems, is too stupid to understand what has happened. He, so to speak, credits Bladderwrack's version of events, and accepts him into heaven. Like the radio plays touched on in the next chapter, this offers in a light and comic spirit matters handled differently elsewhere.

We have looked so far at two forms of closure, moral and intellectual. But *The Hawk in the Rain* is important too for its view of the animal vitality excluded. Hughes has a particular interest, in his first two volumes, in the kind of barrier between man and nature which is not absolute but carries within itself testimony to a deeper underlying link between excluder and excluded. The barrier between land and water is perhaps the most significant example for his later works, but the cage is also noteworthy. A traditional zoo shows two impulses. First, there is a desire to maintain some contact with the rest of animal creation, to bring into our lives the life of other species from which our predominantly urban existence has exiled us; the presence in 'The Jaguar' of the 'mesmerized' crowd answers to this impulse. Second, there is the desire to keep nature at bay, robbed of threat to human dominance, to which the cage answers. The poem is a celebration of what preserves itself from the collision of these impulses.

The opening stanzas might belong to a simple satire, showing us as they do that the life we value in wild animals is destroyed or denigrated by their captivity. The cages either seem empty or dope their occupants into becoming the sleaziest of human stereotypes. The line 'it might be painted on a nursery wall' raises again the charge of immaturity. But the jaguar is different: it maintains its liveliness through an inward-looking spiritual self-sufficiency. In doing so, it creates the powerful separateness characteristic of the animal in Hughes' early nature poems and alerts us to what might be called their overriding purpose. Hughes works towards creating a sense of awe in the face of a life that maintains itself apart from man; he is reintroducing his readers to a nature that possesses a genuine (indeed, the only genuine) power, outside man's control. Several poems share the aim of leading the reader away from the assumption of human dominance and towards a new disposition based on respect for nature as the indefeasible source of reality. Here, every facet of the jaguar Hughes picks out separates it from ordinary humanity – an effect strengthened by the beast's swelling to completely non-human size in the last three lines.

Hughes' long-term concern is to bring his readers back into fruitful contact with nature's indispensable energy. It was an essential first step in that campaign to re-establish nature as independent and powerful, a force worth negotiating with and needing treating with respect. 'The Jaguar' enacts this process of re-establishment by moving towards the dissolution of the bars which represent man's supposed hegemony over it: 'there's no cage to him'. The cage, here and in 'Macaw and Little Miss', is a mismanagement of the meeting between mankind and natural vitality, but the poem has established nature as a necessary focus of attention, a strength undiminished even in the least favourable of conditions. In other conditions, such as those prevailing in 'Wind' and 'Meeting', Hughes is able to do more to undercut humanist confidence.

The first, and one of the most important, successful meetings of man and nature in Hughes is 'The Thought-Fox'. The success comes through the unitive power of the imagination. Hughes' faith in this power is perhaps the most consistent component of his aesthetic. His work is based firmly on a belief in the capacity of his words to invoke nature's necessary energies on behalf of his readership; 'The Thought-Fox' provides a paradigm of this invocatory process. For Hughes, the poet is not in the first instance a craftsman in words. The first duty is to get the imagination working freely, and successful poems come from a state of total concentration on the object written about, not on the words used to write about it. In *Poetry in the Making*, his primer of creative writing for schools, Hughes uses the present poem as an example of his conception of the poet's task. He speaks first of how the best words for poetry are those rooted in the five senses, and of how, in bad poetry, the various sensory associations of the words clash rather than complement each other, a fault which can be avoided by complete imaginative participation in the being of the object or creature concerned. In 'The Thought-Fox' all attention goes to the fox and its vivid realisation (very much in words rooted in the senses); it is only at the end and almost as a by-product of this imaginative re-creation that the page gets printed, the poem written.

The poem, written after a period of writer's block, is the meeting point of several memories concerning foxes: a sudden face-to-face meeting with one at the top of a river bank in childhood; a warning dream at university in which a terribly burned fox-headed man induced Hughes to give up the destructive critical study of literature; and a Swedish film, seen not long before the writing, in which a fox walked towards a farmyard in winter. The qualities required of the poet to bring all of this into poetry are not verbal skills, but an attunement or discipline of the whole mind. As we shall see, Hughes' prime and recurring metaphor for the process of writing is angling. But here some of the qualities of concentration which the angler–poet of 'Pike' displays have been transferred to the fox itself: the delicacy, the combined wariness and boldness, the brilliance, the concentrated self-absorption of the fox are also the poet's qualities of mind in the act of imagination, which is itself to remain for Hughes the central act of a fully functioning human maturity.

The fox is not just an analogy for the poetic process: it remains a real fox, and the poem a bringing of the reality of outer nature into the inner world of poet and reader, to light the otherwise 'dark hole of the head'. This is what grants the process its value. If the fox were merely a metaphor for poetry, then the poem would operate in a closed circuit like the Egg-Head's; but it is not, and in the poem, to borrow a formulation from Hughes in *Writers, Critics and Children*, 'the full presence of the inner world combines with and is reconciled to the full presence of the outer world' (p. 92). The sharing of attunement between poet and fox, the steady coming-together (culminating in the switch from sight to scent), the oneness of snow and page, of footprint and page print, and of fox's lair and head – these local felicities enhance this reconciliatory effect.

II

The nature poems of the first volume seemed mostly to work at creating a sense of awe at the power of the elements and animals. Awe remains an appropriate word to use of *Lupercal*, but the poems now remind us that awe includes horror. In a number of poems, Hughes relinquishes the close-range view of the powerful individual beast for an encompassing view of the cycle of processes throughout nature, as in 'Relic'. Inevitably this brings him up against death, which in the first volume had been looked at mainly in the war poems, but is now seen in the animal and plant kingdoms too. In those other nature poems which here maintain the close-range focus on the individual there is a new concentration on predatoriness compatible with this awareness of death.

The water symbolism of several poems here extends the map of the psyche provided by the cage in *The Hawk in the Rain* (and here by the byre in 'The Bull Moses'). 'Pike' and 'An Otter' are the most central. The former opens with four stanzas evoking the pike as predator; the style is like that of 'View of a Pig' – a much simpler diction and syntax than in *The Hawk in the Rain*, and much use of facts and figures. The human scale of measurement is brought out, only to be rejected in favour of that of the pike themselves, so that their grand menace may be realised in full. They are not a stage in a process of ameliorative evolution, but 'perfect . . . The jaw's hooked clamp and fangs/Not to be changed at this date'. Their total absorption in the single activity of hunting, and the oneness with natural processes which this entails, are economically suggested: a pike is 'a life subdued to its instrument' – the fish is the instrument by which life sustains itself, and this instrumentality gives the fish its power over life; like 'The Hawk in the Rain', which 'suffers' death in both senses, permitting and undergoing, the pike is both master and slave. The shift from the obvious prose word order 'the gills and the pectorals kneading quietly' to the line as printed is sufficient to enforce the sense of silent waiting and interlude; everything between kills is aftermath or preparation.

'Pike' now moves to personal anecdote and reminiscence. Hughes' memories are presented so as to create a symbolic context in which the pike can be placed in some relationship with man. He begins with a memory of three fish, kept in a tank at school, which ate each other; a further intensification of predatoriness comes with the next memory, in which the killer instinct is taken to the limit of self-destruction (as also with the shark in 'Thrushes'). The final, longer memory can be read in a number of ways. First, it clearly carries out the overriding function of all the early nature poems by creating awe in the reader. The 'legendary depth' of the pond, the destruction of the solid monastery, the immensity of the pike, the coming of the night – all these features are comminative, making nature seem more and man less powerful than he likes to think himself. But we are also invited by the closing lines to read the story as a metaphor, like 'The Thought-Fox', for the coming-together of conscious and unconscious. In *Poetry in the Making* Hughes uses fishing as a paradigm of the imaginative act:

> All the little nagging impulses, that are normally distracting your mind, dissolve . . . and . . . you enter one of the orders of bliss.
> Your whole being rests lightly on your float, but not drowsily: very alert, so that the least twitch of the float arrives like an electric shock. And you are not only watching the float. You are aware, in a horizonless and slightly mesmerized way, like listening to the double bass in orchestral music, of the fish below there in the dark. At every moment your imagination is alarming itself with the size of the thing slowly leaving the weeds and approaching your bait. Or with the world of beauties down there, suspended in total ignorance of you. And the whole purpose of this concentrated excitement, in this arena of apprehension and unforeseeable events, is to bring up some lovely solid thing like living metal from a world where nothing exists but those inevitable facts which raise life out of nothing and return it to nothing.
> So you see, fishing with a float is a sort of mental exercise in concentration on a small point, while at the same time letting your imagination work freely to collect everything that might concern that still point. (pp. 60–1)

Hughes has many poems about fishing, concentrating on this psychological aspect of it, especially in *Remains of Elmet* and *River*, where he looks at the beauty of the living metal of the fish, rather than the alarming size and ferocity of the *Lupercal* pike. His emphasis is rarely, if ever, on the landing and kill; his interest is in the changed states of mind the angler enjoys and in the discharge of energy up or down the line. The bite is a moment of communication between two realms. Such communication is also the theme of 'An Otter'.

Like 'Pike', 'An Otter' is a marvellous evocation of the spirit of the creature itself. But it develops out of this an image of the man of imagination. The main focus of attention is the otter's relationship with the two elements in which it can move. Is it a land creature, or a water creature, or both, or neither? The poem shifts between the various possibilities, beginning on a note of alienation and deprivation: 'neither fish nor beast is the otter: . . . Of neither water nor land. Seeking / Some world lost when first he dived, that he cannot come at since'. Hughes is here drawing on what Henry Williamson also tells us of the otter: that it is a displaced beast (Williamson is one of the most important influences on Hughes' vision of nature; both belong to a line of nature and sunlight worshippers going back to Richard Jefferies). Tarka's forebears 'had been hunters in woods and along the banks of rivers, running the scent of blooded creatures on the earth, like all the members of the weasel race to which they belonged . . . otters have not been hunters in water long enough for the habit to become an instinct' (*Tarka the Otter*, pp. 31–2). The decision to hunt in water becomes in Hughes' poem a losing of the world of the land, and, since the water is not yet a new instinctive home to the otter, gained by way of compensation, the result is that he belongs nowhere. But there are already suggestions that this alienation is not all disadvantage:

> Takes his changed body into the holes of lakes;
> As if blind, cleaves the stream's push till he licks
> The pebbles of the source . . . .

The otter has the hero's role of diving down into the deeps as if to recover some boon or treasure. Similarly, 'from sea / To sea crosses in three nights / Like a king in hiding' (recalling Lawrence's 'Snake': 'a king in exile') invests the otter with magical powers of swift and secret movement which prepare the way for the later suggestion that by being of neither land nor water he eludes the normal rules of both and achieves immortality.

The second part resolves the tension of the first by showing how the otter's not being of either element allows him to use his keen senses to escape man, and, by implication, all destructive forces, including time. The poem becomes another celebration of the independence of nature, different from but akin to those found in *The Hawk in the Rain*. The power in the otter is not only outside man's sphere, but now also beyond the rules which bind man as individual. The otter is king not on land or in water, but in a third almost immaterial realm as insubstantial (and thus as invulnerable) as a meniscus. From this base he makes his forays into other realms where he has special powers precisely because he does not belong. The closing lines seem to suggest that, even when he is caught by the hunt, he is not: his essence, the spirit of otters, escapes and goes off elsewhere, leaving only an empty skin. This is a kind of immortality, and it leads into the notion found in Hughes' later nature poetry of a goddess who is the life force which at once inhabits and transcends any individual creature; Williamson's Salar is similarly 'a passing act in the everlasting action of its racial immortality' (*Salar the Salmon*, p. 12). In its picture of highly sensitive creatures able to penetrate to the source, belonging nowhere and everywhere, free to move between worlds, this poem provides another analogue for the shamanic or Romantic poet which complements Hughes' principal one, of angling.

Most of Hughes' portrayals of types of human character measure their subjects for their ability to remain open to the natural energies. The poet in all of us is the chief character seen as successful at this; others are seen as failing. An interesting exception is the tramp, who, in a number of poems of this first phase of Hughes' career, has found civilisation impossibly constrictive and chosen to live beyond its bounds, closer to the natural, more nakedly. This way of life makes the tramp doubly symbolic, as Hughes explained in a review of Philip O'Connor's *Vagrancy*:

> Our common dream, as archetypal as any, of the two-way journey toward Reality – toward the objectless radiance of the Self, where the world is a composition of benign Holy Powers, and toward the objective reality of the world, where man is a virtuoso bacteria – goes in the aspect of a tramp, rejecting ego and possessions, claiming equality with all life, as Shakespeare went in the aspect of mad Lear and as Tolstoy went in person. . . .
> For the good citizen . . . even after he's thoroughly investigated the lives [tramps] lead, and knows what emptied wretches they mostly are . . . persists in finding in them the symbol of the Holy Pilgrim, the Incorruptible Soul, the all-sufferer, the stone the builders reject again and again.
>
> (*New Statesman*, 6 September 1963, p. 293)

In *Lupercal* Hughes stresses the tramp as 'virtuoso bacteria', the man living successfully on nature's terms, as his civilised counterpart, complacent and degenerate, can not. This contrast between tramp and social man becomes explicit in two pieces. In 'Things Present', the tramp, living a completely physical life, dreams of the human past. He is the end-, or rather by-, product not only of human history, but also of the evolutionary process of which history is a part. The gradual establishment of higher human values such as honour and hope is accompanied by a loss of a fear seen as positive because in the pre-civilised phase it kept man alive to the threat of the environment; the constant possibility of death brought fear and with that sharpness. The growth of civilisation by which man 'step / By step got into stout shoes beneath / A roof treed to deflect death' is thus a progressive withdrawal from confrontation with exactly those dangers the challenge of which would have brought out the best in man. The stupidity of this withdrawal is underscored by the fact that death cannot really be deflected or withdrawn from.

In 'November', the most important of the tramp poems here, a man is walking down a lane with ditches full of rain, aware of himself as separate from the scene around him, hearing the clatter of his boots breaking the general silence. He comes upon a tramp who is his opposite in nearly every way – not moving but still, not aware but asleep, not separate from the scene but part of it:

> In a let of the ditch a tramp was bundled asleep:
> Face tucked down into beard, drawn in
> Under its hair like a hedgehog's.

The contrast between the two figures deepens. The hedgehog simile is the first sign that the tramp, like 'Dick Straightup', can live on nature's terms. When 'a wind chilled' he did not shiver or sneeze: 'a fresh comfort tightened through him'.

When the rains return, the man is able to look on only long enough to register what the tramp shares with the other components of the scene, before he feels he has to dash for cover:

> I thought what strong trust
> Slept in him – as the trickling furrows slept,
> And the thorn-roots in their grip on darkness;
>
> And the buried stones, taking the weight of winter; . . .
> Rain plastered the land till it was shining

Like hammered lead, and I ran, and in the rushing wood

Shuttered by a black oak leaned.

The nature which the tramp and all the other creatures are open
to and trust includes death, at its most powerful in this season.
The observer does not have such trust and, the moment he displays
this by running from the rain, he is struck by images of death on
the keeper's gibbet. But even here there is evidence of the quality
he lacks; some of the gibbeted creatures

>   still had their shape,
> Had their pride with it; hung, chins on chests,
> Patient to outwait these worst days. . . .

This patience is another aspect of the 'strong trust' earlier in the
poem, an acceptance of all aspects of the cycle of natural processes.
The tramp is a figure who has continued to fascinate Hughes; and
the Lumb of the *Gaudete* Epilogue, who roams the hills of western
Ireland, is his ultimate heir.

Part II

2

Wodwo, the Radio Plays, and *Crow*

I

Wodwo, one of the important fruits of that ferment of thought and broadening of religious and political horizons which was the 1960s, is a pivotal volume in Hughes' career, and asks of the reader familiar only with the earlier books an especially large readjustment of focus. Appearing seven years after *Lupercal*, it shows a deeper vision, a more thoroughgoing calling-into-question and an increased burden of 'agony' – perhaps the key word for *Wodwo* and *Crow* – which amounts to an implicit rejection of much, but not all, of what the first volumes offered.

It shows a shift in poetic strategy: Hughes now sets his observations and experience in a redemptive and re-creative pattern to which he alerts us in the Author's Note, which speaks of a 'single adventure', and in the division into three parts. This single adventure is the first clear manifestation in the major works of the pattern of psychological transformation (a mental, emotional and spiritual unmaking and remaking) which is to provide the narrative and dramatic structure of Hughes' later sequences through to 'Adam and the Sacred Nine'.

Despite the Yeatsian organisation of the first two volumes, with poems offering each other mutual support, check and criticism, those poems in *The Hawk in the Rain* and *Lupercal* which deal with different fundamental moods or dispositions remain in themselves static, discrete units. At one pole lies the mentality of the Egg-Head, rejected and satirised; at the other lies the harmonious openness and acceptance of the poet's mind in 'The Thought-Fox', uniting inner and outer worlds in the creative moment; but it is not the chosen business of the early poems to chart a path between. *Wodwo*, by contrast, is constructed so as to guide and channel the reader's response and shifting morale towards a new fundamental mood; and this process is quite as important as the ostensible

33

subject matter of the poems. In the sequences of the 1970s subject matter and process coincide. But here the pattern is by no means schematic or smooth or even everywhere equally obvious. Nevertheless it is discernible: the poems in Part I lead downwards, through a radical stripping-away of existing beliefs and orientations, towards a confrontation in the last four pieces with death; those in Part III, especially towards the end, lead upwards toward reaffirmation of the value of life and a renewed zest and buoyancy. The darkness of the nadir touched on this curve combines with the fact that the pattern is intermittent (leaving the volume partway down the road that has led Hughes from the short lyric to the narrative and dramatic sequence) to link *Wodwo* and *Crow* (where narrative is likewise only partly achieved) in forming what might be called Hughes' second period.

At the heart of *Wodwo* is an urgent prompting towards the asking of fundamental, even impossible questions. The volume's repeated assaults on the invisible barrier separating us from the foundation of reality are what make it a profounder achievement than its predecessors. 'A Wind Flashes the Grass' provides a good example, using a stormy autumn day to join every component of its scene in fear of physical transience; Hughes tries to hear the meaning of the day:

> We cling to the earth, with glistening eyes, pierced afresh by
> the tree's cry.
>
> And the incomprehensible cry
> From the boughs, in the wind
> Sets us listening for below words,
> Meanings that will not part from the rock.

What does the sound the wind makes mean? What does rock mean? These are characteristic *Wodwo* questions, with the directness of a child's worrying at the universe, but darkened by the shadow of adult experience and the burden of history. Here they issue in this vision of death and ephemeralness:

> the ploughman grows anxious, his tractor becomes
> terrible,
> And his memory litters downwind
> And the shadow of his bones tosses darkly on the air.

The volume does not move towards an answering of its questions, but, like Wordsworth's 'Ode: Intimations of Immortality', towards gradually relieving them of the oppressiveness they at first generate, so that, as we leave *Wodwo*, an initial horror has been augmented by wonder.

The presence of the pattern of unmaking and remaking means we must read in a new way; symbols and images, fixed and equivalent in *The Hawk in the Rain* and *Lupercal*, now assume shifting import according to where in the volume they are encountered. 'Still Life', 'Sugar Loaf' and 'Mountains' centre on the durability of stones and hills. The first comes early in the book, where Hughes is negotiating for us a transition between the vision of *Lupercal* and *Wodwo* proper; beneath the manifest and complacent durability of stone, it says, lies, even in a harebell, the greater power of life and change. The second is also a Part I poem, but coming later is more radical, calling into question the value of material phenomena, including natural ones, as 'Still Life' does not; it is full of things less present than we would usually take them to be, things halfway out of existence; the natural world, previously asserted, is now itself becoming insubstantial, questionable. 'Mountains' belongs to Part III and, as we shall see, uses the same components to conjure a new detached calm constitutent of the final phase of reintegration.

At the same time as Part I throws into doubt the faith in natural processes, it also concerns itself with undermining beliefs in purely human ends and motives; Hughes extends his critique of contemporary Western society. The title 'Boom' is the key to the shift which structures the poem (from sales boom to atomic explosion) and to the way the poem works on its reader, being itself a little creative explosion of recognition achieved by its last line. We begin with the sales boom:

> And faces at the glutted shop-windows
> Gaze into the bottomless well
> Of wishes. . . .

We are tempted to think in terms of only one of the senses of the title, thus enacting in our minds an equivalent of the blankness as to consequences with which the poem deals. We read the next short passage as revealing the failure of acquisitive materialism to satisfy our deepest needs:

> Like rearlights away up the long road

> Toward an earth-melting dawn
> Of the same thing, but staler.

We note how the sameness and staleness reveal the glittering promise of the 'earth-melting dawn' as false, but, until we have the last line and its filling with ashes, we do not see that this passage has been also about consequences, and the dawn that of the final nuclear disaster itself. The cheap romanticism of the phrase has been twice undercut, once in an entirely expected fashion, and again at the close as it gives us the other sense of the title. The poem insists that the atom bomb is not unique and unprecedented, except in the scale of destruction it brings, but is rather the final consequence of the kind of thinking which dominates the cultural phase to which it belongs. In *Poetry, Language, Thought* Heidegger writes,

> Man stares at what the explosion of the atom bomb could bring with it. He does not see that the atom bomb and its explosion are the mere final emission of what has long since taken place, has already happened   (p. 166)

and

> What is deadly is not the much-discussed atomic bomb as this particular death-dealing machine. What has long since been threatening man with death, and indeed with the death of his own nature, is the unconditional character of mere willing in the sense of purposeful self-assertion in everything. What threatens man in his very nature is the willed view that man, by the peaceful release, transformation, storage, and channeling of the energies of physical nature, could render the human condition, man's being, tolerable for everybody and happy in all respects.   (p. 116)

Hughes and Heidegger are here united in a critique deeper than can be offered by any position on the spectrum of mainstream, orthodox politics – a critique which, indeed, establishes a level at which political factions who would believe themselves utterly opposed may be seen as infected with exactly the same mentality, which sees nature as a subordinate, an object or standing-reserve available to man as subject, for his technological exploitation or management in the spiritless concern with external well-being.

'Public Bar TV' shows that the blankness as to consequences is self-reinforcing and makes us incapable of seeing it for what it is. So that when Hughes picks on an image from a cowboy movie which, as it were by chance, captures our vacancy and the wasteland we have created both outside and inside ourselves, we must see him as unique amongst the spectators in taking its significance. For the others, this picture is just another part of 'their dream', their fantasy of escape from the nullity this side of the screen.

The group of poems about death which closes Part I is amongst the most remarkable of Hughes' many daring and ambitious undertakings. His aim is to recover our sense of the biological reality of death, to confront it in its fullness and without our usual unthinking acceptance of the traditional frameworks of mediation. In the end, the steadiness of his gaze at the simple physical fact precipitates something of more than purely biological significance; we are prepared, in Heidegger's terms, for authentic Being-towards-death. The four 'Stations' make a short series of meditations on the road to an understanding of death, on the model of the Stations of the Cross. The thought which informs them and the style in which they are written are so unusual in English poetry that they can seem terse to the point of impenetrability; yet they are also statements of a deeply touching simplicity and directness. The first begins with the moment of death as an exposure to a formerly ignored reality, a physical confrontation. The consciousness of the man during his life is seen as an amnesia, a mental barrier against the biological fact.

> Before the funeral service foundered
> The lifeboat coffin had shaken to pieces
> And the great stars were swimming through where he had
>   been.

The coffin is a lifeboat in that it attempts to by-pass or cheat death, to preserve the body for resurrection and after-life. That the sea of death should overcome this effort is implicit in the opening section, where consciousness (of which the coffin is a product) was expunged by death. What supervenes after the smashing of the coffin and the failure of the ritual of which it is a part, is a vacuum – both man and boat have become nothing.

Death has already stripped away consciousness, the hope of resurrection, and the fabric of meaning provided by ownership and kinship, bringing in their place nothingness. In the second section the lifeboat metaphor is applied not to the coffin but to living men:

> I can understand the haggard eyes
> Of the old
>
> Dry wrecks
>
> Broken by seas of which they could drink nothing.

The opposition here is deeper than that in the first section, where we were concerned with the conflict between death and man's attempts at circumvention; this is the eternal opposition between death and life itself. Old age is a Tantalian torture, and it is the combination of the impossible and the inevitable in their situation which gives the old ones the gauntness and privation of their 'haggard eyes'. Our view of them is all the more harrowing because the reuse of the boat metaphor indicates that death begins to invade them long before the moment itself. 'I can understand' has a strangely double effect: it is at once the first fruit of the confrontation with nullity in the opening section, a new and deeper imaginative contact with the being of others, and also a statement so flat, bare and plain that it devalues itself in the utterance. It seems almost to invite the callous response 'Yes, but how does your understanding alleviate the situation?' The answer, within the poem and at this stage of *Wodwo*, is that it doesn't. The understanding seems to lead nowhere, and to be only a further excrescence of the consciousness which death universally annihilates. It stands alone, a curious trophy and a cul-de-sac.

'Haggard', originally a hawking term, meant wild-looking. The third section begins with the 'wild look' of a blackbird 'out of an egg / Laid by your absence'. In turning away from the merely human to nature, away from one wild look to another, the poem turns also to a new conception of the relationship between life and death; death ('absence') becomes the mother of life, the layer of the egg – the two states issue into each other and alternate. More important, in the blackbird they coexist, and without disabling the bird. Absence is symbolised by the snow of 'Emptiness'; presence by the bird's black body. The bird is without any mental framework to set up around death; it simply acquiesces in reality, letting the world get on with its work:

> you, from the start, surrender to total Emptiness,
> Then leave everything to it.

Indeed, any mental framework would destroy the bird's blissful ignorance:

> If you could make only one comparison –
> Your condition is miserable, you would give up.

This is the ignorance of Egg-Head's champions 'Forgetfulness, madness', and of 'A March Calf' in *Season Songs*, a highly practical blindness to mortality shared by all animals, here transmuted and lifted into a type of religious enlightenment which has come to terms with the nothingness which is death, the nothingness out of which life grows and to which it returns. To speak of coming to terms with is to use the pathetic fallacy where the poem does not; it insists on the difference between the human and the natural. But the bird's song nevertheless seems to contain and encompass both death and life in a way we cannot help comparing with our own grapplings with the problem posed:

> It is your own
> Absence
>
> Weeps its respite through your accomplished music,
> Wraps its cloak dark about your feeding.

The blackbird's music does equal justice to both life and death, presence and absence; it gives them both due regard and brings them together for resolution in harmony. There is a balance not present in the previous human approaches to the problem. 'Respite' captures this perfectly, divided as it is between suggesting delay and rest.

The final section of 'Stations' seems to take up the blackbird's example and jettison conceptualisation in a new, naked realisation of death as an inevitable biological fact:

> Whether you say it, think it, know it
> Or not, it happens. . . .

Death is a pre- and post-verbal reality which cannot be disarmed
or pre-experienced; it is sudden, final, unique on each occasion:

> it happens, as
> Over rails over
> The neck the wheels leave
> The head with its vocabulary useless,
> Among the flogged plantains.

Appropriately enough these lines bring us the only description of
the moment of death in the whole poem. The attendant concerns
of the three preceding sections have all been preparing us for this
unembellished realisation, spiralling down towards this nub. Who
is it that dies here? Man or woman? What did he (or she) own? To
whom was he related? Why did he die? Where did this occur? In
what context, social or religious, ought we to set the event? It is
the achievement of the poem that we don't ask. We have been
brought to gaze silently and steadily on the moment itself.
    'The Bear' is a guide and helper on the journey into death
towards which Part I has been moving:

> The bear is a river
> Where people bending to drink
> See their dead selves . . .
>
> He is the ferryman
> To dead land.
>
>
> His price is everything.

If the coffin in 'Stations' was a false lifeboat, there are nevertheless
genuine boats to ferry us on the journey into (not to escape) death.
The last line of the poem develops out of previous suggestions
that the bear exacts 'his price' by eating the flesh of the candidate
for the journey. It seems that death itself is the price that must be
paid for further progress in the confrontation with death. The bear
is the acceptor and agent of a necessary self-sacrifice.
    A key to the understanding of this aspect of the poem is given
by the anthropological background. This is a shaman's account
of his initiation, as recorded in Joan Halifax's *Shamanic Voices*
(p. 109):

We rowed off and came to the cave; the old man told me to take my clothes off, and I do not deny that I was somewhat uncomfortable at the thought of being devoured alive.

I had not been lying there for very long before I heard the bear coming. It attacked me and crunched me up, limb by limb, joint by joint, but strangely enough it did not hurt at all; it was only when it bit me in the heart that it did hurt frightfully.

From that day forth I felt that I ruled my helping-spirits. After that I acquired many fresh helping-spirits and no danger could any longer threaten me, as I was always protected.

This is a metaphor for a necessary crisis of self-sacrifice (pp. 12–13):

The often terrifying descent by the shaman initiate into the underworld of suffering and death may be represented by figurative dismemberment, disposal of all bodily fluids, scraping of the flesh from the bones. . . . The bones are all that remain of the shaman, but like seeds, the bones have the potential for rebirth within them. These bone-seeds are covered with new flesh, and the shaman is given new blood. In this transformed condition, the resurrected one receives knowledge of a special and sacred nature and acquires the power of healing. . . .

Shamanic initiation demands a rending of the individual from all that constitutes his or her past . . . the shaman's sacrifice of self.

The dismemberment is a way of speaking about a psychological breakthrough, a sacrifice of ego in order to found a new self, as in Jung. 'The Bear' is a symbolic culmination to the stripping-away undertaken in Part I, and points also to an interpretative context in which the confrontation with death is not an end, but a stage in the quest for new inner strength. It is this newly dynamic view of death which has been precipitated by the closing poems of this stage of *Wodwo*, and which provides the key event in Hughes' portrayals of a growth towards maturity in the later works.

The radio play *The Wound* is of particular interest, amongst the pieces in Part II of *Wodwo*, for displaying the general pattern of the volume, with its descent to dynamic confrontation with death followed by renewed upturn. The soldier Ripley, wounded and delirious, is trudging along when his derangement causes him to suffer an imaginative descent to a Houseful of Women in the land of the dead. Every other soldier present is himself dead, but Ripley is there by mistake. He witnesses a feast, a dance of death, and a dismemberment at the hands of the women not so much initiatory, as in 'The Bear', as a revenge for previous mistreatment; the women are getting their own back. Despite his puritanical qualms, Ripley is rescued from being caught up in this series of events by a girl who represents life and leads him back to it. Ripley's descent to witness death parallels the movement of Part I. The leading back to life parallels that of Part III.

Ripley's last words to the girl before he resumes ordinary consciousness and is rescued by other soldiers include these: 'If ever I get back to streets do you know what I'll do? I'll marry you.' This is one of many hints in the play of themes which Hughes is to take up and develop in his major works of the 1970s. The mud and slaughterhouse imagery of *Gaudete* can be traced back partly to here; so too can the figure of a wounded or mutilated female; most important, perhaps, is the pattern of the story itself – the movement out of ordinary reality into another dimension, and then back to ordinary reality, but changed – which clearly relates to that of Hughes' later narrative and dramatic sequences.

Hughes' other radio plays of the mid and early 1960s look forward to *Cave Birds* and *Gaudete* even more clearly. Perhaps the most important of them in this respect is *Difficulties of a Bridegroom* (unpublished), in which the motif of marriage assumes a centrality it is also to achieve in the 1970s. The protagonist is involved in a minor road incident which (as with the Hairy Hands episode in *Gaudete*) triggers a shift in his consciousness, thanks to which he is faced with his difficulty – how to see his bride-to-be whole. He is a man not unlike Shakespeare's Adonis with his 'Calvinist spectacles, which divide nature, and especially love, the creative force of nature, into abstract good and physical evil', as Hughes says in his Note to *A Choice of Shakespeare's Verse*. He can see her as either bodily and sensual, the Lady of the Literal, or as abstract and mathematical. But this division of her, the index and product of his own disposition, prevents union: out of high-mindedness he refuses the bride in her bodily aspect; and his own unrecognised physical side prevents him from achieving the abstraction of himself which would permit union with the abstract aspect of her he has himself created. At the end, no reunion of the two halves of the image of the woman is effected.

Sullivan's refusal of the physical aspect of her injures and wounds the woman as the *Cave Birds* protagonist's crime wounds the female presence there. The woman presents her own injuries as what Sullivan is 'in for', thus implying what *Cave Birds* makes plainer: that the man's crime against the woman is against himself – he too suffers its consequences. We have here the main elements of *Cave Birds* (male and female, crime and marriage) articulated in a similar fashion and within a similar field of meaning.

The two realms in *The Wound* and in *Difficulties of a Bridegroom* answer to the two dimensions (human and bird) in *Cave Birds*, and to the two realms in *Gaudete* (the village and the spirit world). It is this essentially dramatic device which is to be one of Hughes' chief ways of taking the prolonged look at altered states of consciousness which the shorter lyric forms of his first two volumes could not encompass.

Dogs: A Scherzo (unpublished) is equally important for Hughes' later development. It gives us a preview of the mentality of the *Cave Birds* protagonist. Again we have the two realms: the mundane reality of lodgings and libraries which the central character inhabits, and the mental underworld which keeps breaking into it. Here the disjunction between the two, which is to be so compelling a feature of *Cave Birds*, occasionally becomes the source of an almost flippant humour which undermines the seriousness of the subject matter.

Marcus is an academic archaeologist, an Egg-Head. He is working in the Reading Room of the British Museum. Our first clue that his mentality is suppressing and excluding from consideration some important aspect of his life, that (in terms which are to become familiar to the reader of later works) he has committed a crime against the feminine, is perhaps suggested by the recent death of his mother. As he sits reading in the library, he is suddenly switched to the mental underworld where, as in *Eat Crow* (a work available only in a limited edition published in 1971, but written in 1964), the protagonist is put on trial:

DEFENCE. Mr Marcus.
MARCUS. Yes?
(*Instantly, as if his word had unloosed the avalanche, the voices as before.*)
FIRST. Your feet have caught up with you.

SECOND. Your fingers are first witness.

THIRD. Your blood's signed.

FIRST. Your ribs have given you up.

SECOND. Your skin's got you taped.

MARCUS. (*Begins to laugh, to drown the voices, forcing his laughter*).

THIRD. Your shadow's sucked you dry, it's spitting the rag out.

FIRST. Your shadow's finished with you, it's sick of your thick-
ness.

SECOND. The nightmare, the nightmare, the nightmare

THIRD. She's stamping you to bits.

FIRST. She's kicking your top off.

SECOND. Guilty! Guilty! . . .

MARCUS. (*Slightly complaining*). I asked for help.

DEFENCE. This is the defence.

MARCUS. I'm not charging anybody. I'm being . . . asked to be
defended.

DEFENCE. This *is* the defence.

MARCUS. But whose? Whose defence? (*Shouts*) Whose defence?
(*Silence*)
(*Whispering to himself*) Mother!

Marcus's intellectualism has made him amnesiac about the life of
his own body. Like the *Cave Birds* man he has forgotten (Hughes
is undoing the dismissal of memory in 'Egg-Head') that the wheel
of the galaxy lies in his own abdomen. The force trying to break
through this barrier of ignorance is 'the nightmare', figured, as in
'The Rain Horse', as a real horse.

Marcus's trial does not produce the positive outcome of *Cave
Birds*; he suffers the occult crossover Hughes mentions in his
Shakespeare Note, the inundation by the previously excluded
force. He himself half notices it happening: 'Dionysos is my special
study. . . . At first I was interested in *it*. Now it's interested in
me.' The first evidence of the enantiodromia comes when Marcus
touches a Chinese girl reading nearby; this, in the terms of the
Shakespeare essay, is a Tarquinised Adonis threatening to destroy
'Lucrece (and himself and all order)'. Marcus flees the Reading
Room in embarrassment, and has a few drinks, but he is soon
back on trial. As in the *Cave Birds* poem 'After the first fright', his
attempts at self-justification only re-enact his crime in front of his
judges: 'What have I done now? (*Self-justifying*) Whatever I've
done, I've done in the name of sanity. Yes, I can say that. There

are standards to be kept.' At the play's end Marcus has made no progress; he is finally possessed by what he had rejected – he starts to turn into the dog he has always hated, and shoots himself. The works of Hughes' third period are to slow and control the moment of possession so that it becomes creative.

These plays are of obvious interest to the student of Hughes' development. Despite their limitations, they suggest that, for a time in the early 1960s, he was able to deploy and articulate in the drama, more than in poetry proper, some parts of the vision which informs his later masterpieces. From amongst these plays, *The Wound* is the appropriate choice for *Wodwo*, partly because it not only leads down into death but also back up into life. It is this second phase of the volume's pattern which remains to be examined in relation to the poems of Part III.

In 'Kreutzer Sonata', the you addressed is both Tolstoy and Pozdnyshev, his puppet. It is, first at least, an attack upon Tolstoy's ultra-puritanism and its consequences. The quotation in the fifth line brings Othello and the other Shakespearean Adonis–Tarquin figures into alignment with Tolstoy, so that the poem calls on the pattern of shifts in the English *Zeitgeist* suggested in the Shakespeare Note.

No evidence is brought forward in Tolstoy's story that adultery has been committed. For neither Pozdnyshev nor his author does this matter. The murder is justified, or at least excusable, on moral grounds (the story has an epigraph from Matthew 5:28). And, when Pozdnyshev concludes by asking forgiveness, it is not for the murder, but for having unwittingly conspired in his wife's fall into sin. Hughes reminds us of the supposedly moral reasoning about the murder:

> A sacrifice, not a murder.
> One hundred and forty pounds
> Of excellent devil, for God.

But he does so only after having made the focus of the poem Pozdnyshev and his psychological disorder, so that the lack of evidence ('all absence of facts') becomes a pointer to the real springs of the murderer's action. The morality, the puritan justification, ceases to be what it was for Tolstoy – real and proper – and is condemned by its association with the warped psychology of the murderer.

The stupidity of both murder and morality lies in their doing nothing to resolve Pozdnyshev's problem. Actually, they only put it into its final and worst form. For the murder is also self-murder; the poem invites him to 'Say goodbye' not only to his wife as she dies, but to and for himself as well, since her death marks a final intensification and crystallisation of the death-in-life which his extreme puritanism imposes on him. After his acquittal, Pozdnyshev refuses to have anything whatever to do with sex. He is in effect dead, and Hughes in the final stanza transfers this death to Tolstoy himself, again pointing up the implicit self-contradiction:

> Rest in peace, Tolstoy!
> It must have taken supernatural greed
> To need to corner all the meat in the world,
> Even from your own hunger.

The anti-sensualist message has been reduced to self-defeat.

The poem's thoroughgoing condemnation of extreme puritanical repressiveness makes it, by implication, a poem of commitment to life and sexual vitality. This is the first major upturn in Part III, a renewal of faith to be contrasted with the bleak view of sex offered in 'Her Husband' and 'Reveille' in Part I.

A number of poems in this final section share a pattern of an explosive outburst of destructive behaviour followed by a diminished and restricted aftermath. 'Kreutzer Sonata' is one; 'Out' and 'Warriors of the North' are others – in their cases we note an effort at transcending the detritus of history and penetrating back to a concentration on the development of individual consciousness. (We shall see a reflection of this movement in the shift between main Narrative and Epilogue in *Gaudete*.) This effort is accompanied by the introduction of other new elements. 'Song of a Rat' maintains the confrontation with death achieved in Part I, but now sets it within a group of themes and tendencies which define the affirmations the volume is working through to. The effort to see things whole and nakedly, including the least pleasant aspects of life, continues. With this goes a reopening of the gates to imaginative sympathy with other creatures, a calmness of perception, a balance of view, and the sense of the need for sacrifice.

The calmness is evident in 'Mountains', especially when the poem is compared with its Part I counterparts, 'Sugar Loaf' and

'Still Life'. The opening lines seem to belittle the human presence by destroying the speaker's confidently expressed picture of reality. He says, 'I am a fly if these are not stones', not intending to put himself at risk. Immediately, however, *Wodwo's* characteristic anthropomorphism asserts itself and the mountains become a giant recumbent body:

> If these are not stones, they are a finger –
>
> Finger, shoulder, eye.
> The air comes and goes over them as if attentively.

Unwittingly, the speaker has gambled away his self-image, his ego, in the opening line, and he now finds that the centre of importance has shifted away from himself (suddenly tiny and fly-like) to the mountains, huge and masterful, to whom even the air is in service.

In 'Still Life' the mountain's power is undermined. The poet and the reader shared the knowledge, of which the mountain was ignorant, of the harebell and 'the maker of the sea' within it. Here, however, the mountains have been reasserted, perhaps as the source and exemplar of some superior wisdom. What was complacency and inattention in Part I has now become Emily Dickinson's 'quartz contentment'. The simple abiding is whole and genuine, a lesson, like that of the biblical lily:

> They were there yesterday and the world before yesterday,
> Content with the inheritance,
>
> Having no need to labour, only to possess the days,
> Only to possess their power and their presence,
>
> Smiling on the distance, their faces lit with the peace
> Of the father's will and testament. . . .

The final couplet of the poem gives us the nature of their wisdom:

> Wearing flowers in their hair, decorating their limbs
> With the agony of love and the agony of fear and the agony
>   of death.

Their peace is not in despite of the agony of life going on above them, nor in ignorance of it. It includes and transforms the agony, so that the mood evoked in the poem has the same kind of accepting comprehensiveness we first met in the blackbird of 'Stations'. It is true that the repetitions of 'agony', and the descent from 'love' through 'fear' to 'death', serve to remind us of the pains and horrors, but this does not undermine the peace. The agony is exactly what the mountains decorate themselves with. They represent a steady tranquillity subsisting beneath all the turmoil, and the purpose of the miniature exercise in ego-deflation in the opening lines seems to be to prepare the reader for the reception of this mood. The poem must be seen as one of the most positive thus far – not only because the air of achieved calm, which has only so far been hinted at, is now crystallised, but also because we have here a poem in which the psychological act of supplanting (previously violent and of mixed value) has been turned to account, in that loss of ego is followed by the gain of something superior. An achieved calm is to be an important constituent of maturity in 'Prometheus on his Crag', and in *Crow*.

'Gnat-Psalm', which concludes with the first note of out-and-out celebration, is full of a nimble wit and humour recalling Lawrence. And yet, as we move to this poem, there is no sense of dislocation. For, besides being the first of the final group of clearly positive poems, it is also the climax and conclusion of another group. 'Song of a Rat', 'Skylarks' and 'The Howling of Wolves' have all been concerned to explore animal sound and communication. On each occasion paradox has been necessary to encompass what the sound seems to express. The rat's screech meant death and godhead. The wolves' howling could be both agony and joy. And the lark's song was 'Incomprehensively both ways – /Joy! Help!' It is 'Skylarks' which provides the essential link with 'Gnat-Psalm', through the notion that the joy is only to be achieved (as 'The Bear' suggested) through risking everything in an act of self-sacrifice. This is the springboard to the final affirmations in *Wodwo*, and it completes the pattern of psychological supplanting which has run through the volume, by stressing the loss of the old as no longer purely destructive, but instead the essential preliminary for a fresh start.

The sun in 'Gnat-Psalm', as in 'Skylarks', is seen as a destroyer and receiver of sacrifice. The gnats' fearlessness arises out of a sense that they have an energy to match the sun's, and a willingness to sacrifice themselves to it. Theirs is 'a dance giving their bodies

to be burned'. Because they were comparatively substantial creatures, the skylarks had to undertake a tortuous effort of self-
sacrifice in their flight ('Scrambling/In a nightmare difficulty/Up
through the nothing'). Appropriately for their poem's later place
in Part III, the gnats' self-sacrifice is easier, because they are to
begin with so nearly insubstantial. They hear the suffering and
sadness of the life of others, and see the 'utter darkness' that
weighed the howling wolves down, but they are not themselves
irrevocably enmeshed in it. Their triumphant song is bought at the
price of what little body they have. Yet the stress of the poem falls
not on this, but on the ecstasy which it buys:

> Their little bearded faces
> Weaving and bobbing on the nothing
> Shaken in the air, shaken, shaken
> And their feet dangling like the feet of victims
>
> O little Hasids
> Ridden to death by your own bodies
> Riding your bodies to death
> You are the angels of the only heaven!

As this apostrophe suggests, at the end of the poem Hughes
himself is caught up in their ecstasy, abandoning the confines of
the body in a beneficent imaginative dispersal through the scene.
It is the unforseen reward for the collapse of the walls of the ego.

Skylark and gnat are emblems of the necessary sacrifice of the
ego which, important as it is in *Wodwo*, is to become even more
important in the works of the 1970s. This quality of creative
surrender is of growing importance in Hughes' later works, and
perhaps especially in *Cave Birds*, where it is treated as the key to
inner development in man. It is what separates the heroes of
Hughes' great sequences from the Marcuses whose minds are
willy-nilly invaded by what they have resisted. In these true heroes
we see the explosive moment of supplanting slowed and, so to
speak, controlled by submission.

'Full Moon and Little Frieda', the penultimate poem of *Wodwo*,
reverses the earlier 'New Moon in January' in every way. It is kind,
autumn weather now: 'A cool small evening shrunk to a dog bark
and the clank of a bucket'. Except for these few noises, there is a
peaceful silence, in which a baby girl is not numb but 'listening',

fully alive and aware. Hughes' metaphors capture the delicate, lively, expectant, responsive quality of her awareness (and in the process bring the mirror which has featured in Part III to its final cleansing):

> A spider's web, tense for the dew's touch.
> A pail lifted, still and brimming – mirror
> To tempt a first star to a tremor.

Instead of the disintegration in the earlier moon poem, we have here all elements of the scene bound together in a single mood:

> Cows are going home in the lane there, looping the hedges
>   with their warm wreaths of breath –
> A dark river of blood, many boulders,
> Balancing unspilled milk.

The cows belong; their breaths reach out and envelop the rest of the scene; the liquids of the poem partake of each other's natures. The completion of this mood, its fulfilment and expression, comes with the child's exclamation: '"Moon!" you cry suddenly, "Moon! Moon!"' 'Moon' was one of the first words Hughes' daughter Frieda learned from her picture- and story-books. This poem records her shock of recognition at her first sight of the real thing, the moon itself at the moment of rising. It is a paradigm of the vision of the child, seeing freshly and with wonder. By extension it is a paradigm also of the ideal vision of the imaginative artist, who, in the Romantic scheme, has to attain by discipline and good fortune the stripping-away of preconceptions, conventions and habits of thought necessary to bring about the mentality the young possess naturally. The closing lines of the poem remind us of what the child's response implies for the adult:

> The moon has stepped back like an artist gazing amazed at a
>   work
> That points at him amazed.

The lines bind the scene together into a finished creative whole, set off by the astonishment of the human observer.

'Wodwo' is as important a poem as Hughes has given us. It is part of his ongoing tribute to the indomitable, questing spirit of

Henry Williamson's Tarka. It is his attempt at reinstating the half-man, half-beast Caliban, whom Shakespeare, through Prospero, demeaned and relegated to servitude. It is, as we shall see, an answer to Milton, who, in Hughes' view, confirmed Shakespeare's implicit predictions about the movement of the Zeitgeist. And, above all, it provides a suitable climax to the present volume by capturing the feel of the new disposition towards which earlier poems, with their gradual accumulation of nascent positives, have been moving. In 'Hawk Roosting' Hughes allowed us to share the vision of a bird of prey through hearing its imagined interior monologue. In 'Wodwo' he does this with one who might be the first man clearly aware of his own place in the physical world and his own biological inheritance.

In Book VIII of Paradise Lost Milton has Adam recall the first moments of human awareness:

> Straight toward heav'n my wond'ring eyes I turned,
> And gazed a while the ample sky, till raised
> By quick instinctive motion up I sprung,
> As thitherward endeavoring, and upright
> Stood on my feet. About me round I saw
> Hill, dale, and shady woods, and sunny plains,
> And liquid lapse of murmuring streams; by these,
> Creatures that lived and moved, and walked or flew,
> Birds on the branches warbling; all things smiled;
> With fragrance and with joy my heart o'erflowed.
> Myself I then perused, and limb by limb
> Surveyed, and sometimes went, and sometimes ran
> With supple joints, as lively vigor led;
> But who I was, or where, or from what cause,
> Knew not. To speak I tried, and forthwith spake;
> My tongue obeyed, and readily could name
> Whate'er I saw.

There are many differences between this and Hughes' answering soliloquy of primal vision. Adam's speech is to an angel, a representative of a deity who is transcendent of material nature. Wodwo's speech is a monologue, the self-communings of one denizen of a nature which is everything. For this reason, Wodwo's first gesture is downwards, to the ground ('nosing here') whilst Adam's is upward to heaven. Adam's every gesture separates him off from the rest of creation: his standing upright, his ability to speak, his sense of heaven above – all these are presented in that light. And of the creation he is master: it is he who names everything; he sees, hears and smells, but need not touch, because touching can only be done vulnerably and on terms of equality with the touched; his speech is in the past tense, it is a memory, and this in itself implies human specialness and mastery; and everything he says is a statement, carrying some degree of certainty and authority. Wodwo, as his name implies, is part-man, part-beast. He still belongs to nature. Nor has he Adam's mastery, being thrown into a world to which Adam is appointed. His freedom is a mystery to him, a vacuum which doesn't automatically fill with a sense of authority. He does not name things, but instead wonders if they name him. He is present as a participant; 'Wodwo' is a tactile poem. Wodwo speaks in the present tense, as things happen to him, articulating not only his discoveries but also his doubts and errors and worries.

Especially important is the fact that he asks questions (more than a dozen in a speech of only twenty-eight lines). This incessant questioning is the heart of the poem and the climax of the volume. Throughout *Wodwo* we have met questions, and always they have been difficult, probing ultimate mysteries and matters prior to those we usually deal in. Always the asking cost pain. The climax now is not a matter of finding answers; with this kind of question, the sense of having found answers could only be a self-deluding hubris. The vindication for the 'descent into destruction', is this poem which makes the courage to go on asking itself heroic, a quintessential mark of health and openness. Wodwo's unpunctuated rush and tumble of questions makes asking, if not happy, then at least more exhilarating than it has previously seemed. It is the tentative, humble, exploratory nature of the question which links Wodwo with little Frieda, for every child begins in Wodwo's situation, meeting objects for the first time, without knowledge of them or experience to refer to, and he or she responds as Wodwo does with a question. The question is the child's characteristic form of speech. Hughes is trying to reawaken in us a child-like thinking, and he inverts our values when he advocates this over our usual adulthood (seen in this light as childish in the pejorative sense). In his Foreword to *Children as Writers* Hughes says,

Children's sensibility, and children's writing, have much to teach adults. Something in the way of a corrective, a reminder. Theirs is not just a miniature world of naïve novelties and limited reality – it is also still very much the naked process of apprehension, far less conditioned than ours, far more fluid and alert, far closer to the real laws of its real nature. It is a new beginning, coming to circumstances afresh. It is still lost in the honest amoebic struggle to fit itself to the mysteries. It is still wide open to information, still anxious to get things right, still wanting to know exactly how things are, still under the primeval dread of misunderstanding the situation. Preconceptions are already pressing, but they have not yet closed down, like a space helmet, over the entire head and face, with the proved, established adjustments of security. Losing that sort of exposed nakedness, we gain in confidence and in mechanical efficiency on our chosen front, but we lose in real intelligence. We lose in attractiveness to change, in curiosity, in perception, in the original, wild, no-holds-barred approach to problems. In other words, we start the drift away from the flux of reality and so from any true adaptation.

The question Wodwo asks most often is 'What am I?' If Milton's Adam were given to asking questions, he would ask 'Who am I?' For him it is a matter of personality and character, of man separate from the beasts. For Wodwo it is a matter, as it has been throughout this volume, of penetrating beneath these ways of seeing, to the biological reality about which our humanism usually leaves us amnesiac. Wodwo knows what the protagonist of *Eat Crow* and Marcus in *Dogs: A Scherzo* need reminding about. His pristine vision ensures his wholeness and his awareness of it. His being half-animal is symbolic not of his inferiority to the wholly human reader, but of his being in touch with parts of his reality which we too share, but like to forget about. It is the reader who is inferior and divided.

Wodwo's crucial ability to ask questions is to feature equally strongly in 'Prometheus on his Crag' and *Cave Birds*. The protagonists of both these sequences win through to a strengthened mental and spiritual state which owes a good deal to Wodwo. But the more important legacy comes in Hughes' next volume, *Crow*, the central character of which is a developed version of Wodwo himself.

II

The two most consistent elements of Hughes' vision have been his sense that ours is an age of ending, in which a mistaken drift, two millennia long, has finally issued in destruction, nullity and chaos; and, with that, a firm resolve to devote his poetry to encouraging into existence a Turn towards a new and better age. He has sought to assist a rebirth from the ashes of the civilisation destroyed by the Great War. *Wodwo* can be seen as an effort at identifying and getting clear of the old errors and their consequences, followed by a penetration back to an original openness and zest for life figured in Wodwo himself. Wodwo is a new beginning; so too is Crow. As 'Lineage' and other poems tell us, he is what survives the nihilism and the collapse of the foundations of civilisation and emerges ready to try new possibilities. He has the same incorrigibility as Wodwo, who says, 'I'll go on looking'; Hughes describes him as 'Indifferent to all the discouragements of time, learning a little, but not much, from every rebuff . . . being nothing really but a total commitment to salvaging life against all the odds'. This comes from Hughes' 'A Reply to my Critics' (*Books and Issues*, 1, nos 3–4, 1981), where he identifies Crow with the Trickster figure, the embodiment of 'the optimism of the sperm, still struggling joyfully along after 150 million years', who belongs to the beginning of literature, being found in primitive and folk sources, and recommends himself to Hughes because he represents, more clearly than any other archetypal personality, the possibility for a new beginning for human development:

> Trickster Literature is the beginning [and] . . . draws its effects from the unkillable, biological optimism that supports a society or individual whose world is not yet fully created, and whose metaphysical beliefs are only just struggling out of the dream stage . . . out of the womb and the soil, and the bare forked animal has a repertoire for all untried possibilities.

Crow is, then, in terms of Hughes' history, that which survives the Great War and quests for a renaissance of potential. There are a number of poems in which conflict or battle are portrayed; Crow, like his avatar the Celtic Morrigu, witnesses or profits by or is involved in the carnage, which he always survives.

Crow is unfinished. Its subtitle reminds us that Hughes at one

time conceived of a narrative in which Crow would begin in error
and then be corrected by experience. He would have represented
the persistence of our raw potential, and charted its progress
towards fulfilment too. The story began,

> in heaven, where Crow is created, as part of a wager, by the
> mysterious, powerful, invisible prisoner of the being men call
> God. This particular God, of course, is a man-created, broken-
> down, corrupt despot of a ramshackle religion, who bears about
> the same relationship to the Creator as, say, ordinary English
> does to reality. He accompanies Crow through the world, in
> many guises, mis-teaching, deluding, tempting, opposing and
> at every point trying to discourage or destroy him. Crow's whole
> quest aims to locate and release his own creator, God's nameless
> hidden prisoner, whom he encounters repeatedly but always in
> some unrecognisable form.

This, from Hughes' sleeve-note to his recording of the poems,
entails his asking Crow to bear a second role, which he shares
with the protagonists of the other seventies sequences, that of
candidate for spiritual adjustment and inner development. This
would seem to make Crow a remarkably complete image of our
humanity: he is the embodiment of both the primal, immortal
energy of life, which inhabits each of us, and the burden of
consciousness and error and rectification. Crow is exactly what we
are: a part of nature trying to be a man.

But this is not to say that he is an entirely successful narrative
device. It may be that he is overloaded in having these two roles –
for the evidence from primitive literature is that the Trickster
survives precisely by being impervious to change. This contradic-
tion, or paradox, is one Hughes is well aware of (it is indeed
present in 'The Man Seeking Experience' in *The Hawk in the Rain*),
and it has two consequences. The clash of roles produces some of
the most moving moments in the poems, but it also vitiates the
narrative Hughes once intended, and it needed the more complex
strategies of *Gaudete* and *Cave Birds* for Hughes to deploy the two
roles fully. The unfinishedness of *Crow* is a problem or challenge
which those two works take up and resolve. Here, in his 'Reply to
my Critics', is Hughes' awareness of the contradictory elements in
Crow's character:

The morality of the sperm is undeniably selfish. . . . [It is] the

ego of the sign for Mars. But the paradox is, this spirit has at
the same time no definable ego at all – only . . . a single need to
search – for marriage with its creator, a marriage that will be a
self-immolation in new, greater and other life.

Life, seen thus, is the cruellest of conundrums: the same force that
drives towards 'self-immolation' gives also the selfishness of the
survivor. The conundrum may be insoluble, but the problem of
artistic strategy is not. In *Cave Birds* Hughes mutes the element of
pure Tricksterism and survival and concentrates on that of personal
transformation, making his protagonist set out in mental error and
undergo correction; he also creates two realms, one bird and one
human. In *Gaudete* the Trickster-survivor element is present in full
measure in the shape of the substitute vicar of the Main Narrative,
who is 'the optimism of the sperm' personified. But Hughes is
now able to encompass the paradox of the two roles because he
has two vicars, one of whom can die a death which represents the
sublimation of the primal energies. This death is essential to the
inner transformation Hughes aims at, but for Crow it is impossible –
there is only one of him, and that one immortal.

Crow begins with poems about his birth. 'Crow and Mama' is
the most far-reaching, drawing to the centre of attention some of
the most important themes of the book. It is about the impossibility
of escaping the biological roots of life, and thus about the intercon-
nection of all life. None of Crow's actions or gestures will be
permitted the luxury of being judged in isolation. Each one seems
to entail an answering loss and suffering on the part of his mother,
who is nothing less than the whole 'earth-globe' that hatched him
in 'Two Legends' and the 'bedrock atom' from which he was
ripped in 'A Kill'. Crow is not fully aware of the consequences of
his actions, but is nevertheless repelled by the pain and horror he
notices, for he now stops doing anything. A conceptualisation of
his position would run: if participating in life means inflicting pain
and suffering on what has given rise to and supports you, then
perhaps it is better to avoid participating. Instantly, the earth-
mother closes on him 'like a book / On a bookmark'. Those who
refuse to be victimisers become victims; those who refuse to be
predators become prey. This is akin to the blacker poems in *Wodwo*,
where the vegetarian's way out is seen as bogus and there is no
escaping the horrific and issueless cycles of mutual destruction.
But Crow has yet to learn that escape is impossible, so he tries a

succession of vehicles each of which fails, producing only more
wounding in the mother. The furthest he can go only brings him
out 'Under his mother's buttocks'. Heidegger speaks of the travel
which destroys time and distance but cannot bring Being near;
Roszak in *Where the Wasteland Ends* speaks of 'the astronautical
image of man' as 'the quintessence of urban-industrial society's
pursuit of the wholly controlled, wholly artificial environment'
(pp. 18–19); Crow's errors here encompass this latest technology
and, in giving him his second role as candidate for rectification,
implicate us in his quest.

'Crow and Mama' defines his situation and decides what his
subsequent quest shall be. He cannot commit suicide, because he
is incorrigible biological energy. He cannot accept life as it is,
because of his sense of horror at the pain it involves. And the
ubiquity of that pain prevents him escaping to another time or
place where it might be otherwise. These are three unalterable and
impossible terms within which Crow is bound. The only variable
factor is Crow's way of seeing. His quest will thus be not to find
his mother (there is nowhere he could possibly escape her), but to
recognise her as such. This is to say that he must cease being only
repelled by the horror and recognise it as something to which he
is necessarily connected and which can be seen as more than just
horror. In the book as it stands he does not get very far; his gains
are small, and soon rubbed out.

'Crow Alights' shows us a violent death which is a last surge of
destruction after which entropy supervenes, except for Crow, who
'had to start searching for something to eat'. His action is not
chosen callousness, but part of his and our nature. The poem
evokes two equal and opposed facets of our humanity, with the
death seeming to stand for the burden of consciousness and
relatedness grown suddenly insupportable, and the urge to eat
standing for simple biological persistence. The opposites are so
utterly different here that it is hard to imagine their reconciliation
within a single psyche. Yet this is the problem *Crow* is struggling
with, and in succeeding poems we are to meet a number of
different possible orientations which Crow tries or witnesses.

In 'Crow's Account of the Battle' we meet slaughter on the scale
of the Great War. In the face of such an escalation in suffering the
most common orientation in our time might be withdrawal into
numbness such as is the equivalent of withdrawal of moral discrimi-
nation. The draining of significance pointed up later is already

present early in the poem in the terrible equivalence given to 'intestines' and 'pocket-books' by their simple juxtaposition within a list of items, in the way human blood has become no more than rainwater, and in the way killing has become mechanical. This numbness which levels down afflicts participants as much as bystanders, and is found in Hašek's *The Good Soldier Švejk*, an early forerunner of the survivorship of the Eastern European poets Hughes has admired:

> 'I think that it's splendid to get oneself run through with a bayonet,' said Švejk, 'and also that it's not bad to get a bullet in the stomach. It's even grander when you're torn to pieces by a shell and you see that your legs and belly are somehow remote from you. It's very funny and you die before anyone can explain it to you.'   (p. 153)

This debunks a hollow and stupid heroism, of course, but also calls up the unreality and meaninglessness of the war and makes these unfeelings available to curative laughter. Elsewhere in *The Good Soldier Švejk* Hašek picks on a devotional picture in a church for an emblem of the divorce of feeling brought on by the war:

> From another painting on the other side, a martyr gazed open-mouthed at him [Švejk], while Roman mercenaries were sawing through his buttocks. During this operation no suffering could be detected on the martyr's face, nor the joy nor the glory of martyrdom either. He only stared, open-mouthed, as though he wanted to say: 'How on earth did this happen to me? What on earth are you doing to me, gentlemen?'   (p. 88)

It is this sort of nullity which becomes apparent in Hughes' poem after the battle. The succession of images with which he makes the point might easily come from an evening's television:

> And when the smoke cleared it became clear
> . . . shooting somebody through the midriff
> Was too like striking a match
> Too like potting a snooker ball
> Too like tearing up a bill
> Blasting the whole world to bits

> Was too like slamming a door
> Too like dropping in a chair
> Exhausted with rage
> Too like being blown to bits yourself
> Which happened too easily
> With too like no consequences.

The absence of consequences is entirely within; in the outer world of bodies and buildings there is ruin.

This conclusion reflects back on the earlier passage in which the battle is described as reality's lesson. As regards the participants, we now know, this can only be meant with the broadest of ironies. They learn nothing. They only die, or have their inner lives cauterised. What is being undergone here is in one sense not reality at all, because of the monstrous dislocation of human sensibilities which attends it. At the end, when the numbness has become apparent, no resolution of the situation can yet be proposed.

'The Black Beast' may be read as a sequel. Crow tries to externalise the blame. In his neurosis, he invents this beast responsible for the disasters and horrors he has previously witnessed, and sets out to hunt it down. That this is the wrong approach is implicit, of course, in the name of the villain: Crow is himself the Black Beast, and to pretend that guilt lies outside is to ignore one's own nature. Just such ignorance has produced the disasters in the earlier poem. In trying to solve the problem Crow re-enacts and intensifies its causes; in his pursuit of his supposedly external enemy he succumbs to the sickness of the military and scientific mentalities. He is in danger of becoming a St George figure, Hughes' emblem of neurotic suppression of the inner life. Hughes proposes that, rather than killing the dragon, we should accept it and find it a place, which is what he portrays in two of his most charming children's writings, *The Iron Man* and *Beauty and the Beast*. A similar pattern is found in the adult writings. In *Cave Birds* we see the suppressive mentality of a figure akin to St George slowly replaced, through a necessary sacrifice, by a more accepting and negotiative mentality, for which the appropriate metaphor is marriage, as it also is in the similarly patterned story 'The Head'. In 'Crow's Account of St George' there is no such saving upturn; the act of suppression simply reaps its logical reward.

Hughes does not tell the St George story in anything like its original terms, instead making it an occasion for pointing up the presence of the same suppressive and externalising mentality in the modern scientist. As he argues in his 'Myth and Education' essay, the scientific concentration on objective facts in the outer world necessarily involves a severance from the inner world of the imagination, the contents of which grow murderous with neglect. This insight is central to Hughes' work; it is found in Jung too, as part of his model of psychological development; but it is worked out in most detail, as we have seen, and with the fullest sense of its cultural, historical and philosophical implications, in Heidegger. Here is the closure against the inner life, somewhat as we have already met it in the misdealings of Sullivan in *Difficulties of a Bridegroom*:

> He sees everything in the Universe
> Is a track of numbers racing towards an answer.
> With delirious joy, with nimble balance
> He rides those racing tracks. He makes a silence.
> He refrigerates an emptiness,
> Decreates all to outer space,
> Then unpicks numbers.

The product of this mentality is a horrific demon such as we recognise from many a sci-fi movie; the St George figure kills it – an act not heroic as it would be in the film, but merely intensificatory of the suppression; only at the end does he come to his senses and find that like Hercules in his madness he has slaughtered his own family by mistake.

Other orientations towards the problem of Being must be explored or tried. In 'Criminal Ballad' Hughes returns to the question of how to support a raw consciousness which takes in the full range of human experience and suffers a continuous awareness of the interrelatedness of all lives; this is the burden refused in 'Crow's Account of the Battle', where circumstances make it so insupportable that numbness comes instead; here we have the opposite – despite its acute horror the burden cannot be escaped. The poem is an intensification of what we find in Blake's 'Auguries of Innocence', where the wounding of any one life lessens all. Blake speaks of the starving of a dog, the misusing of a horse and the wounding of a skylark, but for Hughes there need be no deliberate wrong committed; he is considering the possibility that any act or event, whether ostensibly violent and destructive or not, involves pain, suffering and loss for some other element of the creation. He recounts a man's life in such a way that this is brought out at each stage:

> when he sucked
> And fastened greedily at the hot supply
> An old lady's head sank sideways, her lips relaxed
> Drained of fuel, she became a mere mask
> Reflected in half-empty brown bottles
> And the eyes of relatives
> That were little circles in blind skin
> And when he ran and got his toy squealing with delight
> An old man pulled from under the crush of metal
> Gazed towards the nearby polished shoes
> And slowly forgot the deaths in Homer
> The sparrowfall natural economy
> Of the dark simple curtain
> And when he clasped his first love belly to belly
> The yellow woman started to bellow
> On the floor

In some other context, bringing these seemingly disparate events back into connection might create a saving sense of cosmic benevolence. 'Sparrowfall' refers us to Matthew 10:29, where Christ is comforting the disciples by telling them that God's providence, his caring scheme of things, covers everything, even the smallest details such as man himself would forget. For Hughes, this is no comfort to the old man at his death; the gentle, euphemistic 'forgot', describing the brain's ceasing to function, strengthens the point, which is further bolstered by the death's being accidental, at a far remove from any sense of salvatory pattern.

The pain, not to be abolished, transfers itself to the consciousness of the adult man:

> And when he walked in his garden and saw his children
> Bouncing among the dogs and balls
> He could not hear their silly songs and the barking
> For machine guns
> And a screaming and laughing in the cell
> Which had got tangled in the air with his hearing

He is acutely aware of the connection between events, which, though ever-present, is usually forgotten; Hughes' purpose in telescoping both time and space is to force the reader to share the awareness. Stephen Crane (whose poetry is an important influence on *Crow*) takes a different route to the same end when he speaks of 'the screams of cut trees'. Forgetting suffering and connection is itself occasionally criminal in Hughes: the amnesia of Marcus in *Dogs: A Scherzo* and that of the *Cave Birds* protagonist are examples. But this is not the criminality of the man here; he cannot escape what they ignore.

It seems likely that the title is suggesting that the man is criminal because he is alive, and for no other reason. This very harsh judgement belongs to the works of Hughes' second period, but has gradually receded since. It is mentioned in 'Prometheus on his Crag' as one of the possible meanings of the vulture; and in *Cave Birds*, though less so in later revisions of the sequence. These last two works are comparatively recent in their trade editions, but have had a prolonged genesis and are rooted in the second period. In 'Crow's Nerve Fails', his own innate animal ego is dinted by this sense of life as guilt:

> Crow, feeling his brain slip,
> Finds his every feather the fossil of a murder.
>
> Who murdered all these?
> These living dead, that root in his nerves and his blood
> Till he is visibly black?

The imagery here is noteworthy partly because it will be reversed at the redemptive climax of *Cave Birds*, where the risen falcon of Horus has wingbeats each of which is 'a convict's release'. Crow has not yet earned this freedom:

> He cannot be forgiven.
>
> His prison is the earth. Clothed in his conviction,
> Trying to remember his crimes
>
> Heavily he flies.

The world of *Crow* is so harsh, and his progress through it so

limited and halting that any moments of stillness and gentleness
come to seem all the more precious; one such is 'Crow's Undersong'. In *Tarka* Williamson pictures a group of swallows resting at
evening after their hectic day: 'They talked in the undersong
voices – which men seldom hear, they are so soft and sweet –
while clinging to the reed-maces' (p. 80). This becomes in Hughes'
poem the notion that beneath Crow's croakiness and the character
it expresses lies hidden some deeper and softer principle. Within
the rough-and-ready survivor is that which survives, the spirit of
the life of which he is only the vehicle:

> She cannot come all the way
>
> She comes as far as water no further
>
> She comes with the birth push
> Into eyelashes into nipples the fingertips
> She comes as far as blood and to the tips of hair
> She comes to the fringe of voice
> She stays
> Even after life even among the bones

The figure evoked here is to become the goddess of *Gaudete* and
Hughes' other later works. In terms of Crow's quest and the
underlying narrative of the book this poem has a curiously double
effect. The title insists that what we meet here is part of Crow
himself; but at the same time the feminising and personification of
this principle offers her, more clearly than at any previous point,
as a somehow separate figure filled with characteristics, including
a naïve vulnerability and reticence, which make her the goal of
Crow's drive towards redemptive union. She is both what possesses
him, what he is, and also what he must search for. In *Gaudete*,
these two roles are divided: the figure possessed is the substitute
Lumb of the Main Narrative; the figure searching for spiritual
union is the original vicar now away in the otherworld. The
present poem accompanies 'Dawn's Rose' to create a stillness and
gentleness which foreshadow the mood of the subsiding energy
and of new calm which dominates the closing poems. As we shall
see, the ending of *Crow* has only a little to do with the story of
Crow's quest, working instead to create a muted version of the
upturn in mood we found at the end of Part III of *Wodwo*. Crow

himself appears only twice in the last nine poems, so the new mood is associated with a dwindling of the Trickster–survivor of the earlier pieces.

Crow contains a group of poems in which laughs, grins and smiles take on an independent existence. These are gestures peculiarly difficult to assign definite significance, partly because they belong in a zone where words and thoughts have failed. *Crow* seems to depict a striving to outgrow a psycho-spiritual impasse itself represented by the twin extremes of numbness and hypersensitivity into which the effort to develop is always deviating. At each renewal of the effort some imbalance enters and we are derailed into an emotional excess, so that a fresh start has to be made. Not all these moods are ascribed to Crow himself – others he witnesses – but taken together they chart the rise and fall of the spirit as we move through the volume. It is here that *Crow* is most clearly paving the way for 'Prometheus on his Crag', which traces and resolves a similar succession of responses to agony, but with greater economy. It is in this light that the wild laughter and tears of *Crow* may perhaps be seen. The sequence takes it as given that the burden of awareness is so massive no rational or verbal formulation can be depicted in the poems as adequate to sustain it. Even laughter itself may or may not help: in 'Crow's Battle Fury' a succession of deaths makes him laugh so much he shakes himself to pieces, but this disintegration is not a prelude to psychological transformation and Crow is put together in his old shape, unenlightened, back at the situation of 'Crow and Mama' where his every step wounded her.

'A Bedtime Story' introduces us to a new type of failure. The man here is 'Almost a person'; his failing is not numbness or excess emotion, but simply the partialness and inadequacy of his senses and mind:

> Somehow he could not quite see
> Somehow he could not quite hear
> He could not quite think
> Somehow his body, for instance,
> Was intermittent

This defective equipment makes him feel out of touch: 'nothing could connect'. This is the reverse of the numbness in 'Crow's Account of the Battle', which came from too great an exposure to pain and suffering; here the disconnection prevents exposure:

> And when he saw the man's head cleft with a hatchet
> Somehow staring blank swallowed his entire face
> Just at the crucial moment
> Then disgorged it again whole
> As if nothing had happened

Having failed to take any real grip on the experience around him, the man has a final gambit: he tries to write himself into contact with events. But a precondition of success at autobiography is truly living through the events described, and this man has not; his life-story would be spurious. In the event it is never written: '"I give up," he said. He gave up. / Creation had failed again.' Hughes must repeat for us the admission of defeat; any statement the man might make has to be corroborated, since all we have learned of him previously would lead us to doubt its validity; he is not to be trusted even in his moment of despair.

'Truth Kills Everybody' returns us to the theme of personal transformation found in 'Crow's Battle Fury' and associated with the second of Crow's roles. It records his mismanaging a meeting with his creator who defends herself with what Hughes in 'A Reply to my Critics' calls 'successive cuttlefish ink-clouds of illusion – composite symbols, each one recombining the various changing factors of the fight, in a progression'. The progression consists in successive alterations in the nature of the symbols, so that they offer Crow's changing view of his goal as it grows steadily less crudely at variance with the goal's real nature. Unfortunately, despite this progression, Crow's basic tactic of simply holding on for all he is worth does not change, so that the refinement is accompanied by an escalation of the energy involved in the confrontation and he is at last destroyed:

> The ankle of a rising, fiery angel – he held it
>
> Christ's hot pounding heart – he held it
>
> The earth, shrunk to the size of a hand grenade
>
> And he held it he held it and held it and
>
> BANG!
>
> He was blasted to nothing.

Crow's disintegration is both promising (in that it represents a jettisoning of the ego that prevented union with his goal) and regressive (in that, like the sudden supplantings of an old consciousness in *Wodwo*, it happens too quickly and out of context). This ambivalence is the product of the basic paradox of his nature as unbreakable biological ego seeking to be broken in union with the source. The paradox has a curious effect on the reader, centring on Crow's death. That Crow has been established in other poems as unkillable means that we cannot believe in his death. 'BANG!', with its capitals and exclamation mark, recognises this, and whilst we are willing to think of Crow in the first of his roles, as we must, nothing is amiss. When we turn to the second role, there is an evident difficulty: the dynamo of Hughes' paradigm of psychological rectification and growth is a sacrifice of the old self made without reserve or expectation of reward, and the only adequate metaphor for this is a death such as is portrayed in 'The executioner' in *Cave Birds*. Crow's immortality prevents the required seriousness and grandeur attaching to his own demise. We cannot participate imaginatively in the self-sacrifice of a being incapable of it. This is not in any sense a criticism of Hughes; it is, rather, yet another statement of the basic paradox of Crow's nature, but this time in terms of artistic strategy and reader response, with a view to explaining why *Crow* should remain incomplete, but have its pattern, transmuted, brought to completion in later works.

The calmer, steadier, wholler vision of the closing poems in *Wodwo* is paralleled in *Crow*. To trace the serpent through *Crow* is to read one of the volume's truest barometers. As the superannuated, incompetent Christian God *Crow* shares with the poems of Stephen Crane fades out, so the serpent, Crow's creator, is seen in truer light. From being 'God's only son' in 'A Childish Prank', and the manifestation of his goal which Crow mismanages in 'A Horrible Religious Error', it has now become, in 'Snake Hymn', a figure linkable with the goddess in other books. Here we have 'the spirit of the sperm' which has possessed Crow seen with fresh detachment. It has become the divine force which is simultaneously transcendent and incarnate in the various transient forms life takes:

> The love that cannot die
> Sheds the million faces
> And skin of agony
>
> To hang, an empty husk.

Whenever Hughes tries to evoke the whole spirit of existence in this fashion, he resorts to paradox, already here in the co-presence of so many deaths and the undying energy which enlivens them, and in the accompanying co-presence of fulness and emptiness; and now also in that of agony and virgin joy:

> Still no suffering
> Darkens the garden
> Or the snake's song.

'King of Carrion' tells us most clearly that the atmosphere of calm (strengthening as we move towards the close of the volume) is to be achieved via the waning of the Crow we have grown used to. If he has been primarily a figure of energy, this poem depicts his entropy; this is a still world of death and vacancy. From this mood the second of the 'Two Eskimo Songs' draws a minimal affirmation. Water makes a series of efforts at living, unsatisfied with being one of the elements from which others make a life. But every effort is repulsed by some counterforce to life. Water reverses its effort and tries to die, to have no part at all in life, but with no more success. Efforts of both kinds produce only a rain of tears. At several points in the collection tears and laughter continue until they have served their emotional purpose and turn into their near opposite or disappear. So now, water cries itself out:

> It came weeping back it wanted to die

> Till it had no weeping left

> It lay at the bottom of all things

> Utterly worn out   utterly clear

'Worn out' corresponds to the entropy of 'King of Carrion', whilst 'clear' gives us the positive the poem is able to make out of this. The water's new-found clarity and stillness come to stand for a mood of poise, serenity and freedom, or, to use the term the title supplies, of play.

The upturn at the end of *Crow* is less marked than in *Wodwo*, since there is nothing here which answers to 'Full Moon and Little Frieda and we are losing our central character, rather than building towards his climactic introduction. Nevertheless, the movement displayed in *Wodwo* included the generation of just such a calm, poised, whole vision as we see traces of at the end of *Crow*. And there is in both works at this point a feeling of healthy detachment from a previous possession. We have seen this in 'Snake Hymn', and it forms the basis of the final poem, 'Littleblood', which is a song or prayer of invocation to a life force now seen as separate, present in all life, but addressable:

> O littleblood, drumming in a cow's skull
> Dancing with a gnat's feet
> With an elephant's nose with a crocodile's tail.
>
> Grown so wise grown so terrible
> Sucking death's mouldy tits.
>
> Sit on my finger, sing in my ear, O littleblood.

Detachment is not an adequate word: this is not a Buddhistic cutting-off from biological life, but a sign of a new consciousness of that life. And in the switch towards this here, at the end of *Crow*, we have the distant seed of the shift from possession to prayer which occurs in *Gaudete* with the death of the substitute Lumb and the Irish priest's transcription for us of the other Lumb's addresses to the goddess.

The Crow project as a whole must be placed in the context of the unfinished Romantic epic, with *Milton* and *Jerusalem*, *The Prelude*, *Endymion* and *Hyperion*. In his *Fearful Symmetry*, Northrop Frye lists three possible courses for the poet wishing to write a new national epic, refounding spiritual roots, together with the objections and difficulties attendant on each: 'His second course is to visualize his mission as a rebirth of a new Orc. . . . But Orc is a circular conception' (p. 316). The relevance of this to the problem of Crow's immortality is striking. Crow is Hughes' Orc, a figure of resurgent energy, and in asking him to be both that circular, ever-renewing figure the Trickster–survivor, and also the pathfinder to a new Holy Ground, Hughes evidently created narrative difficulties best solved outside the existing framework, in the changed artistic strategies of *Gaudete* and *Cave Birds*, which may be seen as in a certain sense making good Hughes' intentions for the original project.

Crow as first conceived would have involved Hughes in telling the whole story in the prose sections between the poems; in the work as it stands not only is the story incomplete but such sections of it as are covered have to be excavated from or read into the poems in a way never entirely satisfying. In *Cave Birds*, the narrative is not absent but fully implied by the very different procedure adopted there, and it is carried through to its necessary conclusion. The protagonist, too, is a more adequate figure than Crow; indeed, crowishness becomes one of the phases he passes through.

In *Gaudete* the new strategy is twofold. Hughes himself withdraws completely from his narrative, offering little or no interpretative comment about Lumb's last day, simply presenting the facts. And he takes narrative only to where it would involve him in portraying some sort of restoration within the fictional world he has created; at that point, facing all the problems of endings which are the lot of a Romantic poet devoted to the dynamic (and therefore unending), he makes a radical shift of focus which takes us away from narrative altogether.

Part III

3

An Approach to *Gaudete*

I

Gaudete begins with a Prologue in which the Reverend Nicholas
Lumb, vicar of a sleepy modern English village, having been
abducted by the spirits and taken to the underworld to perform
the healing of a sick female figure, is replaced in the ordinary
world by a double of himself made from a lopped oak, whom I
shall call Lumb 2. The Main Narrative which follows recounts the
events of this Lumb 2's final day. Though the spirits have made
him resemble the original in appearance, they have given him a
very different nature, that of a fertility spirit whose whole being is
dominated by his sex drive. In trying, desperately, to be both
substitute vicar and fertility spirit, Lumb 2 has formed the women
of the village, both married and unmarried, into a secret society
connected with a new religion. He has sex with as many of them
as possible, explaining when necessary that one of them is to bear
the new messiah. Great passions have been aroused, leading to
murders, suicides and other disasters. The menfolk learn of Lumb
2's sexual exploits with their women and hunt him round the
parish until he is shot dead by one of them, Major Hagen. The
Epilogue consists primarily of a set of short religious poems written
by the original Lumb and centring on the nature of an unnamed
goddess and his experience of her.

Gaudete sets out from the same account of history as *Crow*,
but reflects more fully the movement from the bankruptcy of
Christianity to the inception of a new religion. The Prologue begins
with Lumb embodying the bankruptcy:

> He has no idea where he is going. Or where he is.
> Is it dusk or is it eclipse?
> He urges himself, as if towards solid ground.
> He concentrates on the jolt of his reaching stride and the
> dragging flap of his cassock. . . .

73

> He walks with deliberate vigour, searching in himself for
> control and decision.
>
> (p. 11)

His walk betrays his spiritual emptiness, and like everything else
in the opening pages is simultaneously an image of his own
mounting psychological crisis and a more general statement about
loss of direction and energy in contemporary society. Lumb
encounters a town filled with corpses, passing amongst them,
touching hands and faces in unwitting parody of Christ's healing
miracles. This vision of death and disruption recalls the beginning
of Hughes' adaptation of Seneca's *Oedipus*, where there is a similar
link between the sickness of the community and that of the central
character. It recalls also Eliot's crowd of those undone by death
flowing over London Bridge; *Gaudete* begins in the waste land, and
is, like *Crow*, an attempt to get beyond it. At the heart of the sick
culture is Lumb's own sickness, and the crowded dead are a
projection of his incipient division into two personalities; in *Symbols
of Transformation* Jung writes, 'the crowd expresses violent motions
of the unconscious. Such symbols always indicate an activation of
the unconscious and an an incipient dissociation between it and
the ego' (p. 207). The Prologue now pictures in the most literal
fashion the creation of such a dissociation.

Lumb is summoned (as the protagonist of *Cave Birds* is to be) to
the subterranean world of the spirits to heal the sick female, who
is what will become in the Epilogue the goddess of inner and outer
life who assumes such importance in all Hughes' later works. She
is couched in a 'firelit, domed subterranean darkness' like the
flame-lit, cavernous womb of life visited in Rider Haggard's *She*;
in both writers the fire is that of eternal life-giving energy, and in
the Main Narrative of *Gaudete* a character's disposition towards
this energy is figured as his flame, soft and lambent if he has inner
harmony, fierce and destructive if not. Subsuming these inner
flames is the sun (as important to Hughes as to Williamson and
Jefferies), the source of all energy, which becomes the symbol of
the goddess in the outer life ('the sun . . . Was always here, is
always as she was', says one Epilogue poem). Lumb refuses his
call to the healing task:

> He declares he can do nothing
> He protests there is nothing he can do

> For this beautiful woman who seems to be alive and dead.
> He is not a doctor.   He can only pray.
>
> (p. 15)

This stands in *Gaudete* as a failure parallel to the *Cave Birds* protagonist's re-enaction of his crimes in front of his spirit judges, and it inaugurates *Gaudete's* extended concern with the healing function. In the village, and the modern world it represents, the few necessary regulatory functions one imagines carried out in a primitive tribe have been lost in division of labour and the complicating of the social system. In a tribe, the shaman has care of both souls and bodies, since such dualisms do not pertain; in *Gaudete* (which, like the recent Laureate poems, looks at modern England with an anthropologist's eye) this function has been lost in being split between the doctors, such as Westlake, and the priests. In the Main Narrative all Lumb's deeds are grotesquely over-direct, too simply physical distortions of the healing function. It is only in the Epilogue that we have what approaches its restoration.

Lumb's refusal to heal is a closure against part of his own being, and this brings about the splitting of personalities to which Jung refers – what the ego will not accommodate takes on an independent existence. The whipping of the oak log which brings this about is the first of the motifs *Gaudete* draws from English folklore and legend. Beyond this material lie the Germanic myths of Parzival and the *Nibelungenlied*, and the classical myths of Dionysos to which Hughes also alludes. These supplement what can be gathered from the system of internal cross-references which operates – references from one part of *Gaudete* to another, and from *Gaudete* to Hughes' other works.

Lumb's closure brings into being his *alter ego*, who is the undiluted life force, primal energy denied the mediating and harmonising influence of the other aspects of Lumb's psyche. He is Crow, but with a survivorship now seen as sexual. In the Main Narrative he has, with a Crow-like directness and simplification, turned the gospel of love into the drive to breed and perpetuate the genes.

Before we learn this, we see him consecrated to his doomed and parodic task. He must sacrifice a bull and be baptised or consecrated in its blood and entrails. (Bulls recur throughout *Gaudete* as beasts of the goddess, and act, like the flame, as a test of attunement to her ways.) An important echo of the bull sacrifice comes with Lumb 2's death: as he approaches Hagen's residence 'All the anchored bulls recoil', a small reminder of the Prologue bull's boat-like appearance. The bull is, then, associated with both Lumb 2's birth and his death, and this is foreshadowed in the Prologue ritual:

> And Lumb
> Squeezes the pistol
> Squeezes his eyes shut as the shot slams into his brain.
> (p. 18)

The ambiguity of 'his' allows us to invoke Jung's comment in *Symbols of Transformation*: 'the Mithraic bull-sacrifice is an anticipa-tion of the god's self-sacrifice' (p. 121). It is as though Lumb 2's eventual extinction is preordained, as certain as the setting of the sun whose track across the sky measures out his final day in the Main Narrative.

The healing function rejected in the Prologue and revived in the Epilogue is also glimpsed tantalisingly in what might be called the Hairy Hands episode of the Main Narrative, since Hughes chooses a modern Devon legend of that name to provide the sudden shock which serves to thrust aside one dominant type of consciousness (Lumb 2's) and allow in another (Lumb 1's):

> At a high bend, over the river,
> Stub-fingered hairy-backed hands come past his shoulders
> And wrench the steering wheel from his grip.
> The van vaults the bank. . . .
>
> A toppling darkness, a somersaulting
> Of bumps and jabs, as if he rolled down a long stair . . . .
> (*Gaudete*, p. 98)

The stair suggests a return to the subterranean world from which Lumb 2 climbs at the end of the Prologue. In the vision which follows we receive the main evidence to set beside Hughes' cryptic statement in the Argument: 'It may be that the original Lumb has done the work' the spirits 'wanted him to do'. Here, if anywhere, we see an equivalent to the mutual reconstitution of male and female in *Cave Birds*; Lumb, like Parzival, has been given a chance to undo his 'I am not a doctor':

Lumb bends to the face,
He draws aside the rain-plastered hair.
It is Hagen's wife, Pauline.
Her staring eyes seem not to register his presence.
He calls to her, he speaks to her softly, as to a patient in a
    coma . . . .

(p. 102)

Amongst the village women, members of Lumb's coven, is the
female of the Prologue, the goddess whose first clear predecessor
we met in *Difficulties of a Bridegroom*. In *Cave Birds* the female will
be both mother and daughter to the protagonist; here Lumb and
the baboon woman bring each other to new birth:

He sees himself being delivered of the woman from the pit,
The baboon woman,
Flood-sudden, like the disembowelling of a cow
She gushes from between his legs . . . .

He crawls,
He frees his hands and face of blood-clotted roping tissues.
He sees light.
He sees her face undeformed and perfect.

(pp. 105–6)

But exactly what weight we can give to these lines depends on
their context in the Main Narrative.

II

The most marked stylistic feature of the Main Narrative is its
exercising a minutely detailed and almost absolute control of the
reader's visual imagination, without ever giving clear pointers to
the interpretation of the dictated scene; Hughes tells us what to
see, but not what to make of it. Why should this be?

In *Ted Hughes: The Unaccommodated Universe*, Ekbert Faas records
an interview in which Hughes described his aim:

I became interested in doing a headlong narrative. Something
like a Kleist story that would go from beginning to end in some

forceful way pushing the reader through some kind of tunnel
while being written in the kind of verse that would stop you
dead at every moment. A great driving force meeting solid
resistance. And in order to manage that I had to enclose myself
within a very narrow tone, almost a monotone.   (p. 214)

The combination of stationary and non-stationary features which
Hughes and Kleist share is the stylistic manifestation of kinship of
vision and purpose. At the heart of this lies a desire to test out
and undermine excessive faith in conventional morals and the
social institutions in which they reside. In *The Stories of Kleist: A
Critical Study*, Denys Dyer summarises their repeated shape:

Kleist's *Erzählungen* take place in a world of upheaval and
chaos. In every one of them the settled order of things, the
normal routine, is disturbed by some disaster or unforseen event
that makes a mockery of conventional human responses and
places men and women in situations alien to their normal range
of experience.   (p. 151)

The story by Kleist which comes closest to *Gaudete* is 'The
Foundling', because here the 'disaster or unforseen event' introduced to disturb a corrupt and senescent *status quo* takes on human
form and gives rise to the motif of the *Doppelgänger*. A rich, old
businessman, Piachi has a second wife, Elvira, very much his
junior. There is little sign of happiness in their childless marriage,
and this is true also of the marriages disrupted by Lumb 2 in
Gaudete. The agent of disruption in Kleist is Nicolo, an orphan
picked up on a business trip to Ragusa. Dyer describes him as 'sex
incarnate'; he is the physical double of a Genoese nobleman,
Colino, who had chivalrously rescued Elvira from a fire during her
adolescence, becoming as a result Elvira's unshakable picture of a
sexless, virtuous masculinity. In her arrested inner development
she cannot accommodate anything that conflicts with the values
implicit in the portrait of Colino she hides in her bedroom and
worships.

Hughes' Main Narrative partly records the consequences of the
impossible task the women of the village face in trying to relate
the pictures of manhood presented by their husbands and by the
two Lumbs. But this broad similarity to Kleist masks important
differences. In *Gaudete* the two Lumbs are in the end parts of a

single man. The psychological changes Lumb undergoes in his two
personalities are a major focus of the narrative, giving him a
significance beyond what he would have if he were merely an
agent of disruption and revelation. In 'The Foundling' Nicolo and
Colino are separate men, not the two halves of a developing self.
Their interrelatedness is a matter not of their own inner evolution,
but of Elvira's; they are there so as to bring out her state of mind.
Kleist is focusing here, as in other stories, on the woman's
experience.

But to turn back from Kleist to Hughes is to notice the variety of
female response to Lumb and the insight with which Hughes
presents it. There is the easy-going acceptance Mrs Holroyd reflects
as she sunbathes:

> Closing her eyes
> Concentrating on the sun's weight against her cheek,
> She lets herself sink.
> Her own rosy private darkness embraces her.
> A softness, like a warm sea, undulating, lifts her,
> Like a slower, stronger heart, lifting her,
> A luxury
> Signalling to the looseness of her hips and vertebrae,
> Washing its heavy eerie pleasure
> Through her and through her.
>
> (p. 59)

Mrs Davies shows a similarly happy, sensuous experience of
Lumb 2. These two live in close connection with the land. Others,
more caught up in what Jefferies called 'the pettiness of house-
life', evoked in a succession of sterile domestic interiors, display
reactions more fraught. Dr Westlake's wife's mental crisis, as her
pregnancy forces her to consider suicide, is given in language the
opposite of that just quoted:

> She is gripped by the weird pathos of biochemistry, the hot
> silken frailties, the giant, gristled power, the archaic sea-fruit
> inside her, which her girdle bites into, which begins to make
> her suit too tight.
>
> She feels the finality of it all, and the nearness and greatness
> of death. Sea-burned, sandy cartilege, draughty stars, gull-cries
> from beyond the world's edge. She feels the moment of killing
> herself grow sweet and ripe, close and perfect.   (p. 39)

Lumb 2, in this, like Mr Weston's Good Wine in T. F. Powys's novel of the same name, actualises the pre-existing tendency within each woman. He has no developed human character of his own in the Main Narrative, and is often referred to as an 'absence', an undifferentiated Dionysos staring out of the blank sockets in what was a man's face.

Since it tells of Lumb 2's last day, when his entanglements are reaching a final pitch, the Main Narrative stresses the unhappy and destructive female response to him. In striking this note Hughes is in accord with Kleist. The sudden replacement of an inadequate and desexualised maleness by its opposite is seen in both as the unleashing of a primal energy to which the women cannot adjust. In *Gaudete* they are plunged by Lumb 2 into jealousy, despair, suicide and murder, numbness, the desire for escape and safety and vengeance. The same play of destructive power is found in Elvira's case. Refusing to make any connection between the chivalrous Colino and the lecherous Nicolo, despite their names and their physical resemblance, she has it none the less thrust on her when Nicolo dresses in the clothes Colino wore for his portrait and hides in Elvira's bedroom, behind the curtain which usually conceals the portrait itself. When he is revealed the shock is too great for her: she collapses and dies soon after.

With the menfolk there is a similar concurrence. They are dry and sterile; Piachi, Hagen and Estridge are older men, beyond fatherhood, senex figures in an aborted comic pattern. They hold life at arm's length, Hughes' men preferring to view it through telescopes or binoculars, seemingly unaware that there is a price to pay for the excess of peace and order in which they exist. Each has relegated his marriage or his inner life to a position of insignificance, repressing crucial energies which remain danger-ously cut off from the rest of the psyche. That these energies continue to seethe just under the surface is betrayed by the men's own bodies – Piachi's twitching upper lip, Hagen's nerve 'flickering' on his 'bleak skull' as he watches Lumb with his wife. Hughes spoke to Fass of the characters' bodies as emissaries from the spirit world; it is difficult to over-estimate the significance of gesture and posture here and in the *Moortown* sequences (see Chapter 5).

It is the intervention of the figure of energy, Nicolo or Lumb 2, which works the change in the men, breaking open the wall of suppression and catalysing a reversal of character which jolts them out of de-energised reasonableness so that they become revenge-crazed victims of irrational demonic possession. Like the women, the men are violated by the very energy they have excluded. In Kleist the enantiodromia often kills the men; in *Gaudete* they get off lighter. The irony of the close of 'The Foundling' is typical of Kleist. The story has shown us a man of reason who feels his code of orderly life threatened by an amoral energy-laden outsider; in order to remove this threat he has been compelled towards behaviour involving him in transgressions of his own code far more heinous than those he tries to remove; Piachi finishes in excess, not only murdering Nicolo but also persistently refusing absolution before his hanging so that he can engineer his own damnation and descent into hell, there to continue his vengeance on Nicolo.

The men in *Gaudete* go unpunished. But the Kleist pattern is still present. The quiet, separate lives of the husbands as we first meet them give way, thanks to Lumb 2's revelatory intervention, to the forming of a mob posse at the end of the day. And this sudden change generates the same kind of ironies as in Kleist. By cutting through the laws of monogamy which normally limit disruptive sexual activity, Lumb 2 threatens the energy-excluding system which the village is before his arrival. His threat is sexual, aimed at the most sensitive point in the defensive wall of law, convention and habit. The wall breaks, but without creative results. The men decide to remove the threat Lumb poses to them (not to their wives or daughters – none of them is capable of even the momentary suspension of selfishness which would allow him to ask for the woman's true feelings and needs). In killing Lumb 2 they break the founding principle of their rules by invoking and harnessing energies they would normally refuse to handle. Their meeting in the Bridge Inn at the end exactly parallels the Women's Institute meeting going on at the same time – both groups are seeking to generate a communal energy focused on Lumb. The men's actions in the closing hunt change Lumb 2 from the 'goat-eyed vicar', a figure of rampant natural vitality associated with Pan and Dionysos, to a scapegoat and an occasion for Maytime holiday licence. Only on expelling Lumb do the men come out from behind their cameras, telescopes and binoculars, to form a body.

An enormous range of materials may be adduced in trying to create an interpretative context for the Main Narrative and its characters. It helps to see Hagen as a descendant of 'The Retired Colonel' (in *Lupercal*), and a product of the slow repression of national energies depicted in 'The Warriors of the North' (in *Wodwo*), because to do so is to give him representative force, within Hughes' account of history, as a leftover of Britain's imperial past; and because his being something of a 'Mafeking stereotype' leads us not to expect the kind of rounding of character found in an orthodox novel. (It is part of Hughes' point that the men of the village are most of the time empty, flat stereotypes, and only fill out in moments of crisis such as Lumb provides, and even then in a way unconnected with richness of character). But there are other sources to which we are referred which seem not to offer even this kind of help; in sum, they take away assistance from the reader. We note, for instance, that in the *Nibelungenlied* Hagen's namesake enacts a hero-slaying parallel to the slaying of Lumb 2. The connections between Siegfried and Lumb, centring on their sharing the scapegoat role, feed backwards into those between Lumb and Dionysos (both as he appears in *The Bacchae* and as sacrificed consort of the Frazerian fertility goddess), and forwards into those between Lumb and the May King or Jack o' the Green of more recent folk custom. All of this finds specific echoes in the Main Narrative, but the very welter of associations and resonances thrown up defeats the interpretative effort. We meet the same pattern of action – that of an energy-laden outsider visiting a community from which he is then ceremonially expelled – in so many guises that we despair of ever assigning to it a particular significance. It is an eternally recurrent drama, which René Girard explores in *Violence and the Sacred*, seeing it as a paradigm independent of cultural or historical context and of personal psychology. Speaking of the communal will to expel the outsider he says,

> Each member's hostility, caused by clashing against others, becomes converted from an individual feeling to a communal force unanimously directed against a single individual. The slightest hint, the most groundless accusation, can circulate with vertiginous speed and is transformed into irrefutable proof. The corporate sense of conviction snowballs, each member taking confidence from his neighbor by a rapid process of mimesis. The firm conviction of the group is based on no other evidence than the unshakable unanimity of its own illogic. (p. 79)

Girard's formula for the displacement of violent energy is reflected in the Main Narrative of *Gaudete*. The first hint that this will happen comes with Hagen's killing of his dog: he 'Swerves the full momentum of his rage on to the dog. / He lifts the chair. / This dog is going to account for everything' (p. 35). Later it is Lumb who takes the dog's place: 'Now Lumb will somehow pay for everything' (p. 143). 'Everything' is both intense personal repression and British decline. The absence of a need for evidence which Girard mentions is pervasive, but perhaps clearest in Dr Westlake's re-enaction of an episode from Tolstoy's 'Kreutzer Sonata'; creeping up on Lumb 2 and his wife he finds nothing to support the suspicions he entertains, which nevertheless persist:

> In one flash Westlake understands
> That his accurate intuition
> Has been forestalled and befooled
> By this goat-eyed vicar.
> In spite of what it looks like
> Something quite different is going on here,
> Even under his very eyes,
> And if he could only see clear . . .
> It would be plain
> That her writhing and cries are actually sexual spasm . . . .
> (p. 75)

This scene is to be balanced (or is it cancelled?) in a way typical of the teasing symmetry of *Gaudete*, by that involving Dunworth, titled 'Westlake's grey Daimler' (p. 84). The opening phrase of the passage just quoted reminds us how Garten's photograph of Lumb 2 (itself, in making a specific moment general and permanent, a falsification) becomes progressively more irrelevant to the unanimity of purpose generated at the close of the Main Narrative in accord with the overall pattern of the action.

In using this pattern, both Kleist and Hughes are concerned to create a movement away from the familiar and well-signposted territory of morals and the orthodox character-descriptive vocabulary, towards the more difficult and less well-signposted territory of pre-moral and archetypal cultural patternings. The reader becomes confused and tentative, feeling that his 'right' to judge the people and events in front of him is being denied. Hughes and Kleist want their readers to share, in as deep a way as the experience of reading will allow, some equivalent of the testing to destruction of a system of values which their heroes and heroines undergo. This is the preparatory phase of the imaginative rite of passage both authors put their readers through.

To use this anthropological term here may seem fanciful. But if we bring to mind the psychological crisis which all rites of passage re-enact, birth itself, and then recall once more Hughes' description of the effect he and Kleist aim at, we may see that, in speaking of 'pushing the reader through some kind of tunnel', and 'a great driving force meeting solid resistance', it is the birth process he has in mind, the trauma of loss of attachment and gaining of new independence. Many primitive rites of passage work by calling up in the candidate's mind deep memories of the birth process, making him almost literally die to the old life and be born to the new; the cave paintings of southern France, for instance, were probably approached by long, dark, narrow tunnels for just this reason. For Hughes and Kleist the equivalent process must be created through the twin effects of impetus and inertia in their sentences.

It is comparatively easy to point out the elements of plot which test and destroy the old values, but more difficult to say what replaces them, for the affirmations towards which Hughes and Kleist are working remain implicit. They seek not to replace one system of values with another, but instead to change the reader's sense of the value of all values. They are writing against an absolute and unshakable attachment to any set of values, against the treating of values as though they were part of the data of existence. It is this hubris which produces the energy-excluding rigidity of outlook both seek to undermine. Implicit in their work is the notion that a maturer stance is a strong and open nakedness in which the self, remaining flexible and attuned, is not left to rest exclusively on fixed human values. The *Gaudete* Main Narrative destroys for us the shell of such a system of values.

By the close of their narratives both Nicolo and Lumb have become cut off as scapegoats. This is the mark of their failure as agents of revelation for the other characters: Piachi and Elvira and the men and women of *Gaudete* do not learn from Nicolo and Lumb 2 that they are disastrously excluding from their lives all their deepest energies. The agent of revelation comes into being as an independent entity, taking upon himself a name and a body, only because the energies he represents have been denied; Lumb 2 is the outgrowth of the denial he struggles against, for the mentality which is the sickness of the Hagens and Estridges has first been

found, in extreme form, in the vicar himself. As a last-ditch attempt
at curing this sickness, undoing the denial and righting the balance
of the psyche, the taking of an independent existence is a failure,
because it becomes counter productive by providing the other
characters with an object onto which they can foist all the hatred
and fear generated by their sickness. The close of the Main
Narrative is intensely ironical in this regard (it is an irony quite
unlike that Hughes rejected at the start of his career). A figure
who might be seen as coming into the world to redress the psychic
balance within the individual and within the community leaves it,
having succeeded only in becoming a scapegoat who takes upon
himself and takes away all those pressures which tend towards
the destruction of the *status quo* he sought to change. In short, he
absolves, redeems and reinforces what he came to sweep away.
His rule-breaking example incites others to preserve the rules by
driving him out in a bout of rule-breaking for which he can take
all the blame.

But this failure is such in the world of the narrative only. The
effect on the reader is something different: Lumb 2's death cancels
any expectations we might have for the world of the village; society
there will not be reinvigorated. Instead, the reader is thrown back
on his own inner life; he is prepared for the poems of the Epilogue.
Though Hughes is nothing if not post-Christian, he still shares
with Kleist the Romantic concern with the reversal of the Fall. The
maze-like darkness at the start of each Kleist story, and the
wasteland vision in the Prologue of *Gaudete*, represent our fallen-
ness, which the two writers seek to purge away before creating
something better. Hughes has avoided the temptation of picturing
for us a restored society by bringing the Main Narrative to a close
at the point he chooses and switching modes, for the Epilogue, to
that of the short hymn or prayer; given the problematic nature of
endings in Romantic literature of this kind, this must be counted
one of his most important strategic discoveries. That so many
Romantic epics remain unfinished testifies to the difficulty of
finding a satisfactory answer to the question: how can a terminus
be posited, when the forces being celebrated are incessantly
dynamic? Hughes, in making the field of his myth internal and
psychological, and in tactically abandoning narrative, is rare in
having found an answer.

To see the death of Lumb 2 as purely pessimistic is to ignore the
Epilogue poems, which are integral to the intended effect of the

book. These pieces recognise that the first step in the reversal of the Fall is to be taken in the psyche of the individual, and not at the social or political level. They recognise also that the picturing of ends is self-defeating, since it belongs to the overweening desire to have things known and explicit which runs contrary to the finest values of tentativeness and unceasing flexibility implicit in Hughes' best work. Hughes, like Kleist, withdraws himself from his text, refusing us interpretative assistance, so that the Main Narrative may provide the reader with a stripping-away of attachments and commitments and thus disturb him into openness to the Epilogue.

It is in this light, as radically and deliberately ambivalent, that we must see the Hairy Hands episode and the rest of the Main Narrative. Immediately Lumb recovers from his crash the baboon-woman vision fades: 'already there is nobody. . . . His van sits empty, the doors wide open, as if parked for a picnic'. We are prevented from arriving at any final opinion as to the status of the vision.

III

The Epilogue begins with a picture of the returned Lumb on the west coast of Ireland, like the Wandering Jew or the Ancient Mariner henceforth condemned or blessed to carry the burden of his experience on the fringes of society. He is the most important of Hughes' tramp figures, both casualty and survivor, leaving his message to strike sparks where it may. The poems which embody his struggle towards recovery are hymns and prayers of extraordinary spiritual honesty and intensity. Taken alone or as a group they are remarkable enough; as part of the complete structure of *Gaudete* they represent Hughes' furthest penetration as a religious poet.

Their keynote is humbleness, both in their mood of total subjection to the goddess (the very opposite of the proud, rational humanism Hughes has always attacked), and in their brevity and stylistic simplicity. The latter places special demands on the reader, who must lay aside criteria of linguistic complexity and richness, and follow Hughes in his search for the clear and simple which has jettisoned pretence and which uses words only in vigilant awareness of their tendency to corrupt and deceive. Birdsong and animal cries are the goddess's 'congregations at their rapture', but

Words buckle the voice in tighter, closer
Under the midriff
Till the cry rots, and speech

Is a fistula

Eking and deferring
Like a stupid or a crafty doctor
With his year after year

Of sanguinary nostrums
Of almosts and their tomorrows

Through a lifetime of fees.

(p. 176)

Peter Brook, interviewed by A. C. H. Smith in *Orghast at Persepolis*, took what seems to be a similar view: 'the history of speech has been a withering-away of plenitude, a gradual shrivelling of the entire pianoforte down to a small, thin range of tones' (p. 249). This withering is a cutting-off from the source, so that language ceases to be the holy house of Being, in Heidegger's phrase, through which approach to the mystery must be made, and becomes instead a cheating circuit of interdependent signs closed against reality; Hughes' fistula metaphor, generating the doctor simile, makes speech a system of self-deception – the doctor and his patient are one, and the fees, if paid, come from his own pocket. The Epilogue poems try to open the circuit once more, not by adding new poetic music to words but by cutting them back until the real music which has lain hidden inside them can sound. When this happens they become again an undebased currency and the means by which Lumb, as he himself announces, can make his pain negotiable:

Pain is hardest of all.
It cannot really be given.

It can only be paid down
Equal, exactly,
To what can be no part of falsehood.

This payment is that purchase.

(*Gaudete*, p. 192)

A poem which represents this music particularly clearly is the following:

> The sea grieves all night long.
> The wall is past groaning.
> The field has given up –
> It can't care any more.
>
> Even the tree
> Waits like an old man
> Who has seen his whole family murdered.
>
> Horrible world
>
> Where I let in again –
> As if for the first time –
> The untouched joy.

(p. 194)

After its only completely unstressed syllable, setting off as though brightly, the first line is instantly dragged back by the weight of all that follows. 'Sea' is mimetic in an orthodox way, the *s* sound corresponding to the hiss of waves and spray which we connect with tears or sobs. In the repeated vowel sound, deep and heavy, in the second and third words, we have the swaying of the whole body of water, and an equivalent for the weight and (in the repetition) unalteringness of the emotion; 'grieves' is not stopped-off as 'past' is to be in the next line – the *v* and *s* sounds do not carry within themselves the idea of termination, but instead lead into the second half of the line, which, though also heavily stressed, is as different as might be, a separate rhythmic unit, at one remove from the physical reality of the first half. The second line begins, like the third, with an iambic exactly equal to that in the same position in the first line – the repetition enforces the sameness of the conditions suffered by all components of the scene. 'Is past' echoes the double *s* of the sea in the first half of the first line, but the new *t* sound shuts this off; something, having mounted and persisted, is coming to an end, giving way. The *gr* of 'groaning' (part of the pattern of *g* sounds which further unites all the sufferers in the first three lines) is the syllable which meant devouring, turmoil, destruction in *Orghast*, and deepens the word's person- ification of the wall back into the physical roots of universal suffering. The third line is run-on (the dash joins more than separates) to indicate the collapse of a previous barrier; it quickens and lightens, so that the contrast between the final three syllables here and those in the previous lines is immense – something has snapped, the words no longer try to hold the weight their predecessors clung to. The roughness of the alliteration at the start of the fourth line, together with its drawing on the colloquial, brings the momentary intensity of abandon of a domestic crisis into the poem. 'Any more' is a single rhythmic unit, emphatic by virtue of the contrast in weight between its closing syllable and the other two; it is an ultimatum, a final announcement. The poem's pushing towards an extremity of insupportable suffering is now, however, to be subjected to a twist. 'Even the tree' seems to be just adding another victim to the list, a line which can be left short because familiarity with what has gone before will allow us to finish it for ourselves. But this is not to be the case. The perfectly timed delay of the line-break, together with the poem's first use of a stressed syllable to start a line, throws tremendous emphasis onto 'Waits', with its message that there can be no giving-up or ceasing to care or escape. This is the final intensification of pain in the poem; from here on, its music contains an element to offset the suffering by distancing it. Despite its surface meaning, the simile of the old man already begins to offer this; and, as we reach 'Horrible world', the new element is unmistakable. This short, isolated line is the axis on which the poem turns, a bald statement of what things come down to, the recognition that must be made before the last three lines can be brought out; but, even as it makes this shuddering exclamation, the line is already placing and withdrawing from the physical reality which generated it earlier: 'horrible' is physically weightless, and, just as we saw no blood and heard no cries in the music of the line about murders, so here we find a summary and generalisation which is making possible the very different music of the last section. The heart of the third- last line is 'let in', different in sound from anything found earlier, already delicately speeding and lifting into elation, a mood which is strengthened, as the paradox of freshness and sameness is brought home, by the catching of the breath, in the excitement of epiphany, at the *f* sounds in the penultimate line. The last line, what it speaks of made more special by having been delayed a line, has to balance the whole of the suffering offered in the first section of the poem, and does so not with an answering weight but with ineffable delicacy: the *t* in 'untouched' is given, by the sounds around it, a lightness which, the music guarantees, cannot have been touched by 'grieves' and 'groaning'; and 'joy', a marvellous word to end on, a spreading peal of delight, offers no connection with any other sound in the poem, maximising its virgin separateness even as the poem tells us of its emergence in the only world there is, the world of pain.

Lumb's humbleness or dubiety about the medium in which he writes brings with it a sharp sense of purpose and an enlivening awareness of limitations. His humbleness about his own experience is similarly double in import; what strikes us at first as hopeless or defeatist soon reveals itself as possessing latent strength and drive. The first poem in the Epilogue causes us initially to pause and re-examine our sense of a movement from a moribund Christianity to a neo-pagan renaissance; it seems to be about loss and error, not the founding of a new age:

> What will you make of half a man
> Half a face
> A ripped edge
>
> His one-eyed waking
> Is the shorn sleep of aftermath
>
> His vigour
> The bone-deformity of consequences
>
> His talents
> The deprivations of escape
>
> How will you correct
> The veteran of negatives
> And the survivor of cease?
>   (*Gaudete* p. 176)

Like many Epilogue poems, this refers us backwards, exposing the events and motifs of the Main Narrative to still and silent contemplation. Its sense of loss is balanced by an absence of false hopes or an inappropriate self-reliance on Lumb's part. It belongs, in fact, to a phase after the death of the ego, when everything that ought to be has been placed in the hands of the goddess. And the word 'veteran' (a term Hughes has preserved from his earliest work, but with altered import), whilst suggesting here a long continuance in error, also connotes a toughness and nous which can, in her service, be turned to account.

These poems are typical of the closing phases of Hughes' major sequences; we shall see in looking at 'Prometheus on his Crag' and 'Seven Dungeon Songs' that Hughes' affirmations, his gains and victories, are never matters of irresponsible celebration – part of his spiritual honesty is the circumspection and checked nature of his conclusions.

Another poem helps us delineate Lumb's development, and also brings us closer to the central figure of the goddess:

> I watched a wise beetle
> Walking about inside my body
>
> I saw a tree
> Grow inward from my navel
>
> Hawks clashed their courtship
> Between my ears.
>
> Slowly I filled up with the whole world.
> Only one thing stayed outside me, in the glare.
>
> You beckoned.
>
> (p. 179)

The Epilogue poems may seem the product of a painful striving towards union. This poem seems initially to record a failure to unite with the goddess; she resists incorporation. But it is this very independence of hers which marks Lumb's progress. She is the life force, both inner and outer, and as such is both incarnate in her creatures and transcendent of them – when one dies she moves elsewhere and is eternal; she is Being, which cannot exist without beings, but which is not tied to any one of them. It is this aspect of her which we meet here for the first time, and which allows her to elude Lumb and remain separate from him. In the Main

Narrative, Lumb 2 is a man who, because he has refused the path of introspective self-development, is inundated at the instinctual level by the life force he has sought to close out. He is possessed by primal energy and helpless in his total identification with it. This phase ends with his death, which becomes a major positive only because having two Lumbs allows it to appear as real but other than final, a transformation not an end. We move from Lumb *versus* Lumb, a man suffering the consequences of internal warfare, to Lumb and the goddess; being female she holds out the possibility of union (her beckoning) in a way that the male *Doppelgänger* never could. And, being newly other than Lumb, she is a sign of a sublimation which is a psychological advance. Jung writes in *Two Essays on Analytical Psychology*,

> The only person who escapes the grim law of enantiodromia is the man who knows how to separate himself from the unconscious, not by repressing it – for then it simply attacks him from the rear – but by putting it clearly before him as THAT WHICH HE IS NOT.   (p. 73)

To see the gains Lumb makes we need only turn back from the present poem to the scene beginning on p. 77 of *Gaudete* (chronologically it comes after the Prologue but before the events of the Main Narrative) in which the Lumbs fight over Felicity. In moving between these two phases we shift from male to female, from physical conflict to sensitive negotiation in words, and from inundation by the rejected life force to a yearning detachment from what is now worshipped as the only essential source of health, the goddess.

She is what the Greeks called *zoë*, which Kerenyi in *Dionysos* defines as 'life in general . . . the thread upon which every individual bios is strung like a bead, and which, in contrast to bios, can be conceived of only as ENDLESS . . . *zoë* does not admit of the experience of its own destruction: it is . . . infinite life' (pp. xxxii–xxxvi). Lumb speaks of individual entities as no more than 'the fleeting warm pressure/Of your footfall/As you pace/Your cage of freedom' (*Gaudete*, p. 195). The goddess, by being both immanent and transcendent, gives rise to the tension of opposites on which the Epilogue poems are founded, and thus also to the language of paradox in which many are couched. In the wider body of recent nature poetry outside *Gaudete* it provides

Hughes with one of his recurrent ways of placing individual deaths in a salvatory context; and through this acceptance of natural processes it allows him to forge new links between man and a nature now insistently feminised and personified.

And for Lumb it means that the goddess, the only goal, must remain unattainable: 'Who is this?/She reveals herself, and is veiled.' Heidegger voices the same joint presence and absence when he speaks of Parmenides' goddess of truth, Aletheia, as the unconcealedness of beings which is simultaneously still a concealedness, or when he regards the vast emptiness of the sky as the proof of the god's existence. Except tacitly and vicariously, in the act of writing the poems which invoke her, Lumb cannot take her power to himself. Even when a poem does seem to portray a newly heroic self, it undercuts this incipient sacrilege:

> The steel man, in his fluttering purples,
> Is lifted from the mould's fragments.
>
> I breathe on him
>
> Terrors race over his skin.
>
> He almost lives
>
> Who dare meet you.
> (pp. 196–7)

The steel man is the hero whose creation would 'Put out the sun', but the word 'almost' prevents this, and our sense of Lumb's inner development remains qualified in a way which will be paralleled in the closing poems of *Cave Birds*. The *Gaudete* Epilogue stays true to its sense of grace as a yearning after painful epiphanies of an Other so intense and all-inclusive as to be essential and yet also unencompassable:

> Every day the world gets simply
> Bigger and bigger
>
> And smaller and smaller
>
> Every day the world gets more

And more beautiful

And uglier and uglier.

Your comings get closer.
Your goings get worse.
(pp. 198–9)

This is perhaps the furthest point on Hughes' journey towards the kind of all-inclusive simplicity and clarity that lies on the far side of experience.

4

Cave Birds: The Background and a Reading

'But I'm not guilty,' said K. 'It's a mistake. How can a person be guilty? Surely we are all human beings here, one like the other.'
  'That is right,' said the priest, 'but that is the way the guilty are wont to talk.'

(Kafka, *The Trial*)

Cave Birds: An Alchemical Cave Drama (1978) is a work of collaboration between Hughes and Leonard Baskin, with twenty-nine poems, all but one accompanied by drawings of birds or bird-like beings. It is a much revised and extended version of a limited edition published three years previously and broadcast on radio in June 1975.

In the Note to his *Selected Poems 1957–1981* Hughes says, 'the poems plot the course of a symbolic drama, concerning disintegration and re-integration, with contrapuntal roles played by birds and humans'. The story is about a modern Everyman, a representative product of Western civilisation, first met as he is suffering a psychological crisis, brought about by a long mounting of inner pressures. He soon senses that something is amiss, but cannot understand what, or how it has come about. Answers slowly appear as the sequence develops. Through the cracks in the broken surface of his mind we peer down into the depths of his psyche and witness the dealings and manoeuvres of the large forces of human nature, represented by Baskin's birds, as they resolve the protagonist's fate. The life he has led to date constitutes a crime, for which he is now to be tried. He has murdered a nameless female figure – not in a single act sometime in the past, but day by day, continuously, by means of his way of living. In court he makes the mistake of repeating the crime during his defence. He is found guilty and sentenced to death. What seems his last act is a confession. He has been brought to recognise his guilt and is prepared to pay the price.

95

His execution has surprising results. Rather than just dying, he sets out on a journey. He is in a remote, wild underworld ruled by giant eagles who eventually pick him up and take him off to suffer a second trial. This time the verdict is more favourable. His adventures have brought him through to a new state of nascent inner harmony and attunement. As a result he is able to move forward into a final phase in which he undoes his crimes. He and the nameless female reconstitute each other. The sequence is crowned by marriage and the hero's rebirth as a divine falcon.

Many readers of *Cave Birds* would quarrel with that summary of the plot. This would be partly because it glosses over certain problems, faced in the subsequent commentary. But it would also be because *Cave Birds* does not actually tell its story. The plot is fully implied; the poems guide each reader to his own reconstruction of it.

Cave Birds is in this respect an advance on *Crow*, where the story is substantially absent, and also in its being worked to completion, as the *Crow* story is not (the poems as we have them corresponding to only about a third of the intended epic). The dramatic form adopted for *Cave Birds* brings other gains. Hughes is able to make fuller use than ever before in his poetry of the spoken voice. The speeches of the protagonist in the early part of the sequence make such marvellously apt and exact use of the tones and rhythms of our own speech that they implicate us in proceedings and generate the weight of a definitive judgement on our habits of mind. And when, later, the bird-beings begin to speak, addressing themselves to a 'you' both protagonist and reader, their words have a directness and finality that is wholly compelling.

This dramatic force is enhanced by the presence at various points of poems drawing us back out of the bird realm and into the recognisable world of standard domestic interiors. A parallel alternation of settings operates in *Gaudete*. In both books it creates an uncanny power, insisting on the interpenetration of the two realms, and forcing us towards an abandonment of the collective amnesia which imprisons us in acknowledgement of only the mundane and quotidian. Hughes himself invites us to see this with his word 'contrapuntal' – the two elements seem separate but are essentially parts of a single piece of music.

That Hughes should pick on a musical term is significant in other ways. *Cave Birds* is a drama, but also a poem sequence, and its success stems in part from its adopting a poetic mode of development for which music provides the appropriate metaphor. We have seen Hughes' experiments in the mid-1960s with radio plays and short stories as a struggle to find a way appropriate for saying what could not be conveyed so well by the short lyric poem characteristic of his first two volumes. This is partly a move towards narrative (which he had used with verve as a schoolboy poet). As such, it is only a qualified success in the period of *Wodwo* and *Crow*, and has to wait for *Gaudete* for its vindication. But the same struggle has also thrown up an alternative mode which is to be employed not only in *Cave Birds* but also in the other sequences of the 1970s, notably 'Prometheus on his Crag', 'Seven Dungeon Songs', and 'Adam and the Sacred Nine'. In the place of an explicit narrative we meet the establishment of a core of key symbols and images, followed, poem by poem with their progressive interweaving and development, as the musical argument unfolds, so that each use of a motif carries the resonances of its appearances elsewhere. In all these sequences Hughes manages this procedure with minute care and precision even when working under the exigencies of collaboration.

Since *Cave Birds* is perhaps the most ambitious of the sequences, and its core of symbols and images the most complex Hughes has worked with in this line of writing, commentary may be usefully prefaced by an examination of their origins, and of the themes and patterns with which they are associated.

A start can be made by relating *Cave Birds* to some of Hughes' other works. Three motifs stand out: the idea of a crime and a trial; the disintegration of the criminal and his reintegration; and a divorce between male and female leading to a search for rapprochement which culminates in marriage. Hints of these motifs are apparent in the radio plays previously examined and in *Eat Crow*, published in 1971, but written in 1964, in which, question by question, the prosecution brings the defendant, a Mr Morgan, to the realisation that what he thinks of as himself is really only a tiny portion of the life in him. His inability to carry out a series of bodily functions at will, or to remember at command precise details of his past, remind him of the existence of what Heidegger calls 'the beyond me in me'. Morgan's crime may be the simple fact of existence, or some crucial unawareness, or both. The crime in *Cave Birds* is similarly multiple.

Eat Crow also reflects the negative phases of the next two *Cave Birds* motifs. The prosecution's consistent probing forces Morgan into a disintegration of personality, and his mind is supplanted by a number of other identities, including Morgantwo and Morgan Producer. Simultaneously, we notice a new presence of moaning and lamenting females. Events reach a noisy and dissonant climax. There is then a long pause before a calmer concluding exchange between Morgan and 'She'. There is nothing, however, which might be seen as equivalent to the *Cave Birds* reintegration and marriage. *Eat Crow*, like the radio plays of the early 1960s with which it belongs, is not of itself an entirely successful work; its later phases are obscure and centrifugal, and we need the light cast by *Cave Birds* to help in their interpretation.

Other works also reflect one or more of these leading motifs. We recognise links between *Cave Birds* and the single adventure of *Wodwo* – especially, perhaps, in the visit to the underworld made by Ripley in *The Wound*. We recognise similarities too in Crow's various crimes or errors, and in his search to come to terms with his mother. Prometheus' struggle to fit himself to the pain brought by the vulture is the same story used to explore yet other facets of experience. And the two trials in *Cave Birds* correspond to the two phases of the *Orghast* mythology. The first trial, during which the protagonist persists in his crime, corresponds to the false heroism of Agoluz, a Hercules figure; whilst the second, in which he submits and readies himself for reunion and rebirth, corresponds to the true heroism of Sogis. But the most important links are with *Gaudete*. After the psychological collapse in the Prologue, most of *Gaudete* is devoted to the career of the substitute Lumb. The original is away on a mission in the underworld to try to heal a sick or wounded female figure. What we learn of this healing mission comes in a few visionary episodes robbed of certainty by their context. *Cave Birds* can be thought of as giving us a fuller account, so that the stories of the two works become the complementary halves of Hughes' imaginative ground plan, each with a tone and procedure suited to its chosen territory.

That ground plan is at once quintessentially Hughesian and an age-old expression of the human condition, the roots of which extend far beyond the mainstream of the Western literary tradition. An account of the background to *Cave Birds* necessarily runs back into primitive and occult materials.

I

Perhaps the most primitive reflection of the pattern and imagery
of *Cave Birds* comes in shamanism. A shaman may be called to his
craft by a sickness which brings to an end his participation in the
ordinary life of his community. He may then have a series of big
dreams: 'the same dreams all over the world. A spirit summons
him . . . usually an animal or a woman. . . . At the simplest these
dreams are no more than the vision of an eagle . . . or a beautiful
woman (who marries the shaman).' But they may also involve 'a
magical death, then dismemberment, by a demon or equivalent
powers, with all possible variants of boiling, devouring, burning,
stripping to the bones. From this nadir, the shaman is resurrected
with new insides, a new body created for him by the spirits.' As
we saw in 'The Bear', the shaman's initiatory magic death may
come as part of a perilous journey to the spirit world during which
he is guided by his animal or bird familiar. This first journey
becomes the prototype of his later career as a healer: 'once fully
fledged he can enter trance at will and go to the spirit world . . .
to get . . . a cure, an answer, some sort of divine intervention in
the community's affairs'.

This brief account of shamanic initiation, using Hughes' own
words quoted by Michael Sweeting in *The Achievement of Ted Hughes*
(p. 71), gives us not only the basic pattern of *Cave Birds*, but also
many specific images and local echoes. We can link the initial
sickness to the protagonist's criminality. He is summoned to
transformation by a bird. And his magical death is described for
us in images which seem to owe something to each of the possible
variants Hughes lists: he is devoured by the Raven of Ravens; his
confession is a dismemberment, a stripping to the bone, and ends
with a burning-away of the inessentials. The perilous underworld
journey, the resurrection, the marriage – all have shamanic ana-
logues. Hughes' phrase 'fully fledged' recalls his description of the
end of *Cave Birds* in his Note to *Selected Poems 1957–1981*, where he
says that the hero is reborn as 'a falcon, the full-fledged emergence
of a Horus'.

This same description reminds us that the shamanic pattern was
taken up and used in the myths of less primitive cultures. For *Cave
Birds* the most important of these is the Egyptian myth of Isis and
Osiris and their son, one of the two Horuses, the other being the
god of Edfu who was represented as a falcon and a winged sun

disk; the Egyptians themselves often conflated the two, and Hughes follows suit, so that his risen hero is both the product of a process of resurrection and a divine sun falcon. The myth displays many shamanic elements which are to make their way into Hughes' sequence. The pattern of dismemberment or disintegration followed by a searching journey and then a triumphant reintegration is the most obvious. But there are others which the myth makes more prominent than does the shamanic material: chiefly, the motif of a divorce between male and female and its rectification, but also the incest theme (Osiris and Isis are brother and sister and man and wife) which is germane to 'A Riddle' in *Cave Birds*.

Because Osiris is the god who dies and is resurrected, he becomes the focus of the hopes of ancient Egyptians for an after-life, and his myth becomes the model for a set of rituals designed to help the deceased towards rebirth in heaven. These rituals are themselves reflected quite directly in *Cave Birds*, and have the added importance of lying at the back of the most important of the alchemical texts on which Hughes draws.

What is absent from the Frazerian fertility myths with which the Osiris story belongs (as also from shamanic initiation) is any sense of guilt on the part of the dismembered male; the shaman suffers because that is the path to power, Osiris because of the wickedness of Seth. But in Jung the myths furnish a model of psychological growth towards maturity, and the Osiris figure becomes the guilty one, the error which must give itself up for growth to come about. The male in the pattern is associated with the unredeemed ego, and with a one-sided development of the conscious mind which threatens to suppress and dominate other necessary faculties of the psyche. In principle the one-sided ego can be occupied by an excess of any faculty. In practice, the Romantic diagnosis, with which we are here concerned, has been that the characteristic crime has been Urizenic, the tyranny of the intellect, the rational hubris of which Hughes spoke in his *London Magazine* interview.

Heidegger, like Robert Graves, traces rational hubris ('the most stiff-necked adversary of thought') to its roots in Socrates and the Platonic Idea, which inaugurates the sundering of truth from being, from what is. It is in the light of this analysis of the development of Western thought that we must view *Cave Birds* and the use it makes of the various primitive and mythological motifs identified. Hughes' subtitle was at one time to have been 'The Death of Socrates and his Resurrection in Egypt', and what this emphasises –

the sequence as a dramatic exposé of the errors of abstraction, followed by their correction – remains very much part of the published work, which borrows from the dialogues where Plato describes Socrates' death the hemlock and its steady filling of his body, and which may be viewed as inviting us to take new note of other events in his last days, particularly the recurrence Socrates suffers whilst imprisoned of his lifelong dream calling him to 'practise and cultivate the arts'. Of this dream he says in *Phaedo* 60e–61,

> I used to think that it was impelling and exhorting me to do what I was actually doing . . . because philosophy is the greatest of the arts, and I was practising it. But ever since my trial, while the festival of the god has been delaying my execution, I have felt that perhaps it might be this popular form of art that the dream intended me to practise, in which case I ought to practise it and not disobey. I thought it would be safer not to take my departure before I had cleared my conscience by writing poetry.

Socrates has been brought to the brink of a complete reappraisal of his life effort here. But finally he turns away. The few poems he produces are a hedging of bets, a sop, and he continues on towards a death whose perverse grandeur lies in its being of a piece with the rest of his career. His last hours are spent with his closest disciples, engaged in a last bout of dialectic. Even his closing call for a cock to be sacrificed is a rationalist's characteristically world- and life-denying jest: Asclepius is the god of healing, and a cock the appropriate sacrifice to thank him for recovery; life is a disease for which death is the cure – those left behind ought to arrange the correct gesture.

Hughes gives Socrates a second chance. The 'gloriously beautiful woman dressed in white robes' of whom he also dreamed whilst imprisoned, becomes in *Cave Birds* the overriding female presence bent on ultimate healing. Hughes makes Socrates himself the cock which has to be sacrificed for this to be achieved. And his protagonist takes on the Egyptian underworld journey Socrates speculates about but in essence refuses.

II

When he died, an ancient Egyptian of sufficient rank was

mummified, equipped with amulets and passwords and then undertook the hazardous journey to the underworld, the kingdom of the dead. After an act of obeisance at the threshold, he was escorted by Horus into the Hall of Judgement (sometimes called the Hall of Double Justice), at one end of which sat Osiris, his chief judge. Nearby stood weighing scales flanked by Maat, the goddess of cosmic justice, on one side, and Amemait waiting on the other to devour him should he fail his trials. Forty-two subsidiary judges were in attendance, each concerned with a special area of conduct. The dead man spoke to these in turn, claiming freedom from transgression of the relevant laws. This was the first trial, the Negative Confession. In the second, his heart was weighed in the scales against Maat, or a feather representing her. Provided the pans balanced, the verdict was favourable. Osiris released him to a happy after-life.

The second phase of *Cave Birds*, where the protagonist is picked up by the eagles and weighed in their balance, being judged for both his vices and his virtues, before it is decided that he is worthy of resurrection, follows this pattern and makes use of the attendant imagery: besides the journey metaphor, we have the notion of two possible outcomes, in Baskin's two-headed gatekeeper and in the closing lines of the accompanying poem; and the next poem, 'A flayed crow in the hall of judgment' borrows the Egyptian setting, the weighing scales with their drifting up and down before settling, and the feather of Maat too. The importance of this resurrection ritual is much extended through its being taken up in an alchemical text to which Hughes' sequence refers.

The metallurgical aspect of alchemy, with its progressive refinement of gross or 'corrupt' metals into pure gold, provides some of the imagery for *Cave Birds*, especially in 'The accused' (where we have a reduction by heating which produces 'ore' and 'clinker'), in 'The baptist' (where we meet a dissolving) and in the further heating of the closing poems; but it is as a spiritual discipline, a self-making, that alchemy assumes its deepest relevance. Jung, who assigns inner significance of this kind to the procedures of the adepts, picks out three of the colour phases (corresponding to night, daybreak and dawn) as particularly important: nigredo, albedo and rubedo. The nigredo may be present from the start, or need achieving through a death. In *Cave Birds* the latter is the case and we are some way into the sequence before we meet the Executioner, who fills both Baskin's page and Hughes' protagonist with a blackness which answers to this alchemical phase.

> From this the washing (*ablutio, baptisma*) either leads direct to the whitening (*albedo*), or else the soul (*anima*) released at the 'death' is reunited with the dead body and brings about its resurrection, or again the 'many colours' (*omnes colores*), or 'peacock's tail' (*cauda pavonis*), lead to the one white colour that contains all colours. At this point the first main goal of the process is reached, namely the *albedo* . . . highly prized by many alchemists as if it were the ultimate goal. It is the silver or moon condition, which still has to be raised to the sun condition. The *albedo* is, so to speak, the daybreak, but not till the *rubedo* is it sunrise. . . . The *rubedo* then follows direct from the *albedo* as the result of raising the heat of the fire to its highest intensity. The red and white are King and Queen, who may also celebrate their 'chymical wedding' at this stage.
>
> (Jung, *Psychology and Alchemy*, pp. 231–2)

This gives us some motifs already noted in other contexts: baptism, resurrection and marriage. And the sun symbolism here unites with that of Horus to create in *Cave Birds* a changing climate running through the sequence: we begin with the elements in harsh aspect, the land threatening and volcanic, water frozen and the sun angry; from this we pass into underworld darkness and to primitive, wild, uncharted landscapes where the elements run freely; in the closing phase the sun assumes benevolence and the hero, as he marries, moves into it for a remaking which answers to the alchemical rubedo.

Andreae's *The Chemical Wedding of Christian Rosencreutz*, described by Hughes as 'a crucial seminal work . . . a tribal dream', provides a further layer of alchemical reference in *Cave Birds*. It is a long story, told in seven days and two major phases. First, Rosencreutz recounts his invitation to a royal wedding and his adventures *en route*; then he describes the wedding. At first reading, it is difficult to connect Rosencreutz with the Jungian candidate for inner growth, or with Hughes' protagonist. He seems uninvolved in the transformations going on around him, no more than guest and witness. However, all guests have to undergo various tests of worthiness, and a preliminary weeding-out is announced; the royalty 'resolve without all let / A Wedding PURE to celebrate, / So then the Artists for to weigh, / SCALES shall be fix't th' ensuing day'

(*The Chemical Wedding*, vol. 2, p. 330). This human weighing, described at length, has much in common with both the Egyptian psychostasia and with the second trial in *Cave Birds*. It has the same double aspect, being concerned with both vices (chiefly pride) and virtues. And it has the same twin possible outcomes. Those who fail suffer punishments appropriate to their particular guilt, including stripping and hunting-out. Rosencreutz passes.

In its second phase the book becomes more directly alchemical. A prefatory drama tells of the abduction of the king's son's bride-to-be by the king of the Moors. She is rescued by the king, but wantonly puts herself again under the Moor's dominion. This time the king's son must go forth to fight the Moor for his bride's release. In doing so, he apparently suffers death, but eventually revives and his betrothed is released to him. The two of them appear together in their pomp.

Like *Cave Birds*, this drama has two stages: two abductions here, two trials in Hughes; and the second in each case ends happily and with marriage. In both works the relationship between the sexes is central, and the righting of it the mainspring of the action. The catalyst of the righting is a self-sacrificial act on the part of the male, a death which turns out not to be a death, but magical. A journey of rescue is important in both works too. A major difference must also be noted: in Hughes the guilt for the initial wrongness of relationship is shouldered by the male, in Andreae by the female in the form of her wantonness.

Now follows the 'chymical wedding' itself. Andreae offers a detailed account of the death of the king's son, his subsequent transformations, reintegration and marriage. His initial self-division, symbolised in both *Cave Birds* and the prefatory drama as the temporarily failed relationship between bride-to-be and groom, is now symbolised through multiplication or fracturing – the king's son becomes, in the wedding phase, six sovereigns who have their clothes changed from white to black and find themselves blindfolded in a room draped in black. They are then beheaded. The corresponding event in the prefatory drama is the death of the king's son, and, in *Cave Birds*, execution, possession by Raven.

In the prefatory drama there was a gap between the death of the king's son and his revival. Andreae now fills that, as Hughes does when his hero is in the underworld of the eagles. The bodies of the six sovereigns are ferried by sea to another castle. Since the sea is marvellous and has the power to mitigate and unite opposites, this journey is itself part of the transformation process. It finds its place in *Cave Birds* in 'First, the doubtful charts', where the protagonist has little sense of its importance, and again, in a clearly positive fashion, in 'The baptist'.

The wedding guests are soon to follow the dead sovereigns to the new castle; but first there is an episode of crucial significance. One of the striking features of the book is the strong feminine presence. Rosencreutz is summoned from his home by a woman and the royal castles he visits are peopled by functionaries who are often women; after his success in the weighing he becomes a knight of an order whose president is a woman. Now he is led down clandestinely into the depths of the castle to a sepulchre where a curtain is drawn aside to reveal the goddess Venus naked and asleep. In his *Alchemical Studies* Jung takes this as the central mystery of the work, a katabasis, a dangerous journey into the underworld to recognise afresh the importance of a pagan nature deity and all that she stands for, which has been forgotten or hidden in orthodox Christian symbology.

There are clues that Venus and Rosencreutz are to be more directly involved in the achieving of the final marriage than appears to be the case on first reading. Her chamber is lit by a carbuncle, a synonym for the lapis, the philosopher's stone. During the creation of the new king and queen, which is the marriage so far as we see it in Andreae, the homunculi are compared for beauty with Venus. And behind Venus's bed is a cryptogram on a tablet which translates as 'when the Tree . . . shall be quite melted down, then shall Lady Venus awake and be the Mother of a King' (*The Chemical Wedding*, vol. 2, p. 424). This last clue gives us what is not stated or portrayed, the sexual union which we know must have taken place when we learn near the end that the resurrected king recognises Rosencreutz as his father.

The katabasis, then, offers an insight close to what Hughes is developing more fully in *Cave Birds*: the notion that Christian–Socratic civilisation has suppressed an essential element in its life, an element subsumable under the name 'the feminine'. It is in pointing to this that Andreae's book is for Hughes 'seminal'.

The guests now journey by sea to the castle; their passage is described in more detail than that of the sovereigns, and in a way Hughes is to echo. The new castle is a huge Frankensteinian alchemical laboratory. Here, under female direction, the guests help carry out the opus. The bodies of the sovereigns are washed and dissolved, as Hughes' protagonist is in 'The baptist'. The liquor thus produced is heated, changes colour, and is then put into a globe hanging in the centre of the room. Polished windows reflect the sun onto the globe; the heat forms 'a lovely great snow-white Egg' as in 'A flayed crow' in *Cave Birds*. From this hatches a black bird which turns snow white then multi-coloured. Jung links it with the phoenix, though it is not the final resurrection, just an intermediate bird stage between two human stages – everything that occurs in *Cave Birds* in the eagle underworld, where the protagonist is in bird form, is similarly intermediate.

The bird is now burned, and the ashes are cleansed and made into a dough which is moulded into a homunculus and a homuncula. This corresponds to the gradual mutual reintegration of male and female in Hughes. Quotation will show both how close and how far we are from *Cave Birds*:

> this was our work, we were to *moisten the* Ashes with our fore-prepared *Water till* they became altogether like a very thin Dough. After which we set the matter over the Fire, till it was well *heated*, then we cast it thus hot as it was into two *little* forms or moulds, and so let it cool a little. . . . We having opened our little forms, there appeared two beautiful bright and almost *Transparent little* Images, the like to which Man's Eye never saw, a Male and a Female, each of them only *four* inches long; and that which most mightily surprised me, was, that they were not hard, but limber and fleshy, as other human Bodies, yet had they no Life: So that I do most assuredly believe that the Lady *Venus's* Image was also made after some such way. These Angelically fair Babes we first laid upon two little Sattin Cushonets, and beheld them a good while.
>
> (*The Chemical Wedding*, vol. 2, pp. 458–60)

These figures grow and are then revived by flames. They are placed in bed together, sleep, and wake astonished:

> This happened to them with very great amazement, for they imagined no other but that they had hitherto slept from the very hour in which they were beheaded. *Cupid*, after he had awaked them, and renewed their acquaintance one with another, stepped aside a little, and permitted them both somewhat better to *recruit* themselves. (p. 464)

This periphrasis is Andreae's only mention of the culminatory sexual union. With Hughes it blossoms into 'Bride and groom lie hidden'.

The review of background materials in myth, ritual, philosophy and alchemy provides support and guidance in the interpretation of a work which might otherwise, for many readers, prove alien and difficult of access. It is helpful, but not indispensable. The substance of *Cave Birds* is man, woman, nature, sun, moon, snow, darkness, burning, death, decay, the journey, the power of the bird of prey, the yearning for growth and union. No shaman, god, alchemist or philosopher is mentioned. What we meet is drawn direct from the common stock of human experience through the ages, and that we should have met these same symbols in contexts so diverse as those we have been considering suggests as much.

III

Cave Birds is not easy to subdivide; the hero and a few key symbols are ever-present. Its unity is strengthened by a feature we are to meet in all Hughes' sequences. His heroes' progress (never smooth, always by ebb and flow) is embodied in a succession of stages none of which can be designated wholly gain or wholly loss; the worst piece of escapist backsliding contains the seeds of future success, and the greatest triumph grows out of previous errors and does not exclude them in the future. The psyche is seen as dynamic, continuous. Nevertheless, I have divided the work for present purposes into three phases: the first ten poems follow the protagonist through his first trial to the completion of his execution; the next eleven take him on his journey to the kingdom of the eagles, through his second trial, his survival of temptation and into the celebration of his first marriage in 'The scapegoat'; the last eight see him resurrected and married a second way.

In the first poem ('The scream', p. 7) we overhear the man we are later to recognise as defendant and protagonist. He has just suffered a violent irruption of irrational fear and pain, and is at a complete loss to account for it. He thinks of himself as a sane, well-balanced personality, with an outlook that includes both universal sympathy and a capacity to see death and chance disasters as part of some cosmic pattern in which, in the long run, everything is for the best. The event which has so shockingly challenged this self-image comes in the last six lines. The poem, which begins with the expression of a cultivated and seemingly humane sensibility, ends with a drastic outburst of angry energy previously blocked. We are suddenly shifted from a mild today into a world of primitive, almost Aztec, ferocity. Like the defendant himself, the reader now has to go back over the opening lines and test out the philosophy they offer to see if it is genuine and adequate. What does the scream tell us about it?

In *The Achievement of Ted Hughes*, Graham Bradshaw argues that the defendant is 'an unusually sensitive, suffering man' (p. 221) and that his sympathy for other creatures is real. He sees the crime in *Cave Birds* as that sympathy: it is criminal because it threatens to subvert the will to live, the biological imperative we meet in Hughes' 'Hawk Roosting'. But another look at this first poem suggests that the crime is not the sympathy, but the fact that it is not real, not the deeply felt product of experience, but merely a glibly adopted pose. The *Cave Birds* protagonist must be linked with the Egg-Head, whose error is rational hubris. We saw earlier that, when Hughes wants to indicate the folly of the Egg-Head, he pictures it as immaturity, surrounding it with images of a cosy infantility. 'The scream' begins with just such an image, as part of the protagonist's claimed but unearned sense of the benevolence of the elements and natural processes:

> There was the sun on the wall – my childhood's
> Nursery picture. And there was my gravestone
> Which shared my dreams, and ate and drank with me happily.
>
> All day the hawk perfected its craftsmanship
> And even through the night the miracle persisted.
>
> Mountains lazed in their smoky camp.
> Worms in the ground were doing a good job.

The gravestone, as a symbol of the inalienable challenge of each man's death, is recurrent in Hughes' later poetry. In *Cave Birds* we are to meet it again in the two opening poems of the second phase, where the protagonist really achieves a coming to terms with what it implies, and this will reveal as bogus the friendship he claims here in the casual addition beginning 'And there was my gravestone'.

The clichés of these lines signal the shoulder-shrugging complacency of the rational mind in decay; at bottom they are evasive. The touches of the chattily colloquial show us a man not freshly and directly engaged with reality, unaware of the seriousness of his situation. And it is this unawareness which has produced both the shockingly unexpected uprush in the final lines, and his incapacity to deal with it.

We notice also that his sense of the benevolence of natural processes and of fate rests on what is soon to be revealed as the false notion that he, the protagonist, exists beyond them. All the disasters he lists happen to others, not to him: 'When I saw little rabbits with their heads crushed on roads / I knew I rode the wheel of the galaxy.' Later uses of the image of the wheel will undercut this claim to be riding on it instead of being within it and subject to its laws; the wheel is to become the spiral of intestine carried within, a permanent and intimate reminder of the protagonist's inevitable participation in the processes he is here really refusing to acknowledge. Beneath his claimed attunement and sensitivity we hear a coarse note of self-congratulation at his own supposed immunity:

> And the inane weights of iron
> That come suddenly crashing into people, out of nowhere,
> Only made me feel brave and creaturely.

He evinces a kind of mundane conscience which Heidegger, in *Being and Time*, sees as actually preventing the deeper call to Being made by existential–ontological conscience: 'This would be as if Dasein were a "household" whose indebtednesses simply need to be balanced off in an orderly manner so that the Self may stand "by" as a disinterested spectator while the Experiences run their course' (p. 340). The scream signals the end of all this, cancelling the protagonist's easy poise with a savage and involuntary venting of agony. His pseudo-philosophy has missed something out of account, some part of himself which now lets him feel its pain and anger. This sense of the unacknowledged and separate within him is developed in the second poem in *Cave Birds*, 'The summoner' (p. 8), which introduces us to the bird drama and to the idea that a trial is to be staged. It gives us our first sense that the protagonist's maladjustment is an unexpiated crime – the grip at the end is the summoner fetching him to court.

Perhaps the first thing we notice in this poem is how much more genuine is the presence of predation and death. The talk of the hawk's craftsmanship and the efficiency of the worms is replaced by the simple and immediate 'blood-eating', which stands out amongst the other abstract adjectives in the opening group: 'Spectral, gigantified, / Protozoic, blood-eating'. The others do more than provide a heightening contrast: they initiate a set of seemingly contradictory impressions which continue through the poem. Together with the very concrete biological aspect of the summoner goes a sense of ghostly insubstantiality; together with impressive and overwhelming hugeness goes microscopic smallness. The effect is to suggest a force present in all lives from the smallest and simplest upwards, but itself intangible. For the protagonist this paradoxical presence manifests itself as an oppressive, threatening power insistently at the fringe of, or just beyond, his apprehension:

> Among crinkling of oak-leaves – an effulgence,
> Occasionally glimpsed.

> Shadow stark on the wall, all night long,
> From the street-light. A sigh.

> Evidence, rinds and empties,
> That he also ate here.

Immediately after this passage the suggestion of ghostliness is switched from the summoner to the protagonist's own soul, which, it appears has been wandering about in the night and is now returning once more to join with its body. What it sees is part of the summoner, the physical foundation of the protagonist's continued existence, and this 'bronze image' is suddenly now menacing and disturbing, where in the first poem it 'slept in the sun's mercy', or so the protagonist's complacency made him claim.

None of the detailed personification of psychic contents which will people the drama subsequently has yet taken place. Appropriate to the protagonist's starting point, this poem creates a vague but intense terror. The references to out-of-the-body experiences and ghostliness are a necessary bridge to the bird-peopled underworld to follow. They create a sense of the fragmentariness and self-division which is the reality of the protagonist's being at this time, and of the menacing incomprehension with which he faces the problem. The switching of the vocabulary of the spirit world from protagonist to summoner, so that they become confused, serves to point up the fact that the two are really one. In the words of Hughes' radio introduction, 'his own self, finally, the innate nature of his flesh and blood, brings him to court'. The division which the sequence serves to heal is indeed self-division.

'After the first fright' (p. 10) is a poem of bald, direct power such as fits the protagonist's intensifying and hardening situation. He is speaking to us again, in the voice of the first poem. He has lost some of his composure, and loses more by the end of the poem, but is nevertheless inclined to put down the whole business of 'The scream' and the summons as nothing more than a 'fright'. His first reaction is not self-analysis or a commitment to see the judicial process through , but an assertion of freedom:

After the first fright

   I sat up and took stock of my options.
   I argued my way out of every thought anybody could
      think . . . .

What masquerades here as reassessment is really a bid by the intellect to re-establish its autonomy and dominance, to re-establish the comfortable sense that there are in fact options to take stock of. There are not. The changes already under way are a matter not of conscious choice and the exercise of freedom, but of psychological necessity.

The arguing and disputation the protagonist takes part in here is Hughes' transmutation of Socrates' error of committing again in court the crime on which he was arraigned and of the slip Kafka's K makes in my epigraph. Hughes introduced the poem on radio in this way:

he is confronted in court with his victim. It is his own daimon, whom he now sees for the first time. . . . He protests, as an honourable Platonist, thereby re-enacting his crime in front of his judges. He still cannot understand his guilt. He cannot understand the sequence of cause and effect.

Hughes does not offer to re-create for us the substance of Socratic dialectic. The protagonist's continued rationalising of the situation, his attempts at having the problem of himself defused by reducing it to a matter of words – these things issue in a public-spirited appeal such as a politician might make for good sense, 'civilisation' and 'Sanity and again Sanity and above all Sanity', as in *Dogs: A Scherzo*. But these pseudo-talismanic abstractions, our own Socratic inheritance, not only have no power to defend the protagonist; they actually form, in his present circumstances, the substance of his crime. And at each mention of them his victim responds, not with a counterargument or a contribution to debate, but with a violent gesture of self-maiming and self-destruction. Here we see what lies behind the initial scream, and what horrors have been produced by the protagonist's complacent unawareness. Hughes is attacking neither sanity nor civilisation in themselves here: the crime consists in the fact that the protagonist, divided and guilty as he is, makes an appeal to these concepts in protesting his innocence. Bradshaw has seen the poem as indicating 'the relativity of different cultural responses to the facts of existence' (*The Achievement of Ted Hughes*, p. 217). But the poem's primary field of reference is psychological rather than cultural in this sense; in the first place it is about 'the sequence of cause and effect' within the protagonist, and the appeal to civilisation and sanity is criminal because evasive. We are learning about the terribly damaging effects of his self-division: how his complacency, inattention and reflex self-justification have defiled the deepest springs of life within him. By the close of the poem the first inklings of this truth are just beginning to come home to the protagonist himself: he begins to sense the urgency and seriousness of his situation; he knows now that his own fate, that of the ego, is locked into that of his victim. He falls silent, and, instead of trying 'to praise' as he did on a parallel occasion in 'The scream', he thinks on his guilt. In *Being and Time* Heidegger writes, 'The call asserts nothing, gives no information about world-events, has nothing to tell. . . . Conscience discourses solely and constantly in the mode of keeping silent . . . it . . . forces the Dasein which has been appealed to and summoned into the reticence of itself' (p. 318).

In the first poem the protagonist presumed the sun universally merciful. With 'The Interrogator' (*Cave Birds*, p. 12) we discover otherwise. The sun is the symbol and source of all life, and fount of all earthly energies; ultimately then, the protagonist's crime is against the sun, which sends forth an emissary, a vulture, to gather evidence of a guilt which the sequence develops till it includes Heidegger's objectless, pre-moral guilt at being alive. The situation is like that of the seventh poem in the Prometheus sequence, where 'the sun, plundered and furious, / Planted its vulture'. To treat the sun as capable of spying down thus on earthly life is to restore it to something like its Egyptian function; R. T. Rundle Clark, in *Myth and Symbol in Ancient Egypt*, speaks (pp. 220 and 94) of the Eye of the solar deity as 'the Great Goddess of the universe in her terrible aspect', 'The eye is the power of life to defend itself inviolate against dissolution and the spirits of non-being'; in the south of Egypt this striking power was Nekhabet, a vulture goddess.

Hughes' solar vulture is extremely acute, and the protagonist very exposed to view. We imagine a desert scene, every component sharply defined, as the situation crystallises out of the vague ghostliness of 'The summoner'. The protagonist is tied to his shadow, his dark side, as though to bait.

The angry vulture's gender (she is the first female presence in the sequence) will allow us, once we enjoy possession of the sequence as a single imaginative unit, to see her as an aspect of the protagonist's victim and eventual partner. In 'She seemed so considerate' (*Cave Birds*, p. 14) we have his own account of the visit of the interrogator. It is not horrific or terrible in quite the way we would expect. We enter a third stage in the development of the theme of predation and man's participation in it. In 'The scream' the protagonist recalled a time when he confidently felt himself outside such things. In 'After the first fright' and 'The interrogator' this position became untenable; he could no longer argue his 'way out of . . . the stopping and starting / Catherine wheel in [his] belly'. Now the theme has come home to him and occupies all his thoughts, producing a curious and subtly mixed state of mind. He ceases trying to escape or panic or cover his tracks. The problem of mortality weighs so heavily with him that he becomes resigned, unresisting. It seems he cannot be bothered to put up the defensive walls of his rationalism. He has ceased talking and simply listens to 'this bird-being'.

In many ways, this is an advance on his starting point; a valuable humbleness has come about, a subjection to whatever is to take place within him:

Then this bird-being embraced me . . . .

> I was glad to shut my eyes, and be held.
> Whether dead or unborn, I did not care.

Yet these same lines show his succumbing to a danger he is to face again, in the second phase, in the person of 'A green mother'. The process of inner growth he is experiencing cannot, it is true, proceed without the surrender of the old ego and the sacrifice of the excessively rational faculty. But, at the same time, surrender alone is insufficient; an alert and vigilant activity of the imagination is also required, and the protagonist has lost this in the weariness he here suffers.

His position resembles Lumb's when he is summoned to the underworld in the *Gaudete* Prologue (which begins with a vision of universal death recalling the present poem). Lumb too reacts resignedly: 'he declares he can do nothing'. Both he and the *Cave Birds* man assume they have been marked out for extinction: Lumb thinks, 'because I am a priest . . . they will crucify me', whilst the other says, 'I felt life had decided to cancel me'. In fact, both have been summoned to the same healing task of reunion with a wounded female, a task in which they will have to play an active part. It is perhaps not too harsh to see the resignation of this poem as the last manifestation of the rationalism displayed in the first poem; it is like a petulant child who when defeated refuses to go on playing the game; such is its desire for dominance that it is prepared to sacrifice the life which is its vehicle rather than abdicate.

The protagonist faces a number of tests in *Cave Birds*, including overcoming the threat posed in the poem just examined. Hughes gives his reader tests too. The first is 'The judge' (p. 16), which asks whether we can see how the trial here differs from its model in the world outside *Cave Birds*. If Hughes followed the pattern of a real trial in every detail, criticism of the protagonist's resignation would be invalid. In an ordinary trial the accused is completely passive: he stands still in the dock; information is collected from him; all authority and activity lie with the court functionaries; the accused is there only to be exonerated or condemned. The proceedings are a ritual for the renewal of social order; the accused is merely the occasion for this. His subsequent fate is finally incidental, as is shown by our confusion over the purpose of sentencing: the theatrical display of judicial authority in gowns and wigs and appropriate rhetoric is established in the minutest detail, but whether the guilty are imprisoned as punishment, deterrent, protection for society, or to help them reform, we cannot agree, because it is a smaller matter. The only person less important in our courts than the accused is his victim.

In these ways (together with the mixing of civil and criminal terminology), the trial in the real world is different from that in *Cave Birds*, which stresses the rehabilitation of both accused and victim. This is to say that the paradigm of the trial is not available to Hughes without his subverting it. Its whole structure and purpose are on the surface opposed to those of his book, which is immediately concerned with the individual and psychological rather than the social. The necessary subversion is carried out in 'The judge'. From the title we expect to meet one of the supreme bird-beings, perhaps a representative of the sun on behalf of whom the interrogation was carried out. As we read, it emerges that this is a satirical portrait of the guilty one, the rational intellect which incessantly judges, condemns and imprisons the rest of life. The judge is that part of the protagonist which has caused his problems by setting itself above the other faculties of his mind.

Baskin's gross caricature alerts us; Hughes adds his own subtler clues: 'The pondering body of the law teeters across / A web-glistening geometry.' We are concerned with a slow, lazy degenerate form of thought, the protagonist's own complacent rationalism. And the web in the second line recalls the tyrannical intellect in *Orghast*, Krogon (Crow-gone, suppression of primal energy) 'who hangs like a spider in his steel web, in the middle of his prison universe', as Smith reports in *Orghast at Persepolis* (p. 95).

The poem goes on to concentrate on two facets of the judge: his gluttony and his desire to keep things as they are. Gluttony is a way of picturing the excesses of the intellect, draining life of its energies in a literal abstraction, as in 'A Disaster' in *Crow*. The concern with stasis lay behind the protagonist's desire, in 'The scream', to see himself as outside 'the wheel of the galaxy'. This same concern makes the judge 'a Nero of the unalterable', refusing to acknowledge change, fiddling while the city burns, pretending against the evidence that all will continue as before.

The concern with stasis is one of several features which link Hughes' judge with Blake's Urizen, who is similarly concerned with 'cosmic equipoise':

Hidden, set apart, in my stern counsels,
Reserv'd for the days of futurity,
I have sought for a joy without pain,
For a solid without fluctuation.
          (*The Book of Urizen*, chapter ii, verse 4)

In *The Book of Urizen*, as in *Cave Birds*, the desire for stasis is a sign
of failure to come to terms with death (one's own, and the death
one must deal to other lives in order to go on living). Urizen calls
on the other Eternals: 'why will you die . . . ? Why live in
unquenchable burnings?' In place of death and change Urizen
seeks to set up permanence and uniformity; to achieve these he
becomes legislator–judge:

Lo! I unfold my darkness and on
This rock place with strong hand the Book
Of eternal brass, written in my solitude:

  Laws of peace, of love, of unity,
Of pity, compassion, forgiveness.
Let each chuse one habitation,
His ancient infinite mansion.
One command, one joy, one desire,
One curse, one weight, one measure,
One King, one God, one Law.
          (*The Book of Urizen*, chapter ii, verses 7 and 8)

This recalls the *Cave Birds* man's feigned sympathy for others;
beneath this façade there lies, with both figures, the compulsion
for mental power, control and fixity.

Hughes gave none of this away in his radio introduction,
which was perhaps more cryptic than the poem itself: 'the visible
representative of natural law does not partake of its splendour'.
But there can be no doubt that the real embodiment of natural law
is not this judge, but the sun, 'the solar silence', mentioned only
in passing at the end of the poem.

Next, in 'The plaintiff' (p. 18), the court directs the protagonist's
attention to the victim. She is associated with the moon and
darkness, and through these with everything he has previously
failed to take into account, now grown so huge that he can no

longer ignore her. The speaker points out, with powerful irony, that it is the protagonist's very unawareness which has allowed her to grow to such proportions: 'how you have nursed her!' The nursing has consisted of the inflicting of a succession of wounds, so that the plaintiff corresponds to the wounded female Lumb meets in the Prologue to *Gaudete*. But 'how you have nursed her' is not entirely ironical: in a sense, the protagonist has done just that, for without his crime she would not exist as a separate entity; which is as much as to say that there can be no healing without sickness.

The darkness with which the plaintiff is associated is related to that which will overwhelm the protagonist in 'The executioner', but, in keeping with the ambivalence of his nursing her, she is also associated with the opposite: 'This is the bird of light!'; she is 'life-divining' and thus provides the protagonist with the opportunity to cleanse and attune himself for the first time – in the end his guilt will be seen as the source of his salvation.

A further positive sign is that the vague images of self-division in the opening poems have now given way to a split between male and female. However desperate the situation may seem at present, this use of the genders necessarily carries a hope of future union such as could not be implicit in the exclusively masculine world of the first three poems.

The final lines of 'The plaintiff' show us how the balance of power is beginning to shift within the protagonist's psyche. The plaintiff is what he has suppressed; yet, by now, this crime has produced a countermovement, an enantiodromia, so that her feet are

Roots

Buried in your chest, a humbling weight
That will not let you breathe.

Your heart's winged flower
Come to supplant you.

We have reached a point like that at the close of the third of the 'Seven Dungeon Songs', and the image of this terrible flower will eventually be redeemed in 'The owl flower', where a scintillating blossom is celebrated as a crowning achievement of the sequence. But here the atmosphere is threatening. This flower grows, it seems, at the expense of the protagonist (it was 'blood-fed' in an earlier version of the poem). In his Note to *A Choice of Shakespeare's Verse*, Hughes looks to 'Venus and Adonis' and 'The Rape of Lucrece' for the four poles of Shakespeare's imagination, which become established

> as phases in a narrative cycle: Venus (Divine Power in female form offering love) confronts Adonis (the chronic puritan), whereupon Adonis dies through some form of destroying tempest and is reborn, through a flower death, as Tarquin, whereupon Tarquin (Divine Power, enraged after rebuff, in male and destructive form) destroys Lucrece (and himself and all order). (p. 194)

The flower death mentioned here comes at the end of 'Venus and Adonis'; Adonis has failed to accept Venus' supercharged love and is supplanted by a 'purple flower' that springs up in his blood. In *Cave Birds*, the protagonist, descendant of the Shakespearean Adonis, has rejected all that his female counterpart stands for, and now, ignored and repressed, she returns to 'supplant' him. In *Wodwo*, which is the first work to introduce this movement in a systematic way, the supplanting often leads within individual pieces to destruction, just as it does, on Hughes' account, in Shakespeare, who, despite himself, could not help remaining faithful to the spirit of the times as they moved towards the puritan victory in the Civil War and its covert confirmation at the Restoration: 'what Shakespeare records, apart from the agony of all parties, is the gradual defeat of Venus'. Hughes speaks of Venus being 'dragged into court by the young Puritan Jehovah'. *Cave Birds* reopens this trial and seeks to prompt the reversal of its verdict against Venus. Thus its imagery runs in the opposite direction from Shakespeare's, from angry to loving female. The supplanting will this time issue in integration, not destruction. That Hughes should see our time as propitious for such a movement is the clearest mark of his essential optimism, a feature of his work which is the reverse of his generally perceived reputation.

'The plaintiff' portrays the growth of the protagonist's victim to the point where she ceases to be purely a victim. In an earlier version of the poem this growth was seen in non-psychological terms. It was instead pictured as his increasing sense of responsibility for the disasters of world history so glibly assumed as finally right in 'The scream'. Part of the poem listed them, as 'Karma' in *Wodwo* had done. But the list was arbitrary, and the earlier version was as a result insufficiently distanced from the mentality of the protagonist in the opening poem – casual mentions of Herod, Stalin and the death camps turned the sequence prematurely outward. The present version insists more successfully on the close connection between protagonist and victim.

If the protagonist had managed to speak 'In these fading moments' ('In these fading moments I wanted to say', *Cave Birds*, p. 20), he would have been once more re-enacting his crime before his judges, hiding thick-skinned closure behind claimed altruism. But he does not speak. As a result of the supplanting in the previous poem, his voice has been usurped by the victim:

I wanted to say . . .

> But she was murmuring: Right from the start, my life
> Has been a cold business of mountains and their snow
> Of rivers and their mud . . . .

The victim as she has appeared so far might be seen as the protagonist's unconscious, a suppressed part of his being. These lines remind us that she is also the spirit of life outside him. The central female figures of all Hughes' later works have this double or multiple valency, being at once goddess, anima and desecrated nature, at once inner and outer; thus Moa, in the *Orghast* physiology, is shown as both within and outside Pramanath. Psychological, religious and ecological vocabularies are by themselves inadequate; they must be subsumed in a deeper argument such as Hughes offers in his 'Myth and Education' essay, or such as may be found in Heidegger.

The victim seems to be complaining that she has been exiled by the protagonist to the remotest and most inhospitable zones, frozen out, whilst he has formed a cosy social circle ignoring her. But she will not stay relegated. After freezing comes melting and deluge:

> But after the bye-byes, and even before the door closed, even
>   while the lips still moved
> The scree had not ceased to slip and trickle
> The snow-melt was cutting deeper
> Through its anaesthetic

The brown bulging swirls, where the snowflakes vanished
    into themselves
Had lost every reflection.

The idle chatter has not halted deeper processes. The reflections
lost in the newly turbid surface of the water include that of the
protagonist, the self-conscious one, Narcissus mouthing 'I wanted
to say'. These lines foreshadow the imminent extinction of the
protagonist, to be achieved in the next poem, which develops the
present imagery: the turbulent waters here become what fills him
with blackness there, and the loss of reflection here becomes a loss
of sight there.

The terrible sensations of blindness and drowning, out of which
'The executioner' (*Cave Birds*, p. 22) is made, are counterbalanced
by a calm steadiness running through the poem. Death is not an
emptying but a filling; an end, but also a retreat to the beginning.
We hear the dispassionate description by a third party of an
unrelenting but unhurried decreation and return to a primordial
darkness which answers to the alchemical nigredo and provides a
culmination for the imagery of shadows which has appeared so
often in this phase of *Cave Birds*. The mention of hemlock recalls
Socrates' death potion and its slow working through his body; the
defence of the excessively rational ego has ceased, the protagonist
is silent, the verdict of guilty is bringing the accompanying
sentence:

He fills up the mirror, he fills up the cup
He fills up your thoughts to the brims of your eyes

You just see he is filling the eyes of your friends
And now lifting your hand you touch at your eyes

Which he has completely filled up
You touch him

In touching at his eyes the protagonist actually touches the
executioner. Hughes is reminding us that surrender is not enough.
The protagonist is himself the executioner. The sacrifice of ego has
to be volunteered, without reserve, and not merely extracted
against the will, even if passive. A final poem becomes necessary
to conclude this phase of *Cave Birds*. In 'The accused' (p. 24) the

protagonist himself takes the initiative, and this starts the process by which the darkness of 'The executioner' can become the fecund womb of 'A flayed crow'. This potential is there in the closing lines with their 'world / Before your eyes ever opened', but it needs the confession which follows to start its realisation. Jung, in *The Practice of Psychotherapy*, speaks of the efficacy of confession, the laying aside of pride and the admission of fallibility, and sees it as important in the Greek mysteries, where we meet the saying 'Give up what thou hast, and then thou wilt receive' (pp. 58–9). Hughes' imagery for this confession is that of shamanic dismemberment. The accused strips himself to the bone, offering everything, not only the rational intellect but the predatory nature lurking behind it. All is heaped up for the true judge, the sun, and the protagonist's

atoms are annealed, as in x-rays,
Of their blood-aberration –

His mudded body, lord of middens, like an ore,

To rainbowed clinker and a beatitude.

'Annealed' gives us two aspects of the alchemical–metallurgical process, the hardening and the introduction of colour. Bradshaw has also suggested that Hughes' word includes the sense 'given extreme unction', a religious connotation which helps prepare for the final word of the poem.

Confession is efficacious in two ways: by it, we recognise the guilt we have previously sought to evade and know ourselves better; but it also puts that guilt beyond us – and it is an act of separation and leaving behind. So the accused in this poem displays a nascent capacity to free some vital core of himself from implication with his old ego. What is freed by the purificatory firing here is a new motivating centre of energy in him, deeper than the ego, and now, for the first time, able to act. It is of the nature of sacrifice that as he makes his confession the protagonist can have no assurance that this will be the outcome, nor any clue what further adventures will be produced.

The death-which-is-not-a-death that concludes the first phase of *Cave Birds*, and the death of only one half of Lumb in *Gaudete*, make these works tragi-comic like the dramas Richard Dutton discusses in *Modern Tragicomedy and the British Tradition*, at the end of which he says,

The genre as a whole represents a sustained doubting of the concept of the free, rational, purposive individual which is central to liberal democratic societies and was for so long (though perhaps is no longer) the mainstay of the novel as a literary form. (p. 210)

Hughes is less concerned with doubting a liberal individualism moribund before the Great War than encouraging a new and deeper individualism to grow from its ashes. Some residual aspects of the old civilisation he takes as targets. Others he draws back to what underpins them, for remaking: the concern with the rural and organic becomes an ecological vision; the concern with literature as the shaper of values for an elite becomes the concern with the therapeutic powers of the imagination in all of us; the concern with morality gives way to psychology; and liberal even-handedness and doubt become, as the next sections show, Heideggerian openness and questioning.

IV

Hughes' introduction to the opening poem of the second phase of *Cave Birds*, 'First, the doubtful charts of skin' (p. 26), gives us two of the oldest and most widespread of the motifs we traced earlier: devouring and the after-life journey: 'sentenced and swallowed by the Raven, the hero finds himself on a journey which leads him not to death, but to the start of a new adventure'. This entry into scarcely explored and dangerous territory recalls the transition to the kingdom of the dead in the Egyptian burial rituals; the swallowing by Raven puts us in mind of Jonah and the whale too; but most of all this journey is an odyssey by the protagonist back into himself and his past, an anamnesis or creative remembrance. He meets again the skin he has just confessed; then 'the stopping and starting Catherine wheel' of 'the small and the large intestine, in their wet cave'; then the judge's 'web of veins / Where I hung so long / For the giant spider's pleasure'; and even the vague terrors of the first poems of *Cave Birds* – 'the battle in the valley of screams'. He is exploring his own being.

The exploration is accompanied by images of danger and claustrophobic darkness at first, but then there is a shift to freedom and wildness. The protagonist seems to have penetrated suddenly into an archetypal zone:

> I came to loose bones
> On a heathery moor, and a roofless church.
>
> Wild horses, with blowing tails and manes,
> Standing among graves.
>
> And a leaning menhir, with my name on it.
> And an epitaph, which read:
> 'Under this rock, he found weapons.'

In this exposed and energetic landscape, beyond all that is super-
ficial in his personal history, the protagonist is confronting his
death. The mood is a world away from the glib assumption of
friendly terms at the beginning of the first phase.

The association of death with renewed energy joins with the
strongly positive message of the epitaph to presage a favourable
outcome for the protagonist. The epitaph itself, which is to give
rise to the imagery of the next poem, echoes Andreae's 'Now as I
was diligently viewing it, I found a little Seal, whereupon a curious
Cross with this Inscription, IN HOC SIGNO + VINCES, was ingraven'
(*The Chemical Wedding*, vol. 2, p. 292). Hughes gives us the first
clear formulation of one of the deepest insights of *Cave Birds*. We
learned earlier of the stultifying and unhealthy effects of the drive
toward stasis, 'cosmic equipoise', which the protagonist showed
in his criminal phase. Now we are offered the corollary. The
enlivening power exemplified by the wild horses and the windy
exhilarating space of the moortop can only become the protagonist's
own strength through the facing of death and change. This is the
meeting which, as in Jung and the Heideggerian progress from
inauthenticity to authenticity and resolution, cannot be circumven-
ted.

The primacy of change is so important in the closing lines of this
poem that it even invades the setting which lends it such dignity
and force – time has unroofed the church and unsettled the death-
stone. Hughes has gone back to Jessie Weston and the 'tumbled
graves' and 'empty chapel' Eliot borrowed from her and remade
them so that decay and change themselves become sacred.

'The knight' (p. 28) sees the prediction of the epitaph fulfilled.
The setting is the same, among 'the common wild stones of the
earth'. Here we witness the voluntarily undertaken death and
decay of the protagonist. Like 'The executioner', this poem is more

positive than its subject matter would, out of context, lead us to expect. Hughes plays on this reversal of expectations; death is not what it seems, and neither is victory:

The knight

Has conquered. He has surrendered everything.

Now he kneels. He is offering up his victory
And unlacing his steel

In front of him are the common wild stones of the earth –

The first and last altar
Onto which he lowers his spoils.

Victory comes through submission. The battle is won by taking off the steel armour of rationalism and by sacrificing the safe and separate ego. The protagonist becomes a true knight by passing this test. He is answering Lawrence's challenge in 'On Being a Man' to lay aside the 'tight armour of cowardly repression' and to go forth 'unsheathed'. The only possible metaphor for taking this risk is death, because the sacrifice has to be total:

He reserves nothing.

Skylines tug him apart, winds drink him,
Earth itself unravels him from beneath –

His submission is flawless.

Anything other than this triumphant decay (working out the previous pun on 'spoils') would be an incomplete surrender. Some of the old armour would have been retained, and we would be witnessing a concession or compromise by the ego, an adjustment not a transformation, an Egg-Head's peeping.

For this death metaphor to have the required impact on the reader it must become more than metaphor: it must occupy the whole poem, so that the piece is read first as a marvellously courageous acceptance of the fact of physical death, like the close of Whitman's 'Song of Myself'. Only afterwards can we pick up such words as 'patience' and 'vigil' and see this as an analogy for psychological transformation, a defining of a special state of being, 'a vast inner exposure . . . a stillness of affliction' which is on its way to ecstasy (such as Hughes wrote of in introducing Pilinsky's *Selected Poems*).

The protagonist's knighthood places him now in the service of the Lady who was once his victim; he has begun to become her warrior, the one equipped to move between worlds. But he has not yet achieved this, as 'Something was happening' (*Cave Birds*, p. 30) makes clear. We return, to begin with, from the bird realm, to the ordinary world. The mood evoked seems massively regressive. The protagonist seems lethargic, complacent, evasive and fearful. The female presence is again sick or wounded, dying. Her suffering calls forth no sympathy or responsibility in the protagonist, who is numbly frightened, merely persisting through the events around him, unable to connect with their pattern:

> And when I saw new emerald tufting the quince, in April
> And cried in dismay: 'Here it comes again!'
> The leather of my shoes
> Continued to gleam
> The silence of the furniture
> Registered nothing
>
> The earth, right to its far rims, ignored me.

It is not that April is the cruellest month in Eliot's sense: the protagonist is making no statement about the horrors of life renewed by the cycles of the seasons – he is as cut off from that sensation as from any feeling of joy which spring might bring a less jaundiced eye. He is undergoing the tranquillised numbness of disconnection from a suffering which none the less goes on. His dismay, loss of hope and courage, gives the keynote to this phase. 'Ought I to turn back, or keep going?' he asks, and this failure of confidence separates this poem from those others very early in the sequence with which it seems at first to share so much. Guilt and criminality are no longer central. The danger faced now is a paralysing fear. We are discovering that in 'The knight' the protagonist did not solve his problems, but only began to equip himself to do so. The major achievements still lie ahead, and for the moment he seems incapable of facing their perils. Andreae's hero comes to a similar impasse, dithering at a multiple crossroads. He is rescued by two birds which fly down and show him the way. Similarly, in Hughes' poem an outside agency appears in order to set up a new initiative; the radio introduction says that, 'while the hero undergoes his vigil, a Helper begins to work for him, calling on the eagles'. The emotional vacuum in the protagonist is suddenly filled by a being from the bird realm. He and the reader have been thrust back into the wilderness of the previous two poems. The eagle hunter's singing is an advance on the screams, accusations, evasive chatter and pained silences which have mapped the changing quality of sound earlier in the sequence. Baskin's drawing shows us an eagle, still some way off, but being drawn down to the protagonist. The eagles are the supreme powers of the bird realm, the most majestic forces of the unconscious and the imagination.

In 'The gatekeeper' (p. 32) we hear the eagle hunter as he 'wails out' the protagonist's name. As a result the giant eagle, like Sinbad's roc, picks up the protagonist and carries him off to the next stage of his journey. Baskin's picture is what Hughes calls 'A sphynx. / A two-headed questioner.' The second and decisive trial by eagles, based partly on Egyptian and alchemical models, is, given good fortune for the protagonist, about to begin. We have reached the mid-point of the sequence, and this new being is the appropriate symbol: the Egyptian Book of Caverns has an enormous twin-headed sphinx called Aker at the centre of the underworld; in a cavern inside this monster Osiris lies helpless. The gatekeeper seems to ask the protagonist which way he would like to go from here, but the choice is immaterial. The essential issue has long ago been decided, and what happens henceforth is not a matter of the exercise of the freedoms and options of the intellect. His confession, in 'The accused', set in train a process to which these aspects of the ego are increasingly irrelevant; a deep impersonal process is taking place inside him. Only the final outcome remains unpredictable. There is no choice but there are different possibilities:

And a wingspread

Nails you with its claws. And an eagle
Is flying

To drop you into a bog or carry you to eagles.

In relation to 'The knight' we noted that a true sacrifice must be made without hope or expectation of gain; everything must be at risk. The protagonist's ultimate success is not preordained or inevitable. It is quite possible, even now, that the eagle will drop him casually to be absorbed into the bog of uncreatedness. A similar disaster is seen as possible in the Egyptian after-life journey with its dangers *en route* to the Hall of Judgement.

The protagonist is lucky. He is carried to the hall of the eagles, who now weigh him in their balance. This phase of *Cave Birds* is characterised by a nexus of symbols suggesting the uncanny co-presence in the protagonist of, on the one hand, complete exposure and uncertainty, with everything at risk, and, on the other, the feeling of being part of deeper purposes. Being in the grip of the giant eagle, being in the balance, recognising at last a guide who has perhaps been ever-present – these are all ways of speaking of what Heidegger evokes in *Poetry, Language, Thought* when he describes us as ventured by Being into danger and unprotectedness but not into abandonment:

> To weigh or throw in the balance, as in the sense of wager, means to bring into the movement of the game, to throw into the scales, release into risk. What is so ventured is, of course, unprotected; but because it hangs in the balance, it is retained in the venture. It is upheld.   (p. 103)

Later in the same essay he says, 'the daring which is more venturesome creates a safety for us'. It is like the moment in 'The Ancient Mariner' when the Mariner is diced for.

That the result of the weighing will be favourable for Hughes' protagonist is soon suggested: the rising and falling of the pans of the scales has become, in 'A flayed crow in the hall of judgment' (*Cave Birds*, p. 34), the bobbing of a foetus in its egg:

> I rise beyond height – I fall past falling.
> I float on an air
> As mist-balls float, and as stars.

He is describing the sensations of being inside the egg from which he will eventually be reborn. This allows Hughes to do what he is to do in several poems in the last phase of *Cave Birds* (and other sequences): take an image which first appeared in a menacing aspect and relieve it of that. The darkness the protagonist now inhabits grows out of that of 'The executioner' ('It feels like the world / Before your eyes ever opened'), which itself grew out of the shadows found in the very first poems. The egg of darkness is both a fresh start for the protagonist, promising new life in a shape he cannot predict, and the product of the long process of stripping down to an essential core. He is both 'a new foetus' and 'a condensation, a gleam simplification / Of all that pertained'.

In his analysis of the Egyptian Book of the Dead, E. A. Wallis Budge notes one of the capacities the candidate for resurrection had to develop:

> the words *maa kheru* . . . mean 'true of voice' or 'right of word', and indicate that the person to whom they are applied has acquired the power of using his voice in such a way that when the invisible beings are addressed by him they will render unto him all the service which he has obtained the right to demand.
>
> (*Egyptian Religion*, p. 144)

Many of Hughes' heroes win through to a similar truth of voice, to a language to which the spirits will listen without anger, the poet's voice of openness to Being. The *Cave Birds* protagonist is starting to achieve this, cleansing his voice of those elements which earlier signalled to us his unfitness. The casualness, the clichés, the groundless confidence and certainty, the dismay, have all gone. And now, as with Wodwo, Prometheus and the Lumb of the *Gaudete* Epilogue, we hear the speech of one who is touched by the mystery of existence and who has arrived at the thrilling uncertainties of a new beginning – and this speech is made entirely of amazed questions. The cry which struggles in the protagonist's tissues is almost the pre-birth equivalent of Wodwo's excited reconnoitrings, of Lumb's 'Am I killed? / Or am I searching? / Is this the rainbow silking my body? / Which wings are these?' and of Prometheus's final questioning contemplation of the vulture. There are distinctions to be drawn between these instances, but what they share is also important. The man who can ask questions about existence, instead of closing his eyes to the world or erecting a theory in its stead, and who can go on asking without falling into despair or false hope, has achieved one of the major components of Hughesian maturity:

Where am I going? What will come to me here?

Is this everlasting? Is it
Stoppage and the start of nothing?

Or am I under attention?
Do purposeful cares incubate me?
Am I the self of some spore

In this white of death blackness,
This yoke of afterlife?
What feathers shall I have? What is my weakness good for?

To take the kind of questions which inaugurate the climaxes of the
1970s sequences and set them next to Wodwo's questions, is to note
a significant advance. Though all genuine questioning betokens a
thinking which is open and flexible, and thus at a far remove from
confident, assertive rationality, there remained, for Hughes, after
Wodwo, more of the new disposition to discover and articulate.
Wodwo is active, hurried, questing. Later protagonists ask, then
seem to wait and in a spirit of achieved attunement listen for
whatever of Being their questioning vouchsafes. Some hint of this
spirit is already present by this point in *Cave Birds*.

The feather of Maat recalled in the next couplet serves to
announce the lifting of the fearful burden of 'The plaintiff' ('a
humbling weight/That will not let you breathe') and 'The gatekeeper' ('Such fear – your weight'):

A great fear rests
On the thing I am, as a feather on a hand.

I shall not fight
Against whatever is allotted to me.

My soul skinned, and the soul-skin laid out
A mat for my judges.

The protagonist's inquisitive response to his new surroundings
must be taken into account when interpreting his 'I shall not fight'.
'A flayed crow' is about a different mood from that evinced by his
earlier 'I did not care'. His wondering submissiveness is not
egotistical resignation, but a new openness, an attunement to the
large events happening inside him.

'The baptist' (*Cave Birds*, p. 36) grows out of the image of the foetus suspended in its feeding fluid, which now becomes the sea, the cradle of life, in which the protagonist must be cleansed and baptised in preparation for his new life. This washing, the first stage in the eagle judges' answer to his questions about the future, has a double purpose, like the alchemical solutio. It soothes his wounds, the pains of the past, the lacerations he has inflicted, and it completes the stripping-away of his old being. The poem unites an atmosphere of healing and one of a final overcoming of resistance in their last guise of grief for his former self:

The baptist

Enfolds you
In winding waters, a swathing of balm

A mummy bandaging
Of all your body's puckering hurts

In the circulation of sea.
A whale of furtherance

Cruises through the Arctic of stone,
Carrying you blindfold and gagged.

You dissolve, in the cool wholesome salts
Like a hard-cornered grief, drop by drop

Or an iceberg of loss
Shrinking towards the equator

Or a seed in its armour.

Several strains of imagery previously met are here seen in a more positive light. 'Circulation' gives us the wheel image revalued. The melting of frozen water, so threatening 'In these fading moments', brings now the promise of a new warmth which will promote growth. The final line, returning us to the foetal imagery of 'A flayed crow', offers the knight's surrender of his armour as the necessary prelude to a process of germination which will culminate in the blossoming of the owl flower at the end. The curious surreal image of the 'whale of furtherance' cruising 'through the Arctic of stone' may perhaps be set beside a *Gaudete* Epilogue poem, 'Collision with the earth has finally come' (p. 180), which, though less optimistic, seems to portray a similar sense of helpless dependence on impersonal forces and purposes through imagery of sensory dislocation.

In Hughes' retellings of the *Crow* narrative he sometimes describes Crow as initially a shapeless larval being whose quest is to become human. Wodwo, half-man, half-beast, is the forerunner of Crow in this. The protagonist is now such a larval being, an unshaped potential. In 'Only a little sleep, a little slumber' (*Cave Birds*, p. 38) an eagle looks down into the nest and rouses him out of his gagged silence with the question 'who are your . . . ?' He replies, 'I am the last of my kind.' 'Last' seems to look backwards and create a sense of the protagonist as the left-over of a process issuing in death. But balancing this sense is another in which his statement is the first recognition of his own possible specialness, and of his responsibility for the peculiar combination of deep forces which only his species can carry. Only a man could make the protagonist's statement with its self-placing. Only a man can know himself as last – not in the sense of final, but in that of furthest. Only a man can know himself at the growing tip of the evolutionary process, charged with the role of Shepherd of Being. This is to become an important theme in 'Adam and the Sacred Nine' and 'A Citrine Glimpse'. For the moment it is just one part of the protagonist's mixed reaction to his new situation, even if Hughes' introduction highlights it: 'reduced to total dependence on the help of the eagles, the hero begins to feel first stirrings of humanity again'.

The eagles have weighed him, searching him for virtues, to see if he has that within him which will sustain rebirth. In effect, the protagonist's pronouncement here gives us the verdict. Again he has taken the crucial step himself. In 'The knight' he earned his unweapons. Now he has a cause and a direction in which to use them. But next there is a surprising turn. Just as the way seems to have been cleared for·a relatively straightforward rebirth into a strengthened humanity, another phase of his second trial opens. As there were two parts to the Egyptian after-life trial, so here the protagonist is to be searched for vices also. He is to be tempted. If his 'I am the last of my kind' provides us with hope for him in this new test, it is none the less far from being so unambiguous as to guarantee his success.

The figure who tempts him claims to be his green mother and his guide ('A green mother', p. 40). So strong is her temptation, so charming and enthralling the poetry Hughes has granted her, that it is not until 'A riddle' and 'The guide' that we can be sure these claims are false. Like all really dangerous temptations, hers is based on a keen sense of the tempted's possible weaknesses. The green mother homes in on the protagonist's triumphant meeting with death and on his subsequent problem of dismaying fear:

> Why are you afraid?
> In the house of the dead are many cradles.
> The earth is a busy hive of heavens.
> This is one lottery that cannot be lost.
>
> Here is the heaven of the tree:
> Angels will come to collect you.
> And here are the heavens of the flowers:
> These are an everliving bliss, a pulsing, a bliss in sleep.

She offers him not an alternative to rebirth, but what might easily be mistaken for the culmination of the whole process he has been going through. And her offer panders to feelings he is bound to entertain by this stage. After the long hazardous journeying, the trials, the backslidings and restarts, the protagonist must feel the desire for rest, for firmer ground and a comfortable sense of having reached a conclusion. He would surely like to feel that the risks and sacrifices will now bring their reward.

The green mother brings him back to the grave and, calling it 'her breast' and the source of 'endless life', suggests that it might be the point of departure to any of a range of stations on the tree of life:

> And here is the heaven of the worm –
> A forgiving God.
> Little of you will be rejected –
> Which the angels of the flowers will gladly collect.
>
> And here is the heaven of the insects.

From all these you may climb
To the heavens of the birds,
        the heavens of the beasts, and of the fish.

We cannot help but be reminded of the positive interpretation of physical decay in 'The knight'. Why then is this a temptation it would be wrong for him to accept? His struggle has, in one sense, been to come to terms with the implications of the cycles of growth and decay – surely this absorption in them would be a fitting conclusion? Perhaps we are first alerted to the green mother's falsity by the very cornucopia she offers: we have learned by now to distrust the notion of choice; the protagonist's course has been about readying himself for unpredictable but inevitable developments within, not about choice. Then we notice that the bliss offered would be 'in sleep', restful, but, as in poem 12 of 'Prometheus on his Crag', a stupor of inattention, a laying-aside of his hard-won warrior skills; it would be a failure to meet the challenge of attaining a new maturity, a full humanity. The green mother promises no adulthood for him:

                        You shall see
How tenderly she has wiped her child's face clean

Of the bitumen of blood and the smoke of tears.

Compassionate as this seems, it would mean an end to his development, an imprisoning in perpetual childhood no better in some ways than that hinted at in the opening lines of Cave Birds. The same applies to the green mother's other type of offer, of choice amongst the great religious faiths. Here too the protagonist is tested to see if he can recognise this as a shuffling-off of responsibility for his fate, another kind of arrest in his development. In The Practice of Psychotherapy, Jung speaks of 'that ineradicable feeling of being a child . . . which finds meaning and shelter in the bosom of the Church' (p. 98), and distinguishes organised religion from the real thing, a careful and courageous, unending vigilance of attention to the inner life.

The two kinds of offer the green mother makes are corruptions of the material and spiritual aspects of reality. The protagonist cannot choose between them: like Prometheus, he must be the locus of their collision and harmonising, since without each other they are worthless.

When she has shown him all her wares, the protagonist is left alone in a paradise which seems to combine the seductive powers of both types of heaven ('As I came, I saw a wood', *Cave Birds*, p. 42). Trees seem to be partaking in a ritual, along with animals and birds, which he is privileged to watch. It is 'the crowded crossroads of all the heavens' and he is very taken by it. But, just as he is about to succumb, there is a vital inner prompting, a reminder of the essential element in his immediate experience which it took him so long to acknowledge and which he is now in danger of forgetting:

> a voice, a bell of cracked iron
> Jarred in my skull
>
> Summoning me to prayer
>
> To eat flesh and to drink blood.

Within communion lies predation. The ritual has been like a photograph which he saw, but which had no eyes for him; he could not himself step into it and become a part. Staying here would mean placing himself once more outside the wheel. The bell summons him to participation and to consciousness of participation.

Next we meet the female figure who was at first his victim, then his angry interrogator and the paralysing weight of the plaintiff. Though it is at first puzzling, and though the speaker spends time rehearsing her sufferings at his hands, so that we realise she has been with him at every step, nevertheless 'A riddle' (p. 44) is perhaps the highest reach of upturn so far, because in its closing lines the woman announces her future union with the protagonist. She is his daughter, wife and mother, and these relationships, which come to fulfilment in 'Bride and groom lie hidden for three days', are her riddle, her answer to his prayer. The incest motif, present in the Isis–Osiris story, is found in alchemy too:

> Then it was that I first knew my son
> And we two came together as one.
> There I was made pregnant by him and gave birth
> Upon a barren stretch of earth.
> I became a mother yet remained a maid

> And in my nature was established.
> Therefore my son was also my father
> As God ordained in accordance with nature.
> I bore the mother who gave me birth
> Through me she was born again upon earth.
>
> (quoted in C. G. Jung,
> *The Practice of Psychotherapy*, p. 310)

In *Symbols of Transformation*, Jung explains the incest riddle as a 'repulsive symbol for the unio mystica . . . Incest symbolizes union with one's own being, it means individuation or becoming a self' (p. 321). This gives us the general sense of the poem and the light in which we can see the prophecy as immensely promising, but the relationships can be more specifically stated. The speaker is the other, both inside and outside the protagonist; she is thus the flesh from which he originated and the unconscious from which his mind develops; she is his mother. Following his crimes against her, and her consequent disintegration, it is his task to bring her to new birth; he is her father. And, since his task is also a healing of his self-division, a reuniting of opposites, she is also his bride-to-be.

In introducing the next poem Hughes says that the union will 'be the opposite of a physical marriage'. It is to be an event in the soul, and will involve a mixture of participation and mutual responsibility neither element of which the green mother could offer – 'A riddle' reveals her as bogus. For the reader she has been another test, like 'The judge'; for the protagonist she has been his last trial. He will not now remain in her womb-like embrace, but instead be delivered by this other into full independence and an utterly real world.

'The scapegoat' (p. 46) brings the second phase of *Cave Birds* to a successful conclusion with a celebration of the union just announced, consisting of a recalling of the errors the protagonist once committed. They are all brought into the place of celebration, dressed in suitable festive clothes and made to perform tricks. There is a tightrope walker whom we recognise as the obese judge; there are performing animals, a lizard to make fun of the protagonist's trouble in coming to terms with the wheel of the galaxy, and a baboon to ridicule the armour of his intellect; 'the blind swan of insemination' is made to perform; a magician ridicules the ghostly terrors of the opening pages of *Cave Birds*; and there is a card trickster to help the hero laugh at his former irresponsibility towards the life in and around him. The parodic re-enaction of his crimes generates curative laughter in the course of an organised ritual. That it is a ritual of controlled festivity marks this poem off from the events it recalls. The heaping up of errors in 'The accused' was a wholly serious confession, a once-and-for-all sacrifice, without reserve or knowledge of its outcome. The hunting of the scapegoat is different, lighter in tone, a staged ritual of 'riddance', a sign that the protagonist is beginning to develop a system of inner self-regulation. The laughter it produces not only marks the dwindling to insignificance of the former errors; it also voices the protagonist's pleasure at the new health-preserving skills his inner union has started to bring him. That these skills should first be displayed in a bout of calculated irreverence is one of *Cave Birds'* finest surprises.

V

The marriage just celebrated is only a first part of the hero's reunion with his female counterpart. He has yet to bring himself and her together enough for them to enjoy a more physical and human union. In 'After there was nothing there was a woman' (*Cave Birds*, p. 48), a female figure, the equivalent in the outer dimension of the inner female he has just married, is seen as the newly reassembled product of the evolutionary process. She has just emerged, both from the nothingness into which the sequence descended with the hero's execution and from the successive waves of creativity in nature. The first poems of *Cave Birds* saw the protagonist claiming a specialness which was also a separateness; he tried to place himself outside nature. This woman's beauty is a sign of a very different specialness. The protagonist, if he recognised his dues to the rest of creation at all, had felt happy to pay them in the false currency of a few tawdry phrases about universal sympathy. In contrast, every act of this woman, who becomes closer and more real as the sequence draws to its climax, is a remembrance of her indebtedness to the wild dog and the earthworm. She knows herself the still-linked product of the process for which Whitman spoke in 'Song of Myself': 'I am an acme of things accomplish'd, . . . Afar down I see the huge first Nothing, I know I was even there, / Immense have been the preparations for me.' But there is no element of boast in Hughes' portrait. What he stresses are the qualities in the woman which call out to the hero to complete his own reintegration and join her: her beauty, her vulnerability, her tenderness, her reverential wonder at her own body and the world she finds herself inhabiting. Baskin shows her, half-way human, with a large blank beside her which asks the hero to step into it; in accordance with the riddle she is pregnant with him.

To find his way through to this woman who is now ready to accept him the hero must recognise 'The guide' (p. 50), whose appearance confirms the falsity of the green mother's claim to that role ('Where the snow mama cuddled you warm / I fly up'). Although the guide appears this late in the sequence, the poem is perhaps best thought of as presenting the hero's new awareness of that intangible quality within him which has brought him through his adventures; something in him stopped him committing more crimes, gave him the courage to submit to execution, called the eagles to him, and sounded the bell of cracked iron just as he was being tempted. Perhaps it was the guide, the safety hidden in complete risk, the luck that brings the Mariner back to land.

In 'A flayed crow in the hall of judgment' the protagonist spoke of his state within the egg of non-being as a 'fall past falling'. The guide's cheering message is, 'When everything that can fall has fallen / Something rises.' In the *Gaudete* Epilogue poem where Lumb asks 'How far can I fall?' no answering assurance is forthcoming, and he is left unable to choose a direction, confused by 'a needle of many Norths'. 'The guide' is more optimistic:

I am the needle

Magnetic
A tremor

The searcher
The finder

The poem gives a number of reasons for supposing the guide to have been a previously unstated presence. The references to snow take us back, through 'The baptist' to 'In these fading moments'. The lines

Tumbling worlds

Open my way

And you cling.

And we go

Into the wind.

remind us of the protagonist being picked up by the giant eagle. And the various winds now encountered rehearse the process of stripping, emptying and remaking which is now drawing to a temporary close.

The crystallisation of the guide at this point is appropriate because, as Hughes' radio introduction suggests, 'it seems as if his real journey through the heaven of eagles were only just beginning'. He needs a guide now more than ever. Hughes' statement alerts us for what is a marked feature of the remaining poems. Earlier I quoted his description of *Cave Birds* as having 'contrapuntal roles played by birds and humans'. It is perhaps only with the last half-dozen pieces that the reader is forced to ask what it means to have the two parallel dimensions, bird and human, running in tandem. Up to this point they have been interwoven in such a way that the sequence may be read as a single movement. They have functioned together so as to heighten the drama and emphasise the relevance of the action to life outside *Cave Birds*. But now, just at the moment of incipient success, the imagery is to draw the two realms apart. Those poems concerned with the hero's reintegration of himself, his marriage with the physical aspect of woman and his return to humanity, have imagery which is intimate, close-ranged, occupied with the parts of the body. Those which concern themselves with the final question of what form the hero will take at his rebirth from the egg prepared in the realm of the eagles, move out and away from the earth in a journey into the sun; their imagery is cosmic. This divergence (the distant roots of which lie as far back as *Difficulties of a Bridegroom*) is quite deliberate, and gives us in effect two endings. Why, is a question we must return to after examining the poems concerned. To note it now is to avoid the trap of seeing the problem of the ending as merely a matter of the last two lines of 'The risen'.

The next poem, 'His legs ran about' (*Cave Birds*, p. 52), belongs to the marriage group. We first encountered images of physical

reintegration in 'After there was nothing'. Now these are developed
into a picture of a clumsy, fumbling preliminary to the joyous
mutual reintegration to come in 'Bride and groom'. The hero, like
the Iron Man after his fall from the cliff-top, is in living pieces, and
these are blindly shifting about in a too-frantic attempt at reunion
with the female. The parts cling together, but remain parts, not a
whole. The union is an illusion, like the 'hallucinations' of the
'desert staggerer', and is further undercut by the close of the poem:

> As over a new grave, when the mourners have gone
> And the stars come out
> And the earth, bristling and raw, tiny and lost,
> Resumes its search
>
> Rushing through the vast astonishment.

We are reminded that the truth of the primacy of change, learned
in the knight's confrontation with death, remains applicable. And
we may see in this picture of an earth teeming with life and
searching through space for some fulfilment a reminder of the
hero's special responsibility in relation to the rest of nature. But
primarily these lines begin the divergence of imagery into two
tracks, one cosmic, one intimately physical.

In 'Walking bare' (p. 54) the hero sets out, his being reduced to
a tough and precious crystalline core, and the way pointed out for
him by the guide, on a journey into the sun. The being he takes
with him on this journey is the product of all his previous
transformations, exactly what is required and no more. The bird
voices which once summoned him to court and tried him now
'ignore' him; they are 'on other errands'. His fitness has been
proven and he now feels the thrill of passing through a landscape
no longer antagonistic or indifferent:

> The stones do not cease to support me.
> Valleys unfold their invitations . . .
>
> I rest just at my weight.
> Movement is still patient with me –
> Lightness beyond lightness releasing me further.

Together with the pun on 'just' there is the reversal of all previous suggestions of graceless bulk. And suddenly he is flying:

> And the mountains of torment and mica
> Pass me by.
>
> And new skylines lift wider wings
> Of simpler light. . . .
>
> A one gravity keeps touching me.
>
> For I am the appointed planet
> Extinct in an emptiness
>
> But a spark in the breath
> Of the corolla that sweeps me.

'Corolla', a diminutive of 'corona', the astronomical term for the crown of flames around the sun, is used most often of the whorl of plumes that forms the inner envelope of a flower; this combination of botanical and astronomical is the springboard for 'The owl flower'. As he is sucked by the draft of its gravity into the sun, the hero's 'I am the appointed planet' seems to reaffirm his specialness with a new note of resolve. This specialness does not preclude representativeness, nor entail separation.

Before the entry into the sun comes the culmination of the reintegration in the human dimension, in 'Bride and groom lie hidden for three days' (p. 56). The imagery of reassembly gives rise to a union at once marriage and mutual rebirth. The poem thus fulfils, in this physical sphere, all aspects of the riddle. The event is one of the high moments of Hughes' poetry, reverses the *Crow* poem 'Love Song', and is paralleled in *Gaudete*, in its cryptic fashion, by the climax of the Hairy Hands episode with its double delivery of Lumb and the baboon woman. The answering moment in Andreae has already been quoted; Hughes' title actually echoes another alchemist, quoted by Jung in *Psychology and Religion*: 'Take the glass vessel containing bridegroom and bride, throw them into the furnace, and roast them for three days, and they will be two in one flesh' (pp. 238–9). The end of the poem, like 'After there was nothing', makes it clear that the precious thing is found amongst what is deemed of no value:

> So, gasping with joy, with cries of wonderment

Like two gods of mud
Sprawling in the dirt, but with infinite care

They bring each other to perfection.

The insistence on the origins of the perfection in these lines is related to the alchemical notion that the lapis is 'exilis', tossed out on the dunghill; and also to the general sense of the reassembly motif as explained by Jung. In *Psychology and Religion* he says, 'this process of becoming human is represented in dreams and inner images as the putting together of many scattered units, and sometimes as the gradual emergence and clarification of something that was always there' (p. 262). All the later poems in *Cave Birds* carry reminders that what is now coming to pass is rooted in what has preceded it. The sequence, with its near-iterations, its double lookings, insists on the reinstating of memory and the reversal of the amnesia which Heidegger in *What is Called Thinking?* calls 'the high velocity expulsion of Mnemosyne' (p. 30). The development Hughes traces follows Jung's pattern of a gradual emergence of a humanity always present in potential.

Hughes has seen the general drift of Christianity as of a piece with the error of Socratic abstraction. Robert Graves too links these phenomena. In *King Jesus* Christ's life is told as a tragic denial of his ordained role as consort of the goddess. This judgement on Christ is shared with Lawrence, who in *The Escaped Cock* attempts to give Christ the second chance Hughes is giving Socrates in *Cave Birds*: he imagines him taken from the cross too early, surviving, and being drawn back into the world of the pagan fertility cults and resurrected at the hands of a priestess of Isis who finds in him the torn Osiris she needs for her own fulfilment. Both the pattern of the work, and the intention to redirect the reader's religious sensibility, bring it very close to Hughes. And, as in 'Bride and groom', the key moment is an act of love and healing reintegration. However, Lawrence's immediate target is that aspect of Christianity which degraded sex, making it dirty and evil and something to be hidden; there is no hint of asceticism in the criminal phase of the *Cave Birds* protagonist.

The roasting mentioned in the alchemical text Hughes echoes occurs in the poem:

> They keep taking each other to the sun, they find they can
>   easily
> To test each new thing at each new step

These lines are a tantalising hint that his marriage provides a
momentary union of the two sets of imagery, intimate and cosmic.
But it remains unsupported elsewhere, and Hughes' radio introduction is equally unforthcoming about the exact status of this
marriage. Does it belong to both realms, bird and human? 'Somehow the earthly woman has become his bride. They have just
found each other, hardly created yet, on an earth not easily
separable from the heaven of the eagles.' His 'not easily separable'
avoids resolving the question.

In 'The owl flower' (p. 58) we are clearly back in the cosmic
dimension. The hero is descending into the sun, which now at last
assumes in part a more benevolent attitude towards him. He has
become a 'mote', a tiny glowing speck in its flames:

> In the maelstrom's eye,
> In the core of the brimming heaven-blossom,
> Under the tightening whorl of plumes, a mote
> Scalds in dews.

'Maelstrom' and 'whorl' introduce the notion of spinning or rotation
which dominates the central section. The sun is a giant whirlpool
of flames; its spinning, which is to issue now in rebirth, marks the
final positive revaluation of the wheel image met in the first poem.
The hero enters the hub of 'the wheel of the galaxy' and spins to a
reawakening at Hughes' pun on 'stirs':

> A coffin spins in the torque.
> Wounds flush with sap, headful of pollen,
> Wet with nectar
> The dead one stirs.

This re-creative rotation is also an alchemical symbol associated by
Jung with the mandala and the achievement of wholeness. In
Coleridge we meet it in the whirling waters of the bay at the end
of 'The Ancient Mariner', where the hero is making his return
from what Hughes himself has called attention to as a parallel
shamanic journey to meet death. In a *Gaudete* Epilogue poem it

seems to go wrong – 'The coffin, spurred by its screws, / Took a wrong turning' – and it is left to this poem to reverse the error recorded in the *Wodwo* poem 'Cadenza', where 'the coffin escapes'.

Hughes embodies the effect of this successful rotation in a series of revaluations of earlier images. We have for the first time an authentic smile, and it is on the face of the seed met in 'The baptist' as it now starts into growth. The journey metaphor, introduced in 'First, the doubtful charts', comes to an end as the Egyptian after-life 'ship of flowers / Nudges the wharf of skin'. The egg of 'A flayed crow' hatches, and everywhere there are images of blossoming and fruition which reverse their negative counterparts in 'The plaintiff'. Finally, there is the culmination of the metallurgical imagery:

> And a staggering thing
> Fired with rainbows, raw with cringing heat,
>
> Blinks at the source.

This thing is the divine falcon, the Horus of the next poem; it is the shape in which the hero is reborn, and it is the outcome of the long process of refining which has occupied the sequence and which now culminates in an equivalent to the alchemical rubedo. The still-hot falcon emerges from its mould, dazzled by the light.

This image has a counterpart in the steel man of the Epilogue of *Gaudete*; the fluttering purples of the steel man are the rainbows which pass over the cooling skin of the falcon. The steel man is an embodiment of the completely individuated self, the man who has taken to himself the power of the anima. This is a step Hughes refuses; hence the little qualification in that poem of 'He almost lives'. There is a parallel qualification in *Cave Birds*, but it takes a different and less local form, as we shall see.

'The risen' (p. 60) describes the Horus falcon, extrapolating from the qualities Baskin captures in the accompanying picture of a magnificently powerful, serene, alert and composed bird which remains partly covered by the blackness of 'the doorway'. Baskin thus combines the seemingly contradictory impressions of solid presence (the square head-on stance, the broad chest, the planted talons) and ethereal insubstantiality. The poem begins by seeing this combination of impressions as giving us the falcon in the act of rebirth and emergence:

> He stands, filling the doorway
> In the shell of earth.
>
> He lifts wings, he leaves the remains of something,
> A mess of offal, muddled as an afterbirth.

'Offal' carries a subsidiary, metallurgical meaning – the dross which falls off in any process – and therefore gives an emergence which is the product of the alchemical images in the previous poem. The next couplet, 'His each wingbeat – a convict's release. / What he carries will be plenty', picks up the word 'release' in 'Walking bare' and suggests that the falcon's existence is sufficient to set the seal on the process of coming to terms with predation. And, just as the image of the coffin spinning into rebirth in the previous poem marked the reversal of an error recorded in *Wodwo*, so here these lines reverse 'Crow's Nerve 'Fails', where his 'every feather' was 'the fossil of a murder' and in his blackness he flew 'clothed in his conviction, / Trying to remember his crimes', beyond forgiveness. The *Cave Birds* hero has broken through this barrier of amnesia.

The poem now dwells on the falcon's insubstantiality: he is a 'sudden shadow', and like 'music' real but bodiless and unfixed in time or place; even his shape, as he flies near the sun's brightness, is ill-defined and crumbling; he is like an instrument of fate, working to a secret purpose. We are still in the cosmic sphere in this poem, as we are also after the birth of Horus in the Egyptian material: 'as soon as he is born, Horus assumes control of his own destiny. He appears as a falcon and soars up into the sky . . . beyond the stars. . . . He seems to fly out into the vast regions beyond the limits of the divinely created universe and alights upon the ramparts of the eastern horizon' (Clark, *Myth and Symbol in Ancient Egypt*, p. 213). Baskin's falcon has, we note, no human attributes at all. And Hughes' imagery in these last two poems has been kept clear of the human and intimate, being purely cosmic. Behind the sigh (it is not a question) of the closing lines of 'The risen' there is a firm insistence by both artist and poet, mitigated only by the lines in 'Bride and groom' about visiting the sun, that the two endings of the sequence be kept separate. Behind the longing for some single all-inclusive culminatory union lies the knowledge that this cannot be. And this knowledge is something more than the sense given in the little 'Finale' to *Cave Birds* (p. 62) that endings are also beginnings, that nothing is truly final.

Some readers have felt the sequence vitiated by this duality of realms at the end; others, that the absence of the falcon from a man's wrist says much the same as the 'Finale', with its acknowledgement of the unending dynamism of the psyche and of a Being for which there is 'constantly something still to be settled' (Heidegger, *Being and Time*, p. 279). But the division between the two realms is too deep-seated, starts too far back, and is worked into the structure of the sequence too deliberately for either of these views to be acceptable.

Amongst the background material we began by adducing, the Egyptian myth of Isis and Osiris is noteworthy for displaying the same double ending we meet in *Cave Birds*. Osiris's own resurrection and union with Isis is curiously ambivalent for the Egyptians; it is partial, and has to be supplemented by the birth of Horus as falcon. In *The Origins and History of Consciousness*, Erich Neumann takes the Osiris myth as the first instance of the process of individuation. He summarises its importance in three words, 'self-transformation, resurrection and sublimation' (p. 233), the last of which may help us with *Cave Birds*, since it tells us in its most literal sense that some part of the hero must remain beyond the threshold. The falcon form is a symbol of the hero's developed skill in managing his own inner balancing. He has taken to himself the task that the other birds once had to perform for him. But he can only do so by recognising that part of him must stay bird. His power to negotiate with the forces of the unconscious and to go on remaking his psyche in response to new changes depends on his seeing that there are two dimensions within the one world, and that he must move in both. For the sake of his full humanity, he cannot wholly return to the dimension of ordinary humanity, but must stay in part with the eagles. This, perhaps, is the parallel truth to that conveyed in *Gaudete* in the little word 'almost'.

Optimism is the most striking quality of *Cave Birds*. In its managing to bring the telling of Hughes' imaginative ground plan through to its completion in resurrection and marriage, and in its finding an appropriate answer to the problem of form with which he had wrestled in earlier works, it marks, with *Gaudete* and *Moortown*, the culmination of his effort in his most important field. And, in its implicit faith in ours as a time propitious for the radical redirection of our sensibilities along the lines it suggests, it is optimistic in a wider sense. A measure of this might be made by setting *Cave Birds* beside the two classics of twentieth-century literature which most resemble it in pattern and underlying theme (reflected in each case in terms of the relationship between the genders), Camus's *The Outsider* and Kafka's *The Trial*. Hughes' protagonist is a successor to Meursault and to Joseph K., but unlike them he undergoes a trial which ends not in death but in a special kind of redemption.

5
The *Moortown* Sequences

Moortown has many of the qualities of a Collected Poems: size, scope, stylistic variety, and contents drawn from a long period – it goes back as far as 1963 for one piece, 'Heatwave'. Despite this, it is not heterogeneous. Hughes has arranged the poems into a progression: the collection begins with man in working relationship with the earth, moves through an exploration of the quality and types of human consciousness and perception, which questions and tests that relationship, to a reaffirmation of it at a higher level. The movement is that of Baskin's spiral serpent lifting matter into spirit.

The subtleties of psychological and religious adjustment within a single mind form the core of Hughes' long-term exploration of how man can adapt himself to the given and so achieve a new kind of maturity. He has followed Blake's example in constructing narrative and dramatic sequences which achieve this. He names our different faculties and the eternal forces in life and dramatises the shifts in their balance. His hope is that such sequences will draw the reader's imagination, the key to his health, towards new strength and harmony. Each sequence therefore moves from disharmony, evasion, complacency and maladaptation toward harmony, acceptance, rehabilitation and adaptation.

'Prometheus on his Crag' and 'Adam and the Sacred Nine', the two longest sequences in *Moortown*, share these aims and a common format. Each begins with a primeval Everyman figure from one of the great myth systems. He represents the difficult mixture of the divine or spiritual and the bestial or bodily which is the human glory and conundrum. In each case he is lying on the ground. He is faced with the problem of how to come to terms with the facts. As he ponders this question he is visited by a bird or birds, and this affects his thinking. At the close he succeeds in coming through to some reconciliation which grants a type of freedom and maturity, and this is expressed in both cases by his first movement, the gesture of standing up.

These sequences are the two sides of a single coin. But one side

147

is darker than the other. At every turn 'Prometheus on his Crag' is more pain-ridden than 'Adam and the Sacred Nine'. Whilst Adam only lies bemused and 'defeated, low as water', Prometheus's prostration is a total, involuntary paralysis caused by the 'blue wedge through his breastbone, into the rock'. The birds who visit Adam come with examples of ways of living; the bird who visits Prometheus comes to eat his liver. Adam discovers himself through what appears to be a contemplation of choices; Prometheus's achievement is a coming to terms with the fact of pain.

These differences between the two sequences make them appropriate to the positions they occupy in *Moortown*. The brighter 'Adam and the Sacred Nine' forms a suitable conclusion to the volume, because it offers a moment of reconciliatory affirmation which returns in uplift to a point above the book's beginning. The darker 'Prometheus on his Crag', perhaps the finest fruit of Hughes' steadily deepening inwardness with myth, makes a suitable contrast with the previous section of *Moortown*, a group of farming poems that insist on the redeemed life. The farming poems, very different in style, are based on a series of assumptions (that nature is ultimately benevolent, that time heals, that man can find himself in working with the landscape) which 'Prometheus on his Crag' then throws into question and tests. The rich Devon soil gives way to the freezing hardness of a distant mountain peak. Man is suddenly linked to the earth not as Good Shepherd but as sufferer of the knowledge of pain and death. After a bucolic ministry, a spiritual crucifixion.

I

Since his play concerns itself with freedom and loss of it, Aeschylus begins *Prometheus Bound* as the Titan is about to be chained to his mountain. Freedom is important in Hughes' version, but suffering is more so. He begins immediately after Prometheus's binding, when he is alone at night on a distant windy peak, and the driving of the blue wedge through him into the rock beneath has forced him first unconscious and now delirious with agony. As the first poem opens (*Moortown*, p. 71) he is just beginning to come round. The broken lines give us his gasping hesitancy as he begins to explore his first sensations. Pain has brought amnesia. Not remembering what happened, he must rediscover it through the

feelings beginning to filter through him. But, for the moment, the
effort is too great. His faculties have not fully recombined. It is still
as though his face and words were not his own.

Then the questioning renews itself in him and he listens to the
messages brought by his body. Their answer is a surprise to the
reader. This moment ought to be the worst, when the pain is new
and unaccustomed, and the loss of freedom keenly felt. Instead,
there is this:

> Letting his veins venture for him
> Feeling his ice-burned lungs gulp huge clarity
> Letting his laborious chest lift him
>
> Like the wingbeats of an eagle
> and
> 'Am I an eagle?'

Prometheus is both literally and metaphorically in the dark, not
remembering or understanding what has 'altered'. Yet his lungs
'gulp huge clarity'. The act of breathing, and doing no more than
breathing, brings clarity, almost a minimal sort of understanding.
And, just as his darkness is alleviated or counterbalanced by the
simple clarity, so too his terrible immobility is offset by the language
of movement Hughes uses about the events within the body.
Prometheus is fixed, but his 'veins venture for him' and his chest
can 'lift him / Like the wingbeats of an eagle'. With the closing
question this startling image enters Prometheus's own thoughts.
Helpless, imprisoned and earthbound, he wonders if he might not
have altered into the eagle, that symbol of power and the freedom
of the skies. Poems 3 and 4, bringing the vulture's first visit, will
let him know how dreadful is the illusion he has entertained here.

But it is not wholly so. There is something in this poem, and
the next, which looks right forward to the climactic and redemptive
finale in poems 20 and 21. There really is a sense in which simply
feeling alive (and not masking or embellishing the few sensations
which tell of this) is a minimal wisdom. The achievement of the
sequence is to be built on this foundation. The raw tentativeness
here, and especially the capacity Prometheus shows for asking
questions, are positives which need remarking, even if they are
not to come to fruition until the very end of the sequence.

Poem 2 (p. 72) gives fuller play to this feeling of strength beneath pain and helplessness. Dawn comes, and Prometheus can see his situation. Again, what might be a moment for terror and despair emerges otherwise. He 'relaxes / In the fact that it has happened'. This relaxation fills him even though he is (within the as-yet limited range of his consciousness) seeing and feeling things exactly as they are, unmitigated:

> The blue wedge through his breastbone, into the rock,
> Unadjusted by vision or prayer – so.
>
> His eyes, brainless police.
> His brain, simple as an eye.

He is passive, choiceless, mutely registering the sensations associated with his eternal fate. And this produces in him something akin to rejoicing and triumph, again symbolised by eaglehood. The hint of blood soon to be spilled, in the 'reddening dawn', undercuts the exultation, but does not destroy it completely.

In Aeschylus and his sources, Prometheus's strength is his knowledge that the punishment he suffers is not eternal. Zeus will one day need to release him and crave his assistance. Hughes makes no mention of this here. His Prometheus is realising a fate which 'never can be otherwise'. Though the Titan will in the final poem stand up and 'ease free' this will be no escape from his fate, but instead a turning to account of what here, at the start, is established as the permanently given. The final poems subsume and transform the experience portrayed in these first two. Prometheus is, then, a symbol not of some special fate, but of the human condition.

The opening poems have given us, in effect, the birth of consciousness, and, with that, the first symbol of the accompanying pain, the blue wedge. The next two bring a second and yet more terrifying manifestation, the vulture. Poem 3 (p. 73) is a Fall, brought about by the introduction of time, whose symbol the vulture is to become. In the mythology recorded in *Orghast at Persepolis* Prometheus is

> fractured. He is the crossroads of eternal light and ecstasy, and temporal doom, pain, change and death. Conscious in eternity, he has to live in time. And he cannot solve his dilemma. He hangs between heaven and earth, almost torn apart, an open wound, immortal.
>
> (Smith, *Orghast at Persepolis*, p. 94)

Time's advent in the sequence is dramatic, as Prometheus's 'world's end shout' ends the 'holy, happy notions' amongst which is his half-numb and limited sensory attunement of the first two poems. But the Fall is not for Prometheus alone; the rest of creation suffers too. The shout 'brings Prometheus peace / And woke the vulture'.

We think first perhaps of the peace as being the very temporary relief from pain which a shout can bring. In this light, the close of the poem has, like everything else in these early pieces about strength and freedom, a simple and savage dramatic irony: un-knowingly, Prometheus has bought a little respite at the price of himself initiating the worst of his tortures. But there is another, deeper sense in which the irony is absent. There can be no redemption without the need for it. The vulture is ultimately necessary to Prometheus's salvation. It is his final, balanced contemplation of it in poem 20 which constitutes his triumph and which issues in the rebirth of the final poem. This torture is Gower's 'vulnus dulce'. It is not until right at the end of this sequence that such wisdom will be realised by Prometheus, but it is foreshadowed in poem 3.

Poem 4 (*Moortown*, p. 74) describes the vulture's first visit. As in lines 6–7 of poem 2, Prometheus is the passive and accepting victim, merely witnessing his own fate:

> There was nothing for him to do
> As it splayed him open from breastbone to crotch
> But peruse its feathers.
>
> Black, bold and plain were those headline letters.

The line which follows this, despite its plainness and simplicity, is one of Hughes' most effective. The poem steps right outside the mythological setting and the mode of writing that it has generated, and addresses the reader directly: 'Do you want to know what they said?' The vulture embodies a truth so terrible that we are given the opportunity of a pause for self-examination before deciding whether to face its challenge:

> 'Today is a fresh start
> Torn up by its roots
> As I tear the liver from your body.'

The truth carried in the vulture's feathers is a darker version of that embodied in the goblin at the end of *Cave Birds*. As no achievement is final, so, too, none of life's pains is final.

Hughes has stripped down the mythological apparatus of the Prometheus story to a bare minimum for his sequence. Io, Pandora, Zeus, the divine visitors of Aeschylus's version – none of these plays an active part. Why then has he retained this additional symbol of Prometheus' pain? Why have the vulture as well as the wedge and the chains? Its purpose is more than intensificatory. The wedge is permanently present, the vulture repeatedly so. The difference between the two lies, then, in the vulture's association with time and its eternal painful repetitions, and this is suggested by the message of its feathers.

Prometheus's reaction to the vulture occupies the rest of the sequence, which traces a succession of lapses and advances, phases of hope and hopelessness, calm and disturbance. But his first reaction, in poem 5 (*Moortown*, p. 75), is, as with many victims of overwhelming circumstances, to pretend that nothing has happened. The vulture leaves. He falls asleep, and the Calderonian theme of dream and illusion enters the sequence. Prometheus 'Dreamed he had burst the sun's mass / And emerged mortal'. What causes Prometheus's problem is neither his spiritual divine nature, nor his bodily mortal nature. To live either half alone would be comparatively easy. What pains him is having to live both simultaneously. The dream of poem 5 tries, unsuccessfully, to solve his problem by jettisoning his divine–spiritual side. The gesture which will express his eventual success will be a standing upright. The falsity of the dream's solution is therefore given here in an incomplete gesture. He can only raise part of himself:

> He raised his earth-soaked head
> Like a new-born calf. A skirl of cold air
>
> Joggled the flowers.

His dream is of a reversal of the Fall, everything put back into the 'heart's jar'. But just as Pandora, in the original myth, could not return to her jar what she had loosed, so Prometheus cannot undo his deed. He has irrevocably set in motion the succession of events of which he has, it seems, become the victim:

> He had resolved God

As a cow swallows its afterbirth.

But over the dark earth escaped
The infant's bottomless cry, the mother's lament,
The father's curse.

Only the afterbirth is swallowed, not the infant. Who is the infant?
It is man, Prometheus's creation in the version Hughes follows.
But, more centrally, it is Prometheus himself. The cattle-birth
imagery has him as both cow, 'swallowing' God, and 'new-born
calf', the infant which escapes and cannot be resolved away,
but goes on crying. Prometheus's dream solution would be an
impossibility, a suicide, an undoing of the being he is.

He has perhaps partly fitted himself to the constant presence of
the wedge, but not to that of the vulture, the element of time. In
poem 6 (p. 76), after the failure of his dream, his realisation of
the universe as an endless repetition of events all the same, all
painful, all issueless, drives him mad and dumb, making him see
the world stretching down and out from his peak as a sickening
and sickened jumble of meaninglessness. The sun has risen and
its burning heat is cooking him now, as the cold freezes him at
night. All his initial attempts at thinking up an explanation for his
predicament have failed:

The thoughts that basted sweat down his flushed features
And carved his body in a freezing ecstasy
Like a last supper, are dead as Harakhty.

The vulture, burying its head in him to punish him for his crime,
sends him again into delirium, which Hughes evokes with a clutter
of dissonant images. Time lies at the heart of this confusion and
rambling. The images chosen to express it stretch from geological
prehistory (the 'cretaceous') to the present day ('car bumpers and
shopping baskets'). But hidden beneath this dislocation is the
pattern of life and death, the succession of 'corpses and embryos',
which is essentially what the vulture's repeated visits symbolise.
Its ripping of his liver is death; the liver's regrowth, life. We have
only the one death to face, if we choose to face it at all. Even in
grief we may be staying locked in self-pity. Only in rare moments
do our minds move out, through the widening perspectives
provided by the deaths of relatives, the deaths in history, the

deaths constituent in the animal and vegetable kingdom, to face
the ubiquitous presence of death itself. Hughes has made this
journey. So, too, has Prometheus, for it is his fate and punishment
that a confrontation with death is forced upon him by its happening
daily inside him and whilst he remains aware.

Even in this poem there is hope for Prometheus. His thoughts
are 'dead as Harakhty', a minor Egyptian deity. He is dead in the
sense that almost all Hughes' readers will have to look him up in a
handbook of mythology. He is now neither worshipped nor widely
remembered. But his mention here goes with the phrase 'a last
supper' to suggest that present deadness is part of a pattern leading
to ultimate resurrection and triumph. The reader who looks him
up will find that he is often equated with Harmachis, that aspect
of Ra which represents the rising sun, and therefore also with the
solar falcon god, Horus, who in *Cave Birds* is the symbol of rebirth.

Prometheus on his Crag was first published, as a limited edition,
in 1973. Poem 7 (*Moortown*, p. 77) is one of three new pieces written
for the *Moortown* reprinting (the others being 5 and 17). These
poems have been carefully integrated with each other and into the
sequence by means of a few shared images: the sun, chains, flowers
and freedom. Part of their effect is to strengthen the extent to
which poem 21 is prepared for by its predecessors. The notion of
freedom is now present at a number of junctures before the
climactic rising up. And the 'crocus evangels' of poem 21 now
have precursors in poems 5 and 17; whilst here,

> So the sun bloomed, as it drank him,
> Earth purpled its crocus.
>
> So he flowered
> Flowers of a numb bliss, a forlorn freedom –
>
> Groanings of the sun, sighs of the earth –
>
> Gathered by withering men.

This poem, like several others, especially in the middle of the
sequence, is Janus-faced. By its conclusion everything has taken
on a flowerishness – even men, who wither as flowers do, and the
vulture, which is 'planted'. This imagery bespeaks 'freedom' and
looks forward to the final resolution. But the poem also looks right

back to Prometheus's original crime, the theft of fire. And we have to note too that the flowers here are 'groanings', 'sighs' and 'bloody', and the freedom 'forlorn'. It is this poem, with its angry sun and its interrogation of Prometheus's bones, as though his physical existence might itself disclose a guilt, which links the sequence most clearly with the early part of *Cave Birds*.

Having seen the initial situation here reasserted, we now see Prometheus in poem 8 (*Moortown*, p. 78) starting again to make some attempt at understanding. The whole sequence works in just this way, making brief forays out from its basic facts until it reaches error, then recoiling, then starting again in a new direction. Here we have recoiled back to his basic paralysis, symbolic of the human condition, and something Prometheus's acts in the past have failed to prepare him for; he

> Lay astonished all his preparations
> For his humanity
> Were disablements he lay disabled

'His humanity' suggests itself as the men and women he has created, who are to be important in poem 16, but more as Prometheus's own humanity, the duality which became his when he, a god, was nailed to the earth and mortality.

Hughes is not inviting us to condemn Prometheus's past acts. There is a clear sense, in Hughes' later poetry as much as in his earlier, in which reality, in order to be experienced as such, cannot be prepared for. This is expressed succinctly in a short poem in the Rainbow Press *Orts*:

> He found he had been learning a language
> In school.
> Now he comes to the land where it is spoken.
>
> And he understands nothing. And he is dumb.

The drive towards epiphany, the revelation of the real in all its pristine reality, necessitates that the appearance be fresh and naked, the perception raw. The curtain of mental habit and convention must be torn aside. This is one direction in which Hughes' work pushes. The other is towards fitting oneself to the facts, towards being ready to accept reality rather than fleeing it or distorting it. But how can one be ready without anticipating the reality, which means having a pattern of expectations, which means being prepared? And how close that preparedness is to convention and habit! The best of Hughes' poetry pays scrupulous attention to the fact that the major positive of readiness is always threatening to tip over into its enemies, convention and habit. In *Orghast* terms, he is aware that the hero is always about to become the tyrant, Agoluz become Krogon the Second. Hand-in-hand with this goes a vigilance on the other difficult dividing line, that which runs between the Wodwo faculties of openness to experience, tentativeness and wise insecurity on the one side, and a disastrous unreadiness on the other. Keeping these two pairs apart, readiness from habit, and openness from unreadiness, is health, and part of the maturity Hughes offers.

Unreadiness and openness are both present in poem 8, though openness is still subsidiary at this stage. It is present in the renewal of Prometheus's capacity to ask questions for the first time since poem 1. To be able to ask questions rather than make statements and give answers or theorise or fantasise is a positive sign in Hughes' heroes, from Wodwo onwards. It will represent Prometheus' rehabilitation in poem 20. But here it goes wrong. The lineation of the verse has already given the poem a rushed feeling, as though Prometheus were just managing to control a rising hysteria. This swells until it bursts out and overwhelms him, stopping off his spinning questions and producing the terrible final scene:

> Was he new born was he wounded fatal
> An invalid new born healing
> Bone fractures alert alarmed death numbness
>
> Was this stone his grave this cradle
> Nothingness nothingness over him over him
> Whose mouth and eyes? A mother another
>
> Prisoner a jailor? He spoke it was a scream

A flick forward to the achieved calm of poem 20 will show the progress Prometheus still has to make. Any movement out of numbness is at present only into terror. We are still in a phase which recalls *Crow*'s deviations into emotional excess.

In the next two poems Prometheus' hysteria subsides; he is able
to steady himself inwardly and, for the first time, focus and direct
an active attention (different from the passive registrations he
makes in the opening poems) onto what is increasingly identified
as the key to his problem, the vulture. 'The cure . . . will be to
understand this bird and come to some final reconciliation' (Smith,
Orghast at Persepolis, p. 97). This focusing of attention away from
himself and onto the vulture is, then, an important advance. It is
marked by Prometheus's being allowed to address the reader for
the first time (poem 9, *Moortown*, p. 79). Using words is more
promising than the scream of the previous poem, and his speech
avoids the error he is to fall into in poem 15 of placing his hope in
the future (the hope that sustains him in Aeschylus), instead
accepting, albeit a little sourly, that the situation is permanent,
'cannot be otherwise':

> Now I know I never shall
>
> Be let stir.
> The man I fashioned and the god I fashioned
> Dare not let me stir.

There is even a touch of self-esteem here, as though his dual
nature, holding together mortal and immortal, raised him above
simpler beings who are merely mortal or merely divine. Pinioned
and immobile as he is, his consciousness represents a new mode
of being, a new departure for life which has such potential that it
frightens the other beings of creation. Prometheus is a steep torrent
(this water imagery will be picked up in poem 21) so powerful
they must dam it:

> This leakage of cry these face-ripples
> Calculated for me – for mountain water
> Dammed to powerless stillness.

Though he is now stilled, his potential is not extinguished. It is
for the moment lost to him; but that it exists he does not doubt.
That his unrealised power, his secret, should be hidden from him
is daunting and galling. That it should seem to lie in the possession
of the vulture, which brings him such pain and yet leaves things
still so mysterious, is even worse. For the moment, in the face of

this, Prometheus slips backwards into disgust and hatred:

> Only he knows – that bird, that
> Filthy-gleeful emissary and
> The hieroglyph he makes of my entrails

> Is all he tells.

Prometheus's dilemma is so painful and so difficult that (like Crow with his Black Beast) he feels he needs someone outside himself to blame, and the vulture presents itself as the all-too-obvious choice. Nevertheless, he is managing to speak, asking, and looking straight at the vulture. For all the negatives still evident in him at this stage, he has begun to make real gains. Yet, progress from here is to be anything but smooth.

Emotional opposites resemble and generate each other. Having first hated it, Prometheus 'Began to admire the vulture' (poem 10, p. 80) for its serene uncomplicated efficiency. In most respects this is a further advance. A negative emotion has been turned into what seems to be a positive one. Something appears to have been settled or resolved. Yet immediately after this piece Prometheus is to plunge back into escapism, pessimism and despair, which, though mixed with brighter signs, will occupy the sequence right through to poem 16, where the final upturn begins. And the seeds of this regression lie here. Prometheus's admiration masks the danger that, by a sleight of mind, he will step aside from his problem altogether, shift it onto the vulture and thus make it seem to disappear. The poem gives us a new formulation of his basic dilemma, the contradictory facts to which he is struggling to fit himself: 'the gift of life / And the cost of the gift'. Prometheus sees in the vulture a 'balancing' of these two. In the final poem, when he stands up, we are reminded of this: 'He sways to his stature. / And balances.' But it will be his own balance Prometheus discovers there. And the last line of poem 10 surely suggests that there is something which for Prometheus himself would be inappropriate about what he makes the vulture stand for. He can try to understand the vulture, try to reconcile himself to it. But he cannot make an example of it, or try to copy it. Neither the gift, nor the cost of the gift, can ever be 'nothing' for him. He is a creature of developed consciousness, as the vulture is not. Digestion is no solution for his guilt.

This caveat about the dangers behind his admiration must not be overstated. If we look back at the hysteria of poem 8, the insanity of poem 6, and the numbness and passivity of the earliest poems, then the advances of poems 9 and 10 are clearer.

With poem 11 (p. 81) we learn that Prometheus has been dreaming again. It has been a dream of exquisite but trapping beauty. Everything ugly, heavy, imprisoning and unhappy has been turned into its opposite or transformed. Prometheus is just surfacing, and in his half-awakened state seeks to enjoy the dream once more. Safety, the struggle passed to others, and pain transcended by a tender fragile beauty – these are what he dreams. The image of the butterfly, so light it is almost weightless, has grown in his sleeping mind out of the vulture 'balancing the gift . . . and the cost . . . As if both were nothing'. But, as in poems 5 and 15, the closing lines tell Prometheus that his dream is no more than that, a false hope which makes the reality all the more terrible by contrast:

> But now he woke to a world where the sun was the sun,
> Iron iron,
> > sea sea,
> > > sky sky,
> > > > the vulture the vulture.

There has been no real transcendence or transformation. In fact nothing has changed. The world is as Prometheus knew it yesterday. Yet such is the pathos generated by his dream that we cannot condemn him for it, and this is true also of the next error.

In poem 12 (p. 82) he is still in the grips of escapism, this time in the form of a song. To sing is better than to scream. But his song does not do justice to reality. It seems to ignore both his own circumstances and the product of his previous actions. It is a pain-killer, not a cure.

Man, cut off from his benefactor Prometheus, has misused the gift of fire. In Aeschylus, Prometheus traces with pride the growth of all subsequent human technology from this one gift. In Hughes this gift and its development seem to have issued in war and pollution.

The introduction of man at this point provides the necessary conditions for a further shift in Prometheus's consciousness which is soon to begin. We have seen him thus far shifting from initial numbness, through the helpless passive registration of a few near sensations, via various backslidings, into a contemplation of the vulture. There is now to be a renewal of this movement outwards from himself, this time into consideration of his creation, men and women, his fellow beings. This new development, though fitful and accompanied by various negative emotions, nevertheless entails the growth of Prometheus's conception of himself as suffering not absurdly but on behalf of others. The introduction of man here will, that is, soon provide a new focus of attention permitting the growth of sympathy, the turning-outwards of Prometheus' suffering, and this will issue, in poem 16, in his sense of himself as 'THE PAYMENT'. There the trickster, the meddler in creation, becomes the self-sacrificing redeemer. Or, rather, the possibility of that new role is faced, and this permits the final upturn of the sequence in the five concluding poems.

Prometheus's attention is first drawn in this direction in poem 13 (p. 83). Just as his attitude to the vulture started with a negative emotion, so too his first thoughts about man are jaundiced and full of guilt and revulsion. Prometheus is immortal; he can feel death happening inside him, but cannot irrecoverably die. He has no need to breed to perpetuate himself. He suffers the repeated pains of life and death, not as men and women do, but in the speeded-up and intensified, symbolic form of the vulture's visits. But the two fates are essentially similar, as we noted at the very beginning in saying that Prometheus was Everyman. And now Prometheus becomes aware of his kinship. He recognises, first, his own responsibility towards humanity. The fire is not only the energy which has produced 'the smoulder . . . from the cities'. It is, before that, the fire of life itself, the energy which manifests itself first in the drive for biological reproduction, which Prometheus, as creator, also gave man. He is now on the verge of seeing that in giving man life he gave him suffering, and as a result he views the sexual process in a black way reminiscent of *Crow*. Death appears to him with dark associations; and life is no blessing, just a reluctantly followed compulsion. One responsible for such pain must feel guilty, and that his own pains are a punishment:

> And it seemed
> That the vulture was the revenge of the wombs
> To show him what it was like,
>
> That his chains would last, and the vulture would awake him,

As long as there were wombs
Even if that were forever,

And that he had already invented too much.

Perhaps, with the recurrence of vulture and chains, Prometheus's thoughts have recoiled towards his own fate. Nevertheless, the crucial foray, however distasteful to him, into the fate of others has been made.

The revulsion extends into the next poem (poem 14, p. 84); his brief glimpse into the sufferings of humanity has expanded into a vision of ubiquitous pain. Appropriately enough, the metaphor which expresses this fills the whole poem. Pain is in the inanimate. It is in man, to whom Prometheus seems no benefactor; and in all man's associates and efforts. And it is in every aspect of creation between the inanimate and man. Everything from the tiny, humble snail to the earth itself is part of a single pattern of suffering.

From this pessimism Prometheus moves into illusion once more. Poem 15 (p. 85) is the third and last of his dreams, and it is patterned like poem 11: the wish-fulfilling dream of a transcendence or escape from his dilemma, followed by a final line which drags him with three pulls back down into an unaltered reality which shows that his dream is a false solution. But in other respects it differs from the earlier dreams. It brings to the fore again the theme of time, which we earlier identified as distinguishing the vulture from the wedge and the chains. The theme has been present implicitly in Prometheus's consideration of the biological cycles of life and death suffered by mankind. Time, through these cycles, is the cause of man's pain. Through the vulture it is the cause of Prometheus's. But now, in a remarkable turn, his dream presents him with the alluring notion that time, one of the very terms of his pain and imprisonment, might also provide an escape from them. For he sees not only this

                  centre of every aeon,
     Like the grit in its pearl,
     Himself sealed on his rock

but also a second self, upright and mobile:

       wading escaping through dark nothing

> From aeon to aeon, prophesying Freedom –

> It was his soul's sleepwalking and he dreamed it.

Much in Hughes testifies to the danger of splitting oneself thus. It invariably means a failure to face reality. So it is here, as the close of the poem tells us. Time is no escape. To postpone one's hopes, to make freedom the subject of a prophesy rather than making it a present state of mind, is to give up the task of adjustment to reality. Again, this stage is not simple. The dream, escapist and unsatisfactory, contains hints of success to come. The phrase 'advantageous prospect' tells us that his position has real hope. And the image of him as 'the grit in its pearl' suggests that his suffering is to issue in something rich, rare and magnificent. Also, the image of 'himself wading . . . sleepwalking', even though here associated with escape, anticipates the last three lines of poem 21.

With poem 16 (p. 86) the movement towards that final climax is clearly under way. This is true despite a tragic element here. Prometheus at last finds one way of coming to terms with the vulture. He now actively accepts his suffering, undertaking it for the benefit of others; sacrifice has become self-sacrifice, voluntary altruism:

> He yields his own entrails
> A daily premium
> To the winged Death In Life, to keep it from men.

He has become 'THE PAYMENT'. The tragedy lies in the fact that his self-sacrifice cannot achieve the desired outcome, for he is

> Too far from his people to tell them

> Now they owe nothing.

The heroic deed is ignored. It is as if Christ took courage and ascended the cross to redeem his people, but no one was there to notice or record the event, and the gospels went unwritten. The result of this ignorance is that man is condemned to 'misunderstanding and [to] die in suffering as often as he is created' (Smith, *Orghast at Persepolis*, p. 8).

Prometheus's assumption of the role of redeemer is an important moment and it is now (poem 17, *Moortown*, p. 87) marked by a pause and an alteration in the focus of the sequence. Hughes' version of the myth has always been pared down to essentials. Now he takes the daring step of removing even such mythical elements as had been preserved previously. The whole business has just been a way of speaking, and, in so far as the mythological characters and entities come between us and reality, they must be jettisoned. This ancient Greek story with its gods and wedges and vultures is only a metaphor. There is 'No God – only wind on the flower'. Prometheus's chains have been just a way of indicating the burden of mortality we all carry in our bodies: 'No chains – only sinews, nerves, bones'. The vulture too was symbolic of the energy running through time and life. The wound the vulture renews daily is now explicitly described in terms similar to those we saw latent in the close of poem 3. Gower's 'vulnus dulce' becomes 'the vital immortal wound'. Vital in two senses: in that it is vita, life itself; and in that it is necessary to Prometheus's salvation. And immortal in two senses: in that the wound is everlasting; and in that it is the source of his redemption and a new and deeper kind of immortality for him.

At the same time as poem 17 is abolishing the main structural metaphors of the Prometheus myth, it is also reiterating or introducing others. The six closing lines of the poem provide metaphors for the vulture and what it is associated with. New amongst these is this: 'A word . . . One nuclear syllable'. The verbal metaphor is to be important in poem 19, and will come to fruition in the line 'The mountain is uttering' in the final poem (which will reverse the imagery of swallowing and digestion dominant earlier). But for the moment the potential it offers remains balked. The word is still 'unutterable', the syllable bleeds 'silence'.

The next piece (poem 18, p. 88) provides a characteristically Hughesian surprise. After a poem stripping away the mythological apparatus comes one which makes more extensive reference to it than any other in the sequence. Besides Prometheus, we have Epimetheus and Io mentioned and Pandora alluded to. Hughes is using the first eleven lines for an occupatio, the medieval rhetorician's device for signalling that he is deliberately reshaping his material and investing it with new significance. He is recalling these other characters only to point up their absence and make it intentional, so as to lend a special force to the close of the poem:

The figure overlooked in this fable
Is the tiny trickle of lizard

Listening near the ear of Prometheus,
Whispering – at his each in-rip of breath,
Even as the vulture buried its head –

'Lucky, you are so lucky to be human!'

Someone important has been missed out in the previous poems, and not, so to speak, deliberately.

Underlying the ebb and flow of Prometheus's growth in the sequence has been a trend for his attention to be directed outwards from himself to the vulture and then to mankind. The final phase of this movement is now introduced. After mankind, Prometheus must consider his responsibilities for the non-human creation, represented by the lizard. This poem thus provides an occasion for remarking the unity of theme in *Moortown*. The farming poems in its first section have shown us man in working relationship with and responsible for nature. The philosophical or religious basis for that responsibility is now brought home to Prometheus. And in 'Adam and the Sacred Nine' and 'A Citrine Glimpse' this will be further developed. What the lizard invites Prometheus to is not merely a counting of his blessings. It is not just that, despite his awful suffering, Prometheus enjoys an endowment quite beyond the lizard. It is not even the more complex truth that the suffering and the endowment are one and the same. To get the full impact of the poem we must ask why the lizard speaks. It can hear the pain in his breathing, so we cannot take it that the lizard mistakes Prometheus's situation for bliss or freedom. Nor is there any evidence to suggest that the lizard's existence involves a suffering by comparison with which Prometheus's pains appear as luck. The lizard's visit is neither in envy of him, nor to cheer him up. It comes to recall him to a task. It reminds him of his responsibility, as the growing tip of the evolutionary process, to every creature that has gone before him and paved the way for his unprecedented potential. This responsibility involves care for other creatures, as the farming poems have shown. But before that, and more important, is the renewed injunction to go on with the task of discovering what it is to be human, to fight for the actualising of the potential granted, to bring into being the next evolutionary stage. Prometheus's heroic role is to be something more than it would have been had poem 16 represented the final phase of the sequence. Partly this is a matter of his responsibilities having widened out from a too-distant humanity to take in all nature. But of greater centrality is the revelation that self-sacrifice is not enough. To go on simply suffering, even voluntarily and altruistically, as 'THE PAYMENT', is not the highest heroism. Prometheus's responsibility to others must rather be expressed through responsibility to himself. It is through his own inner development that he will carry out his duties to others on the evolutionary ladder.

The core of this self-development is the capacity for thought, the developed higher consciousness that distinguishes the fully, maturely human. The movement of 'Prometheus on his Crag' is towards getting him to think straight, and the poems go to defining what straight thinking of the right kind is. It has been clear since the verbal metaphor in poem 17 that such thinking necessarily involves words; now, in poem 19 (p. 89), with his first attempt at bringing the flame to utterance, Prometheus learns the slipperiness and evanescence of words, the gap between words and experience, as in 'Crow Goes Hunting'. We notice two or three faults in Prometheus's use of words here, to be corrected in the next poem. First, there is an absence of focus. He has not homed in with his newly recognised tool on the area of concern. He is trying to grab everything at once with words.

We are perhaps also justified in seeing these words as of the wrong kind, belonging to the abstracting intellect. The speaker's words must not only be directed outwards, but also take up and resolve what lies inside him. In poem 19 this has not happened: there is still an untapped and unresolved emotion. Prometheus begins with a shout of words and ends dumb and terrified. Something of the previous hysteria is still present.

The opening sentence of poem 20 (p. 90) is enough to remove all these errors: 'Prometheus . . . Pondered the vulture'. Calm, directed towards the vulture, attuned to his own suffering, as well as to outward circumstances, Prometheus has learned to use words in meditation, as a poet or sage does. And, as with other protagonists in Hughes, his new wisdom is partly a capacity to ask questions. These questions are steady and focused, as their predecessors in poem 8 are not. In *Orghast at Persepolis* Smith lists the values attaching to the vulture theme:

To Pramanath it is the open wound, the eternally repeated death in pain (Agoluz's death) of his manifestation in time, and of his punishment by Krogon's conditions in that world. It is Light, his consciousness of his position.

To Sogis it is the agony of the divine Pramanath, which he suffers too, as a crime, as guilt for not having yet solved the dilemma; and, in so far as he shares Moa's sufferings, it is his jailor, the eye of Krogon.

To Krogon it is his prisoners, the earth, his own body, his bond with animal life on one hand, with spirit on the other; a compound crime he refuses to recognise, which is slowly dementing him.

To Man it is his sickness, the call to resolve the mysterious dilemma, as with Sogis; the complex of the crime, as with Krogon; his suffering in time, the commitments of his material body, as with Pramanath; the deprivations of being divided, as with all the personae.   (pp. 96–7)

In the poem sequence, Prometheus brings to mind each of the possible significances of the vulture in turn. They are presented as alternatives. But Smith's listing, where the vulture is all of these possibilities, gives us good reason for seeing Prometheus's questions as a survey and summary of everything the vulture means. None of these now give him the need for dream and escape, or for disgust, hatred, admiration or hysteria. There is not even the need for a final settled answer. Prometheus has arrived at the style of mature thinking Hughes finds in Vasko Popa and kindred poets and expresses in introducing Popa's *Collected Poems 1943–1976*:

In their very poetic technique – the infinitely flexible, tentative, pragmatic freedom with which they handle their explorations – we read a code of wide-openness to what is happening, within or without, a careful refusal to seal themselves off from what hurts and carries the essential information, a careful refusal to surrender themselves to any mechanical progression imposed on them by the tyranny of their own words or images, an endless scrupulous alertness on the frontiers of false and true. In effect, it is an intensely bracing moral vigilance. They accept in a sense what the prisoner must accept, who cannot pretend that any finger is at large.   (p. 3)

Heidegger in *The Question Concerning Technology* defines a kind of reflection which is 'calm, self-possessed surrender to that which is worthy of questioning' (p. 180).

Most of Prometheus's tentative suggestions about the vulture are quite closely related to each other, variants on a few basic themes. Each of them draws out a possibility which has been implicit in the situation as it has appeared in the nineteen preceding poems. The first question establishes the intimate relationship between Prometheus and the vulture, which is no longer to be distanced, either by hatred or by admiration. He and it are recognised as one flesh. But what part of him is it exactly? Is it his physical, bodily aspect, or is it his immortal divinity? Those questions still contain a residual sense of conflict, of the two aspects of his being as damaging each other. The next two begin the turn outwards and upwards, following the pattern of the whole sequence. Through the vulture he recalls his fellow creatures: 'the fates to be suffered in his image.' Next comes the possibility that the pain the vulture inflicts is what has brought him to being, and may even lead elsewhere. Is the vulture a doorway? And then comes the most daunting and basic of alternatives, linking the sequence with *Eat Crow* and with *Cave Birds*. Prometheus begins to ask questions about his guilt, and wonders if his very life might be a crime. The next questions follow from this, and recall poem 13 (where the vulture was the womb's revenge). They ask if life itself is a theft of an energy which then avenges itself by consuming the thief or by stealing itself back from him.

Two of the remaining three alternatives develop more positive possibilities. Prometheus's meditation has brought him to the point where he can see his suffering as neither pointless nor purely altruistic but part of his own responsible inner development. To have been able to ask the preceding questions is to have realised that his pains are part of an educative process, a growth to maturity, an adaptation through error:

> was it the earth's enlightenment –
> Was he an uninitiated infant
> Mutilated towards alignment?

This last line brings to mind the Lumb of the *Gaudete* Epilogue asking his goddess, 'How will you correct / The veteran of negatives . . . ?', and 'The guide' in *Cave Birds* with his tacking and veering. Both Lumb and Prometheus ask extremely humble

questions, and show great circumspection, recognising that most
of their previous experience has been error-ridden and that they
have made only a precious little progress. Neither of them sees
how, or if, things will develop further. Nevertheless, located in
those questions, and in the guardedness of hope they carry, is a
human quality answering to and extending the realism–optimism
Hughes elsewhere celebrates in the animal kingdom. It is seeing
things as they are and refusing to be daunted by them.

That this, even though no more than a tentative question, and
one amongst many possibilities, is a major positive, won through
to, is corroborated by the final question, which sees the vulture in
a new way:

> was it, after all, the Helper
> Coming again to pick at the crucial knot
> Of all his bonds . . . ?

The word 'Helper' is the culmination of the whole sequence. That
Prometheus can use such a word is a sign of the achieved freedom
to be pictured in poem 21. The last lines here give a further
sign: the vulture's orbit traces out a mandala, Jung's symbol of
wholeness, which it has become without ceasing to be what it has
always been.

In poem 21 (*Moortown*, p. 92), as in 'Adam and the Sacred Nine',
the hero's triumph is symbolised in the simple gesture of standing
up. He achieves freedom at last. But, unlike that of his dreams,
this is a freedom within the terms of existence, not outside them.
And he has achieved 'his stature', neither more nor less. He has
accepted his humanity and so brought it to full bloom:

> The mountain is flowering
> A gleaming man.

As these lines suggest, this poem uses a number of other strands
of metaphor, beside the gesture of standing, to convey his achievement. In this it is like 'The owl flower' in *Cave Birds* and 'The
Phoenix' in 'Adam and the Sacred Nine', as it also is in choosing
those metaphors to draw together various pre-established elements
in the sequence's repertoire of symbols.

The dominant strand is of birth, or rebirth. The mountain, once
a prison, is now a mother in the act of delivery. The 'disinherited

figure chained in the mountain's heart' which Hughes speaks about in his Note to his *Selected Poems 1957–1981* has been reinherited. The vulture, once an enemy, is now a midwife, perhaps itself a phoenix. Accompanying the imagery of birth is that of blossoming and fruition. The source of the pain has been transformed, the 'blue wedge' (poem 2) has become 'the blue fig'. Prometheus is himself the product of a 'flowering'; and he is accompanied by 'crocus evangels', one of the hardest worked phrases in the sequence. Evangels are biblical good news. One function of the phrase is, therefore, to recall and revalue the notion of redemption in poem 16. Placing this word in apposition to 'crocus' also serves to link the strand of flowering imagery to another, that of the production of words:

> And the cry bulges . . .
> The mountain is uttering
> Blood and again blood.
> Puddled blotched newsprint.
>
> With crocus evangels.

This is the rounding-off and climax of the verbal metaphor introduced in poem 17. Finally, the phrase 'crocus evangels' refers us back to a detail of the original myth recorded in Graves' *Greek Myths*. In the story of the Golden Fleece,

> Jason was summoned, and swore by all the gods of Olympus to keep faith with Medea for ever. She offered him a flask of lotion, blood-red juice of the two-stalked, saffron-coloured Caucasian crocus, which would protect him against the bulls' fiery breath; this potent flower first sprang from the blood of the tortured Prometheus.   (vol. 2, p. 238)

The implication of this for poem 21 is that through the crocus imagery Prometheus's suffering, his shed blood, has become an elixir, the gift the returning hero brings with him for his people.

The last sentence adapts an image which the alchemists use to indicate the completion of their opus, the achievement of selfhood:

> And treads
>
> On the dusty peacock film where the world floats.

This derives from the alchemical *cauda pavonis*, or peacock's tail. The word 'floats' signals the realisation of the best of the prophetic sleepwalking 'wading' of poem 15, and the final peace of the water in poem 9. With such touches Hughes weaves together the various metaphors of the sequence, so that the climax seems firmly rooted in what has preceded it.

II

Within the great variety of procedure which characterises the 'Earth-numb' section of *Moortown* are to be found five short sequences the poems of which are in each case closely related to one another by either a narrative or a symbolic development of theme. The penultimate of these is 'Seven Dungeon Songs' which shares much with Hughes' longer mythic sequences, especially *Cave Birds*.

The first Dungeon Song, 'The wolf' (p. 123), introduces the two representatives of the colliding forces of 'Earth-numb' which Hughes identified on radio (in May 1980) as awareness and life on the one hand and unawareness and mere circumstances on the other. Here the symbol of life is the wolf, and the symbol of that which will be locked into and bound by unawareness is a human baby. However, it is not until we have a grasp of the shifting symbols and the stylistic strategies of the sequence as a whole that we are able to identify wolf and baby in this way. Our first response is different. The poem strikes us as a fixed picture of some permanent reality, finished and cut off, resistant to translation into other terms, and not at all likely to give rise to any subsequent narrative development. The poem brings together again the main constituents of the *Wodwo* poem 'The Howling of Wolves': wolf and baby, cold, night, stars. But here the baby assumes an importance equal to that of the wolf, so that the poem becomes, from its first lines ('The wolf / Gazed down at the babe') a bringing-together of balanced and equal opposites. This equality is one source of the poem's iconic stasis, part of what subverts its latent dynamism. The unlikeness of wolf and baby provides a very complete contrast. The baby is totally vulnerable, exposed and lost, without the protection of its parents, without physical strength and expertise for survival in a world which includes predation, and without any experience for guidance. It is in every sense naked. The wolf is an exact opposite: by focusing on its mouth and eye the poem cannot but remind us of the wolf's expertise in hunting, and therefore of its being at home in the natural world; it is invulnerable. But the same focusing reminds us also of the pain, the perpetual woundedness, which is the wolf's lot for being so uncomprehendingly subjected to and limited to its role in the cycles of predation. The baby has, instead of this icy agony, the laugh of innocence and potential. This allotment of tears and laughter, so strange in the situation of the first poem, which could scarcely favour the wolf's adaptedness more (there seems only one outcome of this meeting), comes to seem more apt when we read the second poem and realise what has happened to the balance of power between wolf and baby in the narrative gap between the two poems. That gap, we then see, stands for the long-term human failure to develop a potential which lay in the baby as it never could in the wolf. The potential is that which man alone enjoys for transcending the limitations of animal vision and going beyond the wolf's lot – the potential, that is, for higher human consciousness. This potential (and, as with the baby at the end of 'The Man Seeking Experience' in *The Hawk in the Rain*, also its misdevelopment) is implicit in the language used to describe the baby: to call its mind a 'tabula rasa' is to suggest not only its present emptiness of experience, but also its future filling with this, and in a Lockean way; similarly, to call its laugh 'soft-brained' evokes not only present vulnerability, but also future hardening, and not just in the sense of the joining and firming of the skull plates.

Exactly at the point in the poem where the mounting tension the reader cannot help but feel at a juxtaposition of wolf and baby threatens to break into action, the poem takes its steadiest and most obvious step into the calm, distanced, iconic mode. Instead of relieving the pressure inherent in the structuring contrast by channelling it into activity, the wolf's picking the baby up seems merely to complete a static picture. 'Ran among the stars' does not, then, so much evoke a wolf running over the ground on a cloudless starry night as suggest that wolf and burden are at this point wholly symbolic, stepping into the night sky to form the fixed eternal pattern of a constellation. This is the poem's penultimate surprise, and prepares the way for the final one.

Thus far the wolf has been spoken of as the representative of a limited, predatorial participation in life. That it does not attack or consume the baby is the first sign that it is to be associated not only with pain and decay, but also with the overflowing maternal, birth and succour. The she-wolf has become symbolic of the span of natural reality. Like the tiger of the *Gaudete* Epilogue, shortly to be met again in the second Dungeon Song, the wolf stands for the full range of life. She has become the goddess of all Hughes' recent work, though it is not strictly legitimate to make this identification until the seventh poem of the sequence.

In the gap between the first and second poems lies the whole history of the false development of human potential and its disastrous diversion into the sterilities of masculine–scientific–Christian thinking. In that gap the baby has grown into 'her murderer', a figure who belongs with the tyrant Holdfast, Krogon, the God of *Crow*, and the murderous protagonist of *Cave Birds* before his movement to redemption. All of these men are associated to one degree or another with the killing exploitation of material nature by technology, with deadly logical analytical and abstractive thought patterns, with the stultifying pursuit of complete objectivity which has produced our alienation, and with the atrophy of the awareness of nature's unity and sacredness. This is ground established in Hughes' earlier work, and here he exploits that for dramatic purposes. The whole era of Western consciousness is taken as read, reduced to an elision between poems, so that the reader may be directly confronted with its product, the world as we now perceive it within our fallen, derivative sense of space and time: 'Dead, she became space-earth / Broken to pieces'.

In the first poem the balance of power between wolf and baby was tipped entirely in the wolf's favour, and the nascent human presence was utterly vulnerable. Yet the outcome was not a destructive attack. Now, in the second Dungeon Song (*Moortown*, pp. 123–4), the balance has been, seemingly, reversed. And the outcome of the new dominance of masculine human consciousness has, this time, been destruction. The poem has two functions with regard to the development of the sequence: to evoke this destruction and to give the lie to any thought we may entertain that the reversal in the balance of power has been final and irrevocable.

The murderer is described as 'mad-innocent', which links him not only with the Holdfast figures mentioned above, but also with the misguided righteousness and crazed militarist zeal of the related St George figure, the Knight of the Cross. Likewise,

'muttering / It is good to be God' recalls the powerful-sounding but
vacuous language of the senile and incompetent Christian deity of
Crow. The murderer, partaking of the qualities of all these figures,
has carried out his killing over many generations. 'Familiar' means
not only 'well-known', which implicates the reader in these crimes,
but also 'belonging to the family', taken up and used through
the centuries by the overriding murderous purpose which has
encompassed our efforts of building and conquest. In fact, it is
these borrowed hands and mouths that in practical terms have left
the wolf figure dead, since the murderer himself has no substantial
reality, being a style of thought, a mental error, or, to use the
words of the poem itself, 'Being himself nothing'. This line starts
on the second function of the poem, the revaluing downwards of
the murderer's power and a corresponding upswing in that of the
figure of life who was the wolf in the first poem. Despite the
residual sense of potency lying behind her deadness in the earlier
part of the second poem (we note that, though 'dead', she had
'offspring' to take her place, and that her death is associated with
nursing and renewal), the dominance has thus far lain with the
murderer. From the word 'nothing' onwards this is no longer so:

> Being himself nothing
>
> But a tiger's sigh, a wolf's music
> A song on a lonely road
>
> What it is
> Risen out of mud, fallen from space
> That stares through a face.

The murderer is, we can now see, doubly nothing. He is nothing
in the sense, already suggested, of being immaterial, purely ideal.
He is also 'nothing but' another part of the all-inclusive feminine
figure of life. Because she takes in the totality of life and death,
and is, as Hughes put it in talking to Faas, 'the whole works', she
inevitably takes in also this man her murderer. This surprising
(and surprisingly simple) turn has been facilitated by the particular
way in which Hughes has chosen to evoke the murderer and his
crimes. For his using-up of successive human instruments is an
evil but exact parallel of the immortal feminine figure of life's own
repeated reincarnations in her mortal creatures. The murderer

mimics her combination of transcendence and incarnation. Thus at the end of the poem Hughes can allow the murderer's successive incarnations to be taken up, subsumed in and dwarfed by the larger cycle of incarnations which is the feminine figure's life. She is that abiding force which is both material–physical ('risen out of mud') and spiritual ('fallen from space') and 'stares through' every face. The poem amounts then to a reassertion of what the wolf represented, a power which at the start of the poem seemed vanquished.

Here this reassertion means a fresh start, a turn into new hope, and henceforth the sequence concentrates on the faltering attempts at rehabilitation on the part of the masculine presence. He has ceased to be the wilful murderer of the female figure, and now, as in *Cave Birds*, his goal is to escape further repetitions of his crimes and to reach a rapprochement with his former victims.

In the third Dungeon Song (*Moortown*, pp. 124–5) the male figure is allowed to address us directly for the first time. The poem is a monologue, reminiscent of similar pieces spoken by the protagonist of *Cave Birds* (to which it contains several references). It brings the male figure to a waiting prostration comparable in some ways with that of Adam at the start of his sequence. His quiet passiveness seems helpful to his recovery.

As with the first poem, the effect on the reader is initially different from what it becomes when he is familiar with the whole sequence. Though we sense rapidly that the speaker is the male figure who has been babe and murderer in previous poems, we do not gather immediately that a fresh start is now to be made. The first line, 'Face was necessary – I found face', picking up the final word of the previous poem, inevitably raises the question, necessary for what – for more murders? But by line 6 the speaker's candour and simple informality have established an atmosphere the reverse of threatening which in effect answers these questions. His words evoke a modest patience, and the poem begins to stand in our minds as a miniature essay in the 'Bride and groom' vein, telling, in the words of the person who underwent it, of some symbolic reassembly after disintegration and atonement. Surely, we feel, as the poem mounts, adding to the promising disposition of the male figure a new co-operative geniality on the part of the air and sunlight, and turning the maggots of decay into signs of potential rebirth, this rebuilding is for something better; face and hands and so on are necessary for something more fruitful than endlessly repeated crimes. But by the close of the poem these hopes, though not cancelled, have not been fulfilled, and the male figure has not yet outgrown an uncomprehending, directionless, sick criminality we associate not with the late poems in *Cave Birds* but with the first:

> Only still something
> Stared at me and screamed
>
> Stood over me, black across the sun,
> And mourned me, and would not help me get up.

This recalls the vague and oppressive malevolence of 'The scream'; recalls too 'The plaintiff' ('the burning tree / Of your darkness . . . a humbling weight / That will not let you breathe'). In retrospect the lying-quiet cannot be seen as a fully positive sign. It entails an element of unresolved and involuntary immobilisation. This downturn serves to make us aware that what has thus far been reassembled is only the mechanism of the body, and that the soul or animating spirit, which is, so to say, the wolf-figure herself, is still antagonistically separate, is indeed exactly that which stared at him, screamed, blocked the sun and kept him prostrate. (The identity of screamer and wolf-figure is brought out by the near-borrowing of the word 'stared' from the final line of the second Dungeon Song.)

Symbolism of light and darkness has always been important in Hughes' poetry. We recall, for instance, in the first poem in *Crow*, the frustrated effort of 'muscles / Striving to pull out into the light' and of 'the lungs / Unable to suck in light'. This same symbolism enters 'Seven Dungeon Songs' in the penultimate line of the third poem, so that the male figure's aim is now the removal of whatever blocks the light. The fourth Dungeon Song (*Moortown*, p. 125) describes his first, and, as it turns out, mistaken, effort at this.

I have suggested that what stands 'black across the sun' is the she-wolf, the figure of life who has been the victim, and then becomes the ultimate goal, of the male presence. That goal is now pictured as light. In the first line here we learn that she is also 'the earth' (which picks up the delineation of her in line 1 of the second poem as 'space-earth'). The symbolism works to suggest the female figure as both antagonistic retarding force (the blocker of light), evocative of the male figure's present failure of right relationship and lack of accommodation to reality, and as representative of that overriding reality (the sun) which must remain his ultimate goal.

The poem proceeds, like its immediate predecessor, by raising hopes which are not to be fulfilled. Light is established as his goal, so when the male figure sees 'a crack of light' we take it as a positive sign. But it is not, and this is the wrong light. Coming from 'between sky and earth' it seems to belong to neither of them, to neither 'space' nor 'mud' (in the second poem); it seems a diversion from the reality to which he is trying to attune himself. The rest of the poem supports this reading. This light is something the male figure cannot unite with, but can only reduce to words by naming, thus recalling and falling back into an aspect of his former criminality ('he borrowed mouths, leaving names', as the second poem says). And the words he uses to name the light reveal his continuing failure of accommodation with reality. The earth is still for him inimical, a prison, a claustrophobic grave. We realise, as he does not, that, so long as he continues to regard the earth as a barrier and obstacle, a blockage, rather than as part of what he must aim to fit himself to, he cannot hope to make progress.

There are further, subsidiary suggestions of the wrongness of his present course. The word 'reached' in line 7 recalls the baby's reaching towards the wolf, which developed in the gap between the first two poems into murderous action. The male figure's reaching for the crack of light now carries with it, therefore, the suggestion not only of immaturity but also of the rebuilding of criminality. The charge of immaturity is strengthened with the words 'lizard' and 'gills', which suggest a biological or evolutionary immaturity, a state of being (in the words of 'Adam and the Sacred Nine') 'too little lifted from mud'. When we add to these suggestions the male figure's inaccuracy in calling light 'air', and the unpleasant greediness and voyeurism of his actions, the condemnation of his reaching for this crack of light is complete. The closing lines thus return to the prostration and impasse of the previous poem:

> He lay like the already-dead
>
> Tasting the tears
> Of the wind-shaken and weeping
> Tree of light.

The 'tree of light' is the true light, rooted in earth and belonging to both sky and earth, part of the reality to which he struggles, here misguidedly, to attune himself. This tree of light is another representation of the overriding female totality who is to become the goddess. The unity of tree and female figure is enforced by the tree's weeping, which reiterates her mourning in the previous poem, and the local symbolism of light, sky and earth has its own cogency which the newly introduced tree fits and extends.

The fifth Dungeon Song (p. 126) is spoken by the male figure, giving us a further stage in his attempted rehabilitation. As in the third poem, his language is movingly simple and clear of pretence, retaining calm and a certain dignity without being immodestly reserved. Above all it is honest. As a result the speaker's voice seems to convey a hope that lies quite outside the state he describes. The reader comes away from the poem feeling that, though a deep trough has been described, neither the speaker nor the sequence has been overwhelmed by irrevocable pessimism.

The poem works out a single apt metaphor. Again we begin with new hope. After paralysis and prostration, 'I walk/Unwind with activity of legs'. It seems, literally, a step forward. But, as elsewhere in Hughes' work, a mere shifting about, movement for its own sake, is a time- and energy-wasting escapist diversion from the central problem. So this walking soon becomes frantic and aimless: 'Now I rush to and fro'. Without the necessary attunement to the animating, validating and harmonising female other, the reassembly of the third poem has failed. What 'was once the orderly circuit of my body' has become 'The tangled ball' he cannot sort out by himself.

Given a different cast, his realisation that he cannot, alone, resolve his problems might be a positive development, a sign of readiness to be opened to a sense of the necessity of the female figure of life. Instead, the realisation appears as retrogressive, a tendency to shuffle off the struggle for accommodation and the blame for failure onto others. He claims that his body has been tangled 'by some evil will', which recalls the false sense of blaming something outside himself which trammels Crow's progress in 'The Black Beast'. And he turns for help to others, unable to accept the struggle as his own, and unaware of the barbedness of his own word 'undo'. When this fails, rather than pause and change his approach he only redoubles his efforts of the old kind. The concluding image of dangling was used at the close of 'Oedipus Crow' to indicate his abject failure of adaptation at that point, and has a similar function here, where it is perhaps even more appropriate, since it completes the tangled-ball metaphor, leaving the masculine figure a puppet suspended, in a vacuum, from the strings of his own substance. It is a perfect picture of utter self-division and the helplessness that is produced by his disabling inner warfare. Against this there seems nothing to set, except whatever positive we detect in the tone of his voice and the honesty of his confession.

The fifth poem marks the nadir of the sequence. For that reason, or rather because, in it, the masculine figure recognises that he here touches bottom, it also marks the point at which the very curtailed and qualified affirmation with which the sequence will close starts. 'When everything that can fall has fallen / Something rises' says 'The guide' in *Cave Birds*. We have reached a similar stage, and, though there is nothing in the two remaining poems which might be called equivalent to the achieved resurrection in the closing poems of that sequence, there is now a switch to symbolism which at least carries the possibility of similar revival.

The images of the successive phases of his failure have been prostration, a reaching after false light in the attempt at unblocking the sun, and an unwinding walk. The sixth and seventh Dungeon Songs switch to imagery of communication. All communication is a break in alienation and a sign of relationship and accommodation. So, though neither poem actually breaks out of silence and into an exchange between masculine and feminine, and between human consciousness and surrounding reality, this new symbolism inevitably carries hope. We are moving into the realm of Heidegger's communicative reticence.

Thus it is an encouraging sign in the sixth Dungeon Song (*Moortown*, pp. 126–7) that so many features of an earth which before had seemed to the masculine figure to be simply 'a door locked' and a source of 'suffocation' can now be thought of as at least capable of useful and meaning-bearing communication. The earth has at last ceased to be a barrier and become a part of what he yearns to relate to. The oracle, the crevasse, the tall rock, the rubbly dust – all these remain essentially silent, but the very fact that their silence has to be announced presupposes the possibility of some future break in that silence. Hughes seems to highlight the possibility at two points in the poem. To mention 'the oracle' is inevitably to raise the hope of some divinely sanctioned communication of truth issuing from the earth. And there is this eerily evocative passage, telling us as much as we are to learn about what might be communicated:

> the tall rock of the sacred place,
> An instrument, among stars,
> Of the final music,
> The final justice,
> Was silent.

With this picture, and especially with the 'sacred place', Hughes reintroduces to the sequence the notion of religion. And this is clearly religion different from the world-murdering of the figure who could mutter as he killed 'it is good to be God' (in the second poem). It is a religion more in harmony with and accepting of nature (and, it follows, with the feminine figure who is nature), a religion within which a place, part of the earth, can be sacred, and within which the earth can secretly contain (and, perhaps, occasionally divulge) 'the final music', the music of the spheres, the true pre- and post-verbal expression of the ultimate harmony of reality, and also 'the final justice', some acceptance-compelling embodiment of things as they are. The word that best describes the possibilities being raised here is perhaps not 'communication' so much as 'communion'.

However, the positive element in the poem must not be over-stressed. With the mention of every potential speaker comes the insistence on present silence. Neither communication nor communion is achieved. What really gives the sequence such concluding lift as it generates is the seventh Dungeon Song (pp. 127–8), which, itself yearningly hopeful, throws some of that hope back into previous poems at subsequent readings.

This final poem is made up of eleven conditions that would have to be fulfilled for final success. The conditional clauses all bring together parts of the human body (which were falsely reassembled in the third poem, and tangled in the fifth) with parts of nature. The fulfilment of these conditions would amount to a grand harmonising of human potential with nature – not only with her as she is now, but with her purpose as it has driven through the length of geological and evolutionary time. We can speak about this harmonising and union in two ways. The various bringings-together may be regarded as either a reconciliation of the masculine figure with the female, the earth, through his acceptance of her

necessity and of his own inevitable belonging to her; or, placing
the emphasis another way, as a personification of the figure who
has been successively wolf, victim, light and earth, such as would
permit and facilitate relationship between the two figures. If we
choose the latter description, we are seeing the sequence as
working through to a position not unlike that *Gaudete* achieves,
and the last poem here becomes a prayer such as Lumb offers in
the Epilogue. Were these conditions to be fulfilled, the wolf would
truly be revealed as the goddess.

At the same time as the poem offers up the possibility and the
hope of such an outcome, it also draws together and rounds
off the main group of symbols used throughout the sequence.
Especially noteworthy is the line 'If man-shadow out there moved
to my moves', which creates the possibility of a happy resolution
of the light–dark symbolism by suggesting a rapprochement with
and personification of the dark obscuring earth of the fourth poem
and the antagonistic blackness of the third. Similarly, the last two
lines here, in pushing towards a break in the silences of the fifth
poem, complete the communication symbolism. The new harmony
which this speech would mean would entail not simply a coming-
together of two previously opposed entities, but a radical re-
creation of at least one of them: 'The speech that works air / Might
speak me'. Such speech would mean the making of a new self for
the masculine figure, with and out of, rather than against, the
elemental reality he has previously resisted. It would then be as
though he had never truly lived before, but only danced the dance
of unbeing.

The title of the sequence, together with its position in *Moortown*,
suggest the incompleteness of its final upturn, which, however,
through the vital word 'if', with its recognition of the primacy of
the potential over the actual, and of an inherently dynamic Being
endlessly drawing us onwards, comes to answer, in this distillation
of Hughes' effort, to the kind of qualificatory truths which crown
Cave Birds and *Gaudete*.

III

In 'Adam and the Sacred Nine' Hughes goes back to the hiatus
between man's creation and his finding a direction, first pictured
in 'A Childish Prank' in *Crow*, and uses it to create a less jaundiced

perspective. The gap between his physical emergence and his finding a soul becomes an opportunity. Though God is again unable to complete his act of creation, he at least sends messengers to help Adam decide. And Adam is now capable of doing this; the burden of making a soul has been delegated to him, and to fulfil this task he has to break out of the passivity which binds man in *Crow*. He has the active role of interpreting the examples the birds bring him, and of choosing between them.

In Hughes' sequence Adam undertakes a task of self-discovery, ending in recognition of earth as his base, and in the gesture of standing up. In introducing the poems on radio, Hughes spoke of Adam's initial position as fallen, 'as usual', an expression which indicates that the Fall is to be understood not in its biblical sense, as a once-and-for-all event at the start of history, but as a psycho-spiritual metaphor indicating a recurring state of maladaptation and lack of attunement and purpose.

Hughes' birds are mostly messengers by deed not word. We see them selving, to use Hopkins' term, and share with Adam the task of deciding what each of their examples consists in, and what humanity can learn from it. Hughes gives us the birds in their quintessential activities, but his focus does not rest on their physical reality. He uses this only as a basis for teasing out the metaphysical implications of each bird's way of life. The birds become symbolic of a succession of attitudes to the two recurrent poles of the sequence, Life and Death. The poems are unusually skeletal and slow to reveal themselves. At first we recognise a system of contrasts, in which each bird in some way reverses the one just gone. Later, we notice a development of a small group of motifs running through the sequence – sound and silence, light and dark, and planes of flight. And with this comes a feel for deeper contrasts between birds some distance from each other in the sequence. The variety of attitudes explored becomes gradually apparent, and, as balance, participation, devotion to one pole or other, transcendence, joy, pain, the different modes of acceptance, all pass before us, we recognise something approaching a resumé of the various avenues Hughes has explored at each stage of his career. We also see that, though there is no narrative behind these poems, as there is behind *Cave Birds*, Adam is none the less changing with each new visitor, in preparation for his actions in the last three poems; and that the order of the visitors is significant for the preparation.

His initial mood is given in the first two poems. In the invocation

('The song', *Moortown*, p. 159), the song has separated itself off from the physical world, wanting not sky, not earth, not the earth's denizens, and not even the physical reality of its singer. It contains, or is rooted in, both life and death, joy and lamentation, but is straining away from these, looking for something else, a third thing not now actual.

This poem is prefatory, standing a little apart from the rest; neither Adam nor his bird visitors are mentioned in it. But its yearning and its searching clearly relate to Adam as we first meet him. And it also introduces us to what is to be a leading motif in this, as in other Hughes sequences – the changing character of vocal sound. The resolution of 'Adam and the Sacred Nine' in his standing up and placing his foot on warm rock is accompanied by his first speech, which is the culmination of the sequence's movement from this song of yearning, through silence, cries, screams, whispers and laughter, to a final simple expression of acceptance and affirmation.

In the second poem (p. 160) the fallen Adam

> Lay defeated, low as water.
>
> Too little lifted from mud . . .
>
> Of a piece with puddles . . . .

Water is here very much what it is at the start of chapter 4 of *Women in Love* in the passage where Gerald swims in Willey Water, watched by Gudrun and Ursula. Lawrence speaks of Gerald moving 'into the pure translucency of the grey, uncreated water'. In *Thought, Words and Creativity* Leavis comments,

> As, then, life develops and advances towards man and *in* man it seeks to purify, to single out (in a special sense of that phrasal verb) the individuality of the individual; to attain to being pre-eminently *there* in the complete, and completely 'single' human being. . . . Birkin says, 'It's the hardest thing in the world to act spontaneously on one's impulses . . . .' The 'impulses' in question are not those of the ego and its personal will; they come from the spontaneity of one who has achieved singleness, and can act out of his whole unified being. . . . 'Uncreated', in the sense in which Lawrence uses it, applies to living individuals . . . to their having stopped short of 'manhood'. (pp. 68–9)

This delineates Adam's starting point too. He has stopped short of manhood. And union with water is Hughes' chosen metaphor, as it was Lawrence's. Mud carries the same connotations. This is the mud of uncreatedness from which birth takes place in the Hairy Hands episode of *Gaudete*, and into which, with worse luck, the protagonist of *Cave Birds* would have been dropped by his eagle.

The two moods so far deployed, a yearning and a stopping-off of inner growth, come together now to evoke Adam's dislocation from reality. All his dreams are ego fantasies of power. They have run on ahead of his achieved development, and ignore his evident weaknesses and frailty:

> Too little lifted from mud
> He dreamed the tower of light.
>
> Of a piece with puddles
> He dreamed flying echelons of steel.

These dreams are ego-stupefying indulgences, and the gap between them and the reality of what Adam is, which he will have to face eventually, is expressed spatially and kinetically: he is low, the objects of his fantasies are high; he is still, the objects moving. There is of course point in Hughes' recourse to the common products of modern urban–industrial civilisation to exemplify the aberrations. But not all the dreams are equally bad:

> Wrapped in peach-skin and bruise
> He dreamed the religion of the diamond body.

Like the others, this dream is idle wishing; but it holds the promise of inner development too. The achievement of shamanhood is sometimes expressed as the replacement of the soft mortal body by a hard new immortal one stuffed with stones. And higher religions have used the same metaphor to denote attained wholeness. Hughes' expression also appears in the Chinese alchemical text *The Golden Flower*, on which Jung comments in his *Alchemical Studies*,

> The 'diamond body' . . . is a symbol for a remarkable psychological fact which . . . could be best expressed by the words 'It is

not I who live, it lives me.' The illusion of the supremacy of consciousness makes us say, 'I live.' Once this illusion is shattered by a recognition of the unconscious, the unconscious will appear as something objective in which the ego is included. . . . It is as if the guidance of life has passed over to an invisible centre.   (pp. 51–2)

Whatever hope the dream of 'the diamond body' holds out for Adam is not at present being realised. At the moment his dreams are not harnessed to his searching. There is no co-operation between life and source, between conscious and unconscious. Instead, the dreams threaten destruction. Adam dreamed of dominion, but his dreams have come to dominate him, leaving him sick and wounded:

> His dream played with him, like a giant tabby.
> Like a bitten black-wet-mouse, even his morse had ceased.
>
> Open as a leafless bush to wind and rain
> He shook and he wept, he creaked and shivered.

The tree is a symbol for the self. Adam's process of growth has not yet begun: his tree is a bewintered 'leafless bush'. This symbol reappears later in the sequence, notably in 'The Dove came', where her alighting seems to trigger the final phase. Perhaps the most hopeful sign in Adam at the beginning is his woundedness. Bitten, creaking and shivering, sunk in pain as he is, he is nevertheless 'open'.

In his radio introduction to the sequence in May 1980 Hughes spoke of the God-sent creatures of the world visiting Adam to cajole him into action. But what motive is there for the interest of these other creatures? Man has increasingly come to appear in Hughes' more recent poetry as the pinnacle of the evolutionary process – not in the sense of his being lord over creation, able to use and exploit it at his whim, but as life's latest servant, the current growing tip of a single urge. What is special about man is that the directing and furtherance of that urge seems to have been put into his own hands, just as Adam's finding a purpose in this sequence has become his own task. Whereas throughout pre-human evolution life developed as though automatically, now the burden of further development has settled in part onto man's shoulders. He himself has been charged with the task of fulfilling nature in himself. Hughes uses the rest of nature to remind man of his destiny and obligation, as he used the little lizard to remind Prometheus of his superior endowment and potential. Man's role is to be guardian and fulfilment of those who went before him, Shepherd of beings and of Being. This is why the other creatures view Adam's prostration with such horror and impatience. For the birds who visit Adam there is no choice of ways. They can only follow inbuilt instructions along the single path they dictate. For man, the problem caused by the burden of consciousness prevents this 'easy' way.

Adam's first visitor through the sky-crack is a falcon ('And the Falcon came', *Moortown*, p. 161). In *Cave Birds* the falcon is Horus, a bird of the final splendour of resurrection. The falcon here has more in common with the birds of 'Hawk Roosting', and 'The Hawk in the Rain' and the 'Thrushes'. He is the totally efficient predator, the creature attuned to its single purpose of killing and feeding, a gun, fist, bullet. As the roosting hawk suffered 'no falsifying dream', and the thrushes 'no indolent procrastinations', so this falcon 'would not be put aside, would not falter'. What it hunts is life, to use as food for its own life. Its 'bill' is 'tooled' in two senses: carefully made, and also made for nothing but this job.

In some of his earliest poems Hughes celebrates such predatory efficiency in a way which makes man's use of his consciousness seem a disablement by comparison. In 'Karma' in *Wodwo* Hughes questions the point of the endless cycles of killing. Some hint of this pointlessness, the endless, issueless repetition of killing and eating and being killed and eaten, comes in the last two lines of the present poem: 'reconstruction' is only bodily; it is not concerned with the making of the self, and is made to yield the final emphatic position to 'explosion'. The falcon stays bound to the predatory cycle; it too will die.

With the first three birds we pass from male, through neuter, to female, and through a pattern of contrasting flight paths: the falcon stoops straight down; the skylark, the second messenger, climbs straight up; the duck cuts across both.

There are other contrasts between the falcon and the lark. The falcon is a taker, of the lives of others; the lark ('The Skylark came', *Moortown*, p. 162) is a giver, of its song. Hughes had emphasised in *Wodwo* the great effort of the lark's climb towards the sun, but the emphasis now is on the impossibility of the aim the lark gives itself. Its climb and its song try to cover the sun with 'bird-joy' (the earlier lark's song had been 'Incomprehensibly both ways: "Joy! Help!"') and to give the sun its crest. It wants to climb out of and undo what the falcon belongs to. Its effort is 'To keep off the rains of weariness/The snows of extinction'. But it can never quite reach the sun; and, like death, weariness and extinction cannot be annihilated. So its labour is 'a useless excess', a 'lifting what can only fall'. And even what it achieves, the erecting of its bright little song high in the sky, is hemmed in and qualified by the great eternal darkness of earth beneath and space above. The falcon is master. The lark is a slave 'that lives and dies/In the service of its crest'. But both live in bondage to roles that cannot be Adam's. He will learn by remembering them, but only because this will allow him to steer between their extremes.

'The Wild Duck' (*Moortown*, p. 163) seems to offer such a middle way. She is the first female presence in the sequence. And the flight she makes is its first horizontal. She 'came spanking across water' down from the frozen North – not, it appears, to bring Adam her example, but to rouse him into action, as though he had already had enough clues and must now make his choice: it is dawn and the wild duck is 'Quacking Wake Wake'. But there is more than this to her. She is the first harbinger of belonging and birth. She comes from the harshest zones, the cold, dark and windy Arctic. But the snows which to the lark had meant 'extinction', something to 'keep off' in the effort for perpetual sun, are to the duck 'her mother'. The cold, the round zero of frost, means not death but the egg from which she hatches; and the chill before-dawn wind is 'her father'. Unlike the falcon and the lark, fixed in their verticals within single territories, she takes the whole earth as hers, flying across great stretches of land with her message. She is an earth spirit, and this is enforced in the last three lines of her poem, where the deliberately vague syntax makes earth and bird one. She

Got up out of the ooze before dawn . . .

As earth gets up in the frosty dark, at the back of the Pole
    Star
And flies into dew

Through the precarious crack of light

Quacking Wake Wake

The poem is the most obviously positive so far. The next bird with whom the word 'whisper' will be associated is the crow, after whose visit Adam really will awake. And there are echoes too of 'The guide' in *Cave Birds*. The duck's acceptance of the earth is to be paralleled in Adam's 'I was made/For you'. Yet there is also something in her of the green mother who offered the protagonist of *Cave Birds* an easy way out, a cocoon of earth nursing, choosing which would have meant a premature end to his inner growth. There is something childish about the duck.

Each visitor is placed in the sequence to provide the maximum contrast with its predecessor. The swift ('The Swift comes the swift', *Moortown*, p. 164) is an obvious instance. Its flight is not direct, like the earlier birds', but switches as it suddenly tacks and veers. And, unlike the others, it has no time for Adam. He is simply too leaden and corporeal for the swift, who

Casts aside the two-arm two-leg article –
The pain instrument
Flesh and soft entrails and nerves, and is off.

Whilst the others have plied the shining gap in the sky as though keen to obey the instructions of the Creator and bring Adam their examples, the swift uses the gap only to get out. It 'Hurls itself . . . Out through the lightning-split in the great oak of light'.

In the *Season Songs* poem 'Swifts' the birds' movements are too fast for us to catch them for long. The ultra-human rapidity is to form the basis of the present poem, where it is first caught in the typographical arrangement of the opening line: it is as though the bird has beaten the poet to it and got itself mentioned twice in a line where it belongs only once. The swift is too quick for the camera of the eye; it can often only be heard: 'the ear's glimpse/Is the smudge it leaves'. This invisibility makes the bird seem insubstantial and disembodied. Its flight is neither within the realm of death nor within that of life. The key line tells us that it 'shears between life and death'.

The poem describes a swift hunting an insect, 'the nymph of life', as Adam watches. Just as the swift catches up with the insect, it passes in front of the sun and Adam loses it in the glare. This kind of hunting could scarcely be more different from the falcon's, which is solid, by and for the body. The swift's hunting, by contrast, seems only intermittent; even its prey is tiny and invisible, a 'winged mote'. Afterwards, the bird 'rejoins itself/Shadow to shadow – resumes proof'. But the dark shape of its body is no solider than its shadow. And at its stillest and most evident, as it 'nests/Papery ashes/Of the uncontainable burning', it seems as though it might burst into flames, the energy within it too great to become matter and form for more than a few seconds.

The swift, for all its exhilaration and dashing, its magical cutting between the two poles of Life and Death, cannot, as the opening lines suggest, provide an example for Adam to imitate. Like Prometheus he must make his peace with the pains of the solid body he cannot escape.

'The Unknown Wren' (*Moortown*, p. 165) may seem on first acquaintance to mismanage its repetitions, rising to a climax with the line 'Wren is singing Wren – Wren of Wrens!', which leaves no extra power for the final line, which has to resort to capital letters. Actually, the excess of these repetitions gives us a clue to what the poem is about, and forms our first pointer to a surprisingly subtle argument which is advanced a stage at a time by each of the poem's seven sections. In this, it accentuates a feature of many Hughes poems using incremental repetition: lines which seem different ways of saying much the same, a casual catalogue of alternatives, in fact enact shifts and developments as subtle as those provided by a traditional, more developed syntax. The starting point is as usual the physical reality of the bird; the poem is the product of acute observation, and of a sure sense of what may be taken as common ground with the reader in this line. Hughes discovers new depth in the wren's characteristic secretiveness (which makes it more often heard than seen): 'The Unknown Wren/Hidden in Wren, sings only Wren'. The lark's song was an impossible attempt at transcendence through joy – a doomed effort to get above what the falcon dived into. The wren's is a song for power within the world. It is created by the balancing or barely held tension of the opposites it contains. The bird's energy comes from the tension invoked and expressed in the song. The wren is singing its own strength into existence, like troops singing up courage before a battle.

At first this power appears to be exercised against the alien and inimical forces of process in the natural world in order to help this tiny bird muster the big spirit it needs to endure. But the wren is so successful at this summoning that it can scarcely contain the power it has summoned, which threatens to overwhelm it. The singing, designed to help the bird stay as it is, changes it, brings it to the borderline where supercharged life cannot be distinguished from death:

> Wren is here, but nearly out of control –
> A blur of throbbings –
> Electrocution by the god of wrens –
> A battle-frenzy, a transfiguration . . . .

The power has been produced by an effort of self-giving which is without reserve. Everything of the wren goes into the song, and everything comes out in it: 'His song sings him, every feather is a tongue. / He is a song-ball of tongues.' But, besides being a giving, the song is also a monstrous effort of incorporation. The wren is trying to feed the power of the whole world into its song, to make that power its own, and to give itself power over and against the world: 'the head squatted back, the pin-beak stretching to swallow the sky'.

The poem now returns to the theme of death first suggested by the word 'electrocuted'. The wren's access of life energy, its 'battle-frenzy', is scarcely to be distinguished from a 'death-rapture'. If the swift seems to evade both Life and Death, cutting between them, the wren makes itself the king of birds by belonging to both. Its intensity is generated by the unbearable pull and contention of life and death within it, and this is pictured for us, with a humour typical of the poem, as the bird's simultaneous straining towards take off and its tightening grip on its perch. It appears indeed that this closeness to death is the condition for the vividness of life: 'Imminent death only makes the wren more Wren-like'. It lives according to Heraclitus's maxims about the necessity of opposites to each other: 'Disease makes health pleasant and good, hunger satiety, weariness rest', or 'All things happen by strife.'

Everything about the wren's song has been large, inflated. Just when it sings itself into kingship, Hughes reminds us of its tininess:

> Wren reigns! Wren is in power!
> Under his upstart tail.

The exclamation marks are the wren's 'upstart tail'. Despite the delicate undercutting of this picture, the poem ends in celebration. The wren's almost shamanic wizardry works: his song reduces the threat of the world; earth seems smaller and less immediate and overwhelming than 'in the thunderlight' and the battering wind of dawn.

> And when Wren sleeps even the star-drape heavens are a
>   dream
> Earth is just a bowl of ideas.

We note that it is the threat, and not the earth itself, which has been reduced or overcome. In fact, as the sun comes out and the rain stops, the world seems to join with the wren's song, happy to be incorporated in its joy:

> But now the lifted sun and the drenched woods rejoice with
>   trembling –
>
> WREN OF WRENS!

Excess has triumphed.

After the frenzy of the wren, screwing life to a high pitch with its song at dawn, there is again a complete contrast: the sombre stillness and silence of the owl in the night, the third of the hunters ('And Owl', p. 168). The falcon hunted to renew its physical life. The swift hunted within the thin no-man's-land between Life and Death. The owl hunts within Death; it is itself death and allots their deaths to its victims: 'A masked soul listening for death. / Death listening for a soul.' In 'Owl's Song' in *Crow*, the owl's stillness was petrification with fear. Here the owl seems fearless, a master, the calm and omnicompetent instrument of death. It is the rest of the scene which is terrified. The poem's surprises begin with the kill, which is described in curiously ambiguous terms:

> The womb opens and the cry comes
> And the shadow of the creature
> Circumscribes its fate.

Death as the beginning of new life and not a final end is probably not the primary sense given by the substitution of 'The womb'. It seems that we are instead being invited to realise a sensation prior to any such wisdom: we are asked to see death as the supreme pain of life.

The small cry which broke the silence was that of the owl's latest victim in its death agony. This now draws from the owl a corresponding scream. Its calm and mastery are shattered. The pain, we see, belongs to the killer as well as the killed:

And the Owl

Screams, again ripping the bandages off
Because of the shape of its throat, as if it were a torture
Because of the shape of its face, as if it were a prison
Because of the shape of its talons, as if they were inescapable

The repetition functions to suggest the sudden flood of energy and the nightmare of 'again'. The silent floating and listening between kills is a healing destined never to be complete; each kill is a reopening of the wound of existence, as in a Titanic punishment. The owl's scream is agonised, like the howling of wolves in the poem of that name in *Wodwo*. Existence has become universal pain.

'The Unknown Wren' had been the most perky and joyous of Adam's visitors, the bird whose success in living seemed offered in the most positive way and with fewest qualifications. The owl makes a marvellous contrast, dragging us down again into the darkest reaches of the sequence. But there is a deeper contrast to be noted. The owl is the dark side of the falcon. It gives us the predatory process from a different angle. The falcon is a willing, perhaps for Adam too willing, participant. The owl is much less willing. It is imprisoned in a process it would, we can almost say, like to escape, by staying permanently in death.

The dove ('The Dove Came', *Moortown*, p. 167) is Adam's second female visitor, re-establishing light after the owl's darkness, and making colour prominent in the sequence for the first time. Like the duck, she is, as doves traditionally are, a gentle bird. It is her nature to give herself, and go on giving that most valuable of gifts, whatever her reception:

She gave the flesh of her breast, and they ate her
She gave the milk of her blood, they drank her . . . .

The poem reads as a reversal of 'Crow's Song about England', where the all-giving feminine is being rejected and desecrated; this happens so often that she changes sex to be more martial for exacting revenge; then she tries to take her gifts back. But in 'Adam and the Sacred Nine' her giving overcomes the opposition. This is our first clear sign that the sequence is drawing towards a positive conclusion. The feminine has reappeared, without the disabilities we saw in the duck, as the source of life in genial aspect, and she is now united with Adam:

> And the dove alit
> In the body of thorns.

> Now deep in the dense body of thorns
> A soft thunder
> Nests her rainbows.

The imagery is laden with hints of potential.

The penultimate bird is the crow ('The Crow came to Adam', p. 168), the first of them not to perform in front of Adam. Instead he speaks. Tantalisingly, the poem does not tell us what the crow said. Perhaps the phrase 'love-whisper' suggests an encouraging mention of Eve as the crow's means of prompting Adam. We can at least be sure that he wants Adam to stop contemplating the various possibilities he has been shown and get into action, because of an analogous incident in the Norse myth called 'The Song of Rig'. Kon, son of Jarl, son of the god Heimdall, creator of man, wishes like his father before him to learn ultimate wisdom. Jarl initiates him into the secrets of the runes. Still not having found a role in life, and wishing to know yet more, Kon rides into the forest and lures a succession of birds down to him, and listens to each in turn. Then, as Kevin Crossley-Holland retells it in *The Norse Myths*, 'A crow sat on a branch over Kon's head. "Kon," it croaked, "why do you spend your time seducing birds to talk to you? You would do better to set out on your stallion and show daring in battle"' (p. 25). Whatever Hughes' crow said, it was sufficient to break Adam's trance: 'Adam woke'.

The visits of the crow and the dove go hand in hand, the two necessary preliminaries to Adam's resurrection. More of this is suggested by the last bird, the phoenix ('And the Phoenix has come', *Moortown*, p. 169), the traditional symbol of a rebirth achieved through voluntary immersion in the creative–destructive fires of life. This, the only purely mythological bird in the sequence, brings together qualities and imagery associated previously with both male and female birds, and unites them in Adam. Its voice's martial qualities recall both falcon and wren. But the same voice 'dangles glittering/In the soft valley of dew', thus recalling the gentle femininity of the wild duck.

These qualities are joined in the phoenix, where they are melted down and reborn in a new shape:

Flesh trembles
The altar of its death and its birth

Where it descends
Where it offers itself up

And naked the newborn
Laughs in the blaze

The imagery recalls that of the closing poems in *Cave Birds*, where resurrection is also figured for us in terms of a movement into the everliving fire for remaking. It also recalls the ending of Attar's *The Conference of the Birds*, a Sufi text on which Hughes worked with Peter Brook.

It is not, as it is in Attar, for the birds themselves that the creative firing in 'Adam and the Sacred Nine' has taken place. 'And the Phoenix has come' makes fullest sense if we note the laughter which is its culmination as a distinctively human sound. The birds are here united and incorporated in Adam, who is himself reborn. In his radio introduction Hughes spoke of the birds bringing their examples of how to live for Adam to accept or reject. When the remade Adam stands up, ready to explore the world freshly, he carries with him some wisdom derived from each of the birds. We can say that standing and walking are man's way of flying, an equivalent, not an opposite, to the birds' quintessential activities.

What has Adam learned? How far has he travelled in his contemplative trance, as the different birds have appeared to his changing mind, trying to shift his disposition? To measure this we must turn back and remind ourselves of his starting point. In 'The song' the poem's elements were straining apart and away from each other, and there was the pang of the unrealised. In the second poem we met Adam prostrate, weak and fragile, his inner

development negated by the diversion of his energies into a series
of wild power fantasies of world dominion, each of which lay at a
symbolic extreme from Adam himself. We have already seen this
sense of dispersal, fragmentariness and disintegration overcome
with the advent of the phoenix. Reunification now (in 'The sole
of a foot', p. 170) achieves its final expression as Adam, like
Prometheus, stands up, in the happy meeting of foot and earth:

The sole of a foot

Pressed to world-rock, flat
Warm

With its human map
Tough-skinned, for this meeting
Comfortable . . . .

The yearning and dissatisfaction have given way to acceptance,
signified in the word 'comfortable' and in the exchange of greetings.
Defeat and failure and the raw woundedness these entailed have
given way to a new readiness: Adam's foot is 'tough-skinned'. The
gap between dream and reality has disappeared and been replaced
by a recognition of what it is to be human. Adam speaks:

I am no wing
To tread emptiness.
I was made

For you.

and in his words we recognise something of the hard-won clarity
and the stripped simplicity present also in the *Gaudete* Epilogue
poems.

The two aspects of Adam's triumph – his standing upright and
his speaking – are central to the emergence of humanity, initiating
and making possible all later development. But there is a danger
of defining man against the rest of creation, making his specialness
a separation from the world, as the disaster recounted in the short
sequence 'A Citrine Glimpse' shows. 'Adam and the Sacred Nine'
carefully avoids this pitfall. Man and world are here in accord, as
host and guest, and there is full reciprocal communication between

them. Indeed, the poem makes man's discovery of himself the same as his discovery of his environment, through the most intimate of senses, touch. The notion that sensory apprehension of the world is also discovery of the inner self and of the beginnings of purpose is embodied in the pun, so gross as to be noble, on 'sole'.

Part IV

6

Nature and History: *River*, 'The Head', *Remains of Elmet, Flowers and Insects*

The time for Conservation has certainly come. But Conservation, our sudden alertness to the wholeness of nature, and the lateness of the hour, is only the crest of a deeper excitement and readiness. The idea of nature as a single organism is not new. It was man's first great thought, the basic intuition of most primitive theologies. . . . [And] this is what we are seeing: something that was unthinkable only ten years ago, except as a poetic dream: the re-emergence of Nature as the Great Goddess of mankind, and the Mother of all life.

(Hughes, reviewing Max Nicholson's *The Environmental Revolution*, in 'Your Environment', vol. 1 no. 3 (Summer 1970) pp. 82–3)

I

'March Morning Unlike Others', in *Season Songs* (1976), offers a mood new in Hughes. It starts with the poetry of observation, simple registrations, aiming only to offer up such particulars as seem noteworthy and necessary to the definition and evocation of the essence of this day; they appear before us in and for themselves. In the second paragraph these registrations are used as the springboard for metaphors especially satisfying for growing out of the specific details of the first part, which stands as evidence against which it can be checked. Hughes is evoking a day unusually warm and calm for the month, a summer's day arrived too early, but welcomed as a sign of coming improvement:

Blue haze. Bees hanging in air at the hive-mouth.
Crawling in prone stupor of sun
On the hive-lip. Snowdrops. Two buzzards,
Still-wings, each

Magnetised to the other
Float orbits.
Cattle standing warm. Lit, happy stillness.
A raven, under the hill,
Coughing among bare oaks.
Aircraft, elated, splitting blue.
Leisure to stand.

Hughes seems happy simply to let his eyes rest where they are drawn and then to list what he has seen. But to speak of simple registrations does not do justice to the technique, which is here exactly fitted to the task of evoking a warm ease, a stillness within movement, an absence of the dramatic, a peace, given impact by its including the human observer and determining the mood in which he observes. The first paragraph is not merely a list of witnessings: it is the essence of a landscape seen 'through a lens of powerful, rich feeling' (*Poetry in the Making*, p. 78), and this makes it memorable and moving.

Hughes often, particularly in *Crow*, gives special force to the ending of his poems, building them up to a terminal climax. 'March Morning' reminds us that his openings can be equally powerful. 'Blue haze' consists of two exactly equal, balanced vowel sounds, each long and open, and each accompanied not by hard, sharp consonants such as would cut off its spreading power, but by slow, soft consonants which allow it to go on spreading gently. The music of these two words is so precise and right that the rest of the poem seems merely a development or explication of what it conveys.

Hughes rejects the active, energetic forms of the verb here; with the word 'snowdrops' no verb or adjective is needed, and we find ourselves in the position of the March calf (in the poem of that name in the same volume), for whom the simple presence of grass is sufficient – the noun provides poetry enough alone.

The mood is further evoked by Hughes' presenting us (and this is characteristic of his later nature poems) with a whole landscape, seen at some distance, so that the rush and hurry which would be evident at close quarters (as in the *Gaudete* Main Narrative) is subsumed. No single feature dominates; the view is made up of a number of elements, each equally important and given ample space by syntax and the movement of the verse. And yet, all the while, we have in mind the more usual March weather, perhaps not yet finished.

The anthropomorphism of the second paragraph, developing naturally out of the mood of the first, makes the earth something to which we can relate. It gives a purpose to the season: healing. And it makes the return of spring seem an achievement worth celebration. The drive of the poem has been towards this imbuing of an inevitable and impersonal event with human feeling. It seeks to rediscover the primitive's unreserved participation in the seasons, when his own rites and prayers seemed essential to the continuance of sun and fertility, when spring was a young goddess who had to be rescued from the underworld annually. Our being cast as relatives visiting a convalescent implies a human responsibility towards the rest of creation which it is the main task of all these works to advocate, and which gives another and complementary sense to the phrase 'Shepherd of Being' which I have borrowed to adumbrate Hughesian maturity.

The poem exemplifies much that is characteristic in the books touched on in this chapter. In the middle and late 1970s, as Hughes was bringing the expression of his imaginative ground plan to completion in the works examined in Chapters 3–5, he was also developing a nexus of styles which together represent a major shift in his nature poetry, away from the re-establishing of awe for the hard, autonomous power of nature (achieved by, for example, the metallic simile in 'Snowdrop' in *Lupercal*), and, via a new strain of anthropomorphic imagery and the personification of the natural, towards the encouraging of a gentle, practical co-operation between man and natural environment.

The female personification of the landscape is frequent, especially in *River* (1983), so that the poems in which this happens cannot be considered apart from the realignment of our religious sensibilities towards the feminine which is attempted in *Cave Birds* and *Gaudete*. This personification is used sometimes in a very direct way, so that hills become limbs and the river a woman or divinity. And sometimes it provides the opportunity for the use of attendant images of marriage, of winter as a surgical operation, or (as in 'March Morning') of spring as convalescence and healing. It permits the attribution of devotional and epic qualities to fish and animals, so that we admire them as the pilgrims, celebrators and patient victims of the sacred rituals of the goddess, nature, or as warrior heroes. Poems in which fish or birds appear as precious metals,

jewels or treasures have the same reunificatory aim of making
nature seem rich and valuable to us, and stem from the idea of
the sun as the furnace of life and the river as its molten product.
The river appears, too, as the labouring engine or electrical motor
of life, with the fish as the workers of this machine.

All of these images are to be found in *River*, and all of them can
be traced back to the earlier volumes in this group. They are the
lens through which Hughes draws our attention to a cornucopia
of observed details witnessed during a lifetime of river-watching.
River is studded with instances of acute observation, revealed to
us in the light of these few overriding images and ideas. The types
of poem embodying these instances are also common to the whole
group. There are pieces, more akin to the second paragraph of
'March Morning', in which the observed details lie at one remove,
and we are offered a myth or legend, or single dominating
metaphor, which we must ourselves reapply to particular realities.
And there are pieces, more akin to its first paragraph, in which a
special occasion is being recorded for us, so that the concrete reality
of this moment is uppermost, together with the re-creation of
the observer's shifts of attention, and the metaphors appear
subservient. The latter style is related to the farming-diary entries
in the first section of *Moortown*, and shows Hughes, as a man who
has seen, thought and felt differently, engaged in the
Wordsworthian task of redefining the boundaries of poetry to lift
into it subjects, moods and diction previously rare or excluded.
The nature of this undertaking has itself, perhaps, made inevitable a
wide-ranging response amongst readers; but the adverse criticisms
which seem to me occasionally unavoidable are not of the undertaking itself: perhaps partly because he has often been working in
collaboration with a photographer or artist, Hughes has over-
produced, and the repetitions of units of sound and sense both
within the same volume and from one volume to another make it
difficult to read without being put in mind of Hopkins' distinction
in a letter to A. W. M. Baillie (10 September 1864) between a major
poet's best and his Parnassian:

> Great . . . poets . . . have each their own dialect as it were of
> Parnassian, formed generally as they go on writing, and at last
> . . . they can see things in this Parnassian way and describe them
> in this Parnassian tongue, without further effort of inspiration. In
> a poet's particular kind of Parnassian lies . . . his mannerism.

River has roots in Hughes' earlier work. His fascination with water has always made itself felt: 'Pike' is an obvious forerunner of the fishing poems here and in *Remains of Elmet* (1979). And decades previously he planned a long poem about England of which 'Mayday on Holderness' in *Lupercal* was to have formed a part, centring on a river as the bloodstream of England, and an adder as the repressed elemental life of the country. *River* perhaps revives this project (retaining the adder as earth serpent, and the river itself as the blood and lymph of the land's body), enlarging its theme and scope in ways Hughes could not have foreseen when he first conceived it.

The river is now an essential part of the environment and the Greek *zoë*, or, as 'West Dart' has it, life which is 'spirit' as well as 'blood'; this transcendent aspect is illustrated in 'Torridge' (p. 118); 'The river walks in the valley singing / Letting her veils blow – . . . She who has not once tasted death'. As life, both incarnate and transcendent, the immortal source and the mortal manifestations of it, the river is also, as Hughes' religious metaphors imply, the unconscious, the anima, life within. Some of the most interesting pieces in the collection are those which touch upon the spiritual and psychological implications of river-watching and the entry into a riverine landscape – a theme Hughes first broached in 'Pike' and *Poetry in the Making*. Why do anglers persist, when they are comparatively unsuited to the role of hunting in water, and so easily made to look silly by such birds as the cormorant, with which Hughes compares himself in 'A Cormorant'? In 'Go Fishing' he describes the changing states of mind, first mentioned in *Poetry in the Making*, brought about by the angler's concentrating on water. The process becomes a baptism. The opening section is full of the music of peace. The 'nagging impulses' which usually clog it disappear as the healing flow cleanses the mind. The product of the process is a Wodwo rebirth: 'Crawl out over roots, new and nameless, / Search for face, harden into limbs'. Water here is wholly benevolent, and the meeting with it creative or re-creative. 'Last Night', 'After Moonless Midnight' and 'Riverwatcher' show a darker side, whilst two of the finest poems take the ambivalence of the river and its effect on the watching mind, and create out of this a journey into altered consciousness. 'Milesian Encounter on the Sligachan' treats the journey with a new humour reflected in the connotation in 'Milesian' of a fisherman's 'one that got away' exaggeration, and the longest line in Hughes and the deliberate exaggeration of the Celtic names at the end add to the effect.

'Gulkana' also takes a journey into landscape and displays shifts of mind, dramatised and seen from inside in the sequences examined in Chapters 3–5, but now treated with a new freedom, directness and externality; the poem draws on Hughes' visit to Alaska in the summer of 1980. It opens with strange names and an inviting glimpse of mysterious water in a wild, disturbed landscape which is poorly charted and inhabited only by regressed Indians. This territory seems to close in and watch the anglers; it draws them, but remains inimical and threatening. Hughes tries to counterbalance these oppressive sensations by recalling the freedom of a wider landscape beyond. He is like Lumb in the *Gaudete* Prologue, immediately before his psychological collapse, walking 'with deliberate vigour, searching in himself for control and decision'. Lumb's show of personal solidity fails; so now does Hughes' denial of the fear. He begins to feel like a trespasser. The fear contains an awe, which generates the religious metaphor in his description of himself as 'Pilgrim for a fish!'; but in also calling himself 'Prospector for the lode in a fish's eye!' he hints that something less reputable is involved too – greed, giving rise to guilt.

But what is the fear? In *Poetry in the Making* Hughes speaks of our need to refresh ourselves occasionally by escaping the cities and returning to the wilderness which was our environment during the aeons of prehistory: 'it is only there that the ancient instincts and feelings in which most of our body lives can feel at home and on their own ground' (p. 76). We might, then, describe this fear as a sign of Hughes' instinctual being, his other older self, repressed in civilised life, but now rising up as it senses a return to its proper field of action; and he proposes just such a theory to himself now:

> I explained it
> To my quietly arguing, lucid panic
> As my fear of one inside me,
> A bodiless twin, some disinherited being
> And doppelganger other, unliving,
> Everliving, a larva from prehistory
> Whose journey this was,
> Whose gaze I could feel, who now exulted
> Recognizing his home, and who watched me

Fiddling with my gear – the interloper,
The fool he had always hated.

In the circumstances, however, the explanation is useless. It dispels
nothing. It is a product of the intellect, powerless amongst other,
greater forces. Hughes remains subject to the sinister spirit of
place, and must press on until he can meet its purest and intensest
manifestation in the eye of the fish. But everything here is on a
bigger scale than the anglers' equipment and their English minds
can encompass; they are used to a manageable nature, and can
make no impression now. Then comes success. The eye is at last
available for inspection:

What I saw was small, crazed, snake-like.
It made me think of a dwarf, sunken sun
And of the refrigerating pressures
Under the Bering Sea.

Even the gods here are different: wilder, rawer, older. The fish
swim in a religious trance which Hughes shares for the rest of his
stay. Only as he flies out of Alaska does he recover his old identity:
'I came back to myself'. But the sense of reintegration is immediately
undermined. The encounter with the 'small, crazed, snake-like'
god is so deep and real it makes the everyday self seem no more
than 'a spectre of fragments'. Returning to civilisation, Hughes can
capture in poems much of what he saw on his expedition, but the
spirit of place is too primitive and pre-conscious. Whatever imprint
it leaves will be on the instinctual cortex:

Word by word
The burden of the river, beyond waking,
Numbed back into my marrow. While I recorded
The King Salmon's eye. And the blood-mote mosquito.

Hughes' fullest use of the motif of the journey into wilderness
is the fine uncollected short story 'The Head' (published in Emma
Tennant's *Saturday Night Reader*), which shares much with 'Gulkana'
but uses the greater scope and freedom of prose to develop its
theme in detail. Two brothers (more than brothers) go hunting in
the Three Heads country at the mouth of the Sang. The local tribe,
the Slotts, regard this as sacrilege. The animals are gathering 'to

be counted by their Lord', so now would be particularly inauspicious for killing. But the brothers belong to an age of white imperialism; their hubris, their disdain for savages, superstitions and nature, makes them go on, accompanied by a single, crazy, reluctant guide, Dazzled Falcon. The animals come, peaceful, fearless and in such numbers there is hardly the need to aim in order to kill. The slaughter is boundless and stupefyingly pointless. Dazzled Falcon disappears. The brother telling this story has a nightmare: the guide returns to the camp 'skinned and bleeding' and starts to eat the other brother's face. Shocked awake by this, he hears a pained and mournful cry in the distance 'like a woman shrieking'.

Next day the two brothers start to grow apart. One, with an irredeemable criminal–destructive streak to him, continues killing. But the narrator, tired and sickened, has a flash of imagination and sympathy in which he exchanges consciousnesses with a wolf he is aiming at:

> Suddenly I saw the land in intense clarity, microscopic. In front of me stood a man in a brown leather jacket, with the swift slide of the river behind him. I saw the gleaming coppery substance of his features. I saw the three bands of mingled colour in his iris, and felt the pressure of his rifle's aim on my face. Then I was myself again, and the wolf had come to a halt, ten paces away, ears up, tail high, and waving very slightly. (p. 86)

This works a fundamental change in him, to be reinforced by later experiences. For the moment, he recovers his old self and kills the wolf. But it is his last kill.

Later, they find Dazzled Falcon's skinned head stuck on a post on the estuary sands. Walking out towards it, the narrator again suffers a vision – of the beauty and purity of the non-human world. The sight of the guide's head tells him that the killing is a crime not only against nature, but also against his own essential humanity. He is feeling more and more at one with the victims of man. He dreams, 'My brother became a half-witted wolf and attacked me. . . . My whole being was saturated with animal wounds and animal pain and animal death' (p. 89). Waking terrified, he runs from his tent, only to see a ghostly woman enter it, take his rifle, and disappear beneath the surface of the river.

The other brother is becoming demented by the excess of his

killing. He has shot a giant female of an unknown, half-human, half-ape species. She had approached wanting only to embrace him, but he had gone on firing till she dropped. He starts to act wildly, so the narrator makes an escape.

At dawn he returns to camp, to find his brother torn to pieces. But the still-animated, speaking head follows him everywhere, despite his attempt to shake it off. He buries it and walks back to the Slotts' village. The enraged head gets out and attacks the village, killing an innocent Indian in the gloom. The chief decrees that the narrator must expiate this death by going out the following night to fight the head, which, in the struggle, turns into a beautiful, naked girl who is wounded. The narrator's previous visions of imaginative sympathy have prepared him for the necessary act of compassion:

> I bent low and felt about over pine needles and roots and groaned aloud as my hands came to the slender naked body of a woman.
>
> I picked her up and her moans stopped. I thought, she is dead. And I thought nobody could have survived those cuts. I listened for a while, to hear her breathing and also to detect any new manoeuvres of the head-bird. Everything was silent and still, and the girl draped over my arms seemed as loose and lifeless as cloth.
>
> I carried her back to the village, and it did not occur to me that if she was dead this could be the second death I would have to account for. I thought only that she might be alive, and before anything else I must keep her alive. (p. 98)

The moment may be set beside the healing unions in *Gaudete* and *Cave Birds* and the Ancient Mariner's blessing of the sea creatures unawares.

The Slotts' prediction about the hunting expedition had been proven right. This land is theirs, and they are alive to its sacredness. But they can only see things within the framework of their traditional beliefs, which this latest event seems to violate. The narrator is forced to look after the woman himself. She is the final manifestation of a single female presence in the story – the spirit of nature, the goddess we meet everywhere in *River* and in Hughes' later vision of nature. At first she was wounded and mournful, but always patient and optimistic that these hunters would eventually be corrected. Only after many rebuffs does she become angry and vengeful towards the brother who refuses to open himself to her love. But with the narrator her patience is rewarded by his new sympathy for nature. And this in turn is rewarded by her return to a more friendly and co-operative form in which the two can be united in marriage. 'The Head' is an important adjunct to *Gaudete* and *Cave Birds*, because it gives us in a very direct way a third aspect of the feminine in Hughes' later works. *Gaudete* portrays the movement towards rebirth and a new sensibility in a religious context. With *Cave Birds* the context is psychological; the marriage is a realignment of the hero's psyche. These two contexts overlap and imply each other. They also imply what becomes obvious in 'The Head': an external element to the feminine, generating a new awareness of the environment. The story makes it clear that Hughes' goddess has an ecological aspect, as well as a psychological and a religious.

II

Hughes has chosen for *Remains of Elmet* a time-scale which carefully guides our responses to events in the region of his birth. It is not the short scale of a lifetime where the deaths of the chapels and mills and of individuals might create resentment and pessimism; nor the rather longer scale on which the many decades of dehumanisation and sacrifice of the working people would suggest an equally black view; nor, at the farthest extreme, is it the geological scale of millions of years on which seas swell and shrink and mountains rise and fall. Hughes' scale lies between the social historian's and the geologist's, so that man's tiny but real efforts come and go as interludes in the dominance of a stable nature. This anthropologist's or prehistorian's scale shows men not as named individuals, but as part of a corporate entity, 'mankind', which, like the goddess, is both transcendent and immanent. It suggests a periodisation which runs broadly parallel to the main phases of the process of psychological development portrayed in the sequences dealt with in Part III: an original unity of man and nature is followed by a separation and fall into the phase of the Industrial Revolution; the Heideggerian Turn, back towards nature, is now beginning.

The poems regret the decline of the traditional industries and the collapse of their communities, and find distasteful the veneer of respectability assumed in the quietened aftermath. But *Remains of Elmet* is also clear that the industrial past was itself an equivocal matter, since it was based on the enslavement of both nature and man. 'Hill-stone Was Content' shows the men and women 'conscripted', like the stone itself, into the mills, for 'they too became four-cornered, stony'. Industrialisation, bringing with it urbanisation, was a declaration of war on what was ultimately no enemy: a 'long, darkening stand / Against the guerrilla patience / Of the soft hill-water' – a war against the Mother, and so one which can only be lost.

It was the Great War which, quite literally, robbed the region of its virility, and Hughes sees the whole region as still in mourning for it. But, though it goes on to reiterate the sense of aftermath met elsewhere, 'First, Mills' closes on another note:

> And now – two minutes silence
> In the childhood of earth.

The time-scale suddenly lengthens; the horror is subsumed in an optimism founded on a faith in nature implicit in the personification of earth. In 'The Trance of Light' this faith comes to the centre of the poem, again through manipulation of our sense of time. The industrial period recedes in importance until it becomes only nature's temporary abeyance or sleep. The poem celebrates her reawakening; she is imagined as a beast that 'Stretches awake, out of Revelations / And returns to itself'. The furthest Hughes goes, in *Remains of Elmet*, in emphasising the dominance of nature through the ages is in the poem entitled 'In April'. There the same creature is seen reawakening itself, but man is not mentioned at all: his efforts have receded to vanishing point.

To speak of the landscape as maternal is, of course, not to exclude harshness. In the poems about moors, exposure on the moor-tops has two aspects. On the one hand, and perhaps more obviously, it entails the sparseness and emptiness of 'Heather' and 'Widdop'. But, on the other, it entails a powerful sharpening and enhancing of the forces of both life and death which makes the moors a continuously working laboratory of the forces man must relate to, and which his periodic civilisations rise out of and collapse into.

The time-scale, which is still partly used to create the same meaning it had in 'October Dawn' in *The Hawk in the Rain* (the sense of the huge forces beside which man's civilised efforts fall into a new perspective), now has other purposes too. It ameliorates anger at the waste of human potential by providing a perspective against which an exclusive attachment to the present and its hopes and fears is no longer possible. The human is now set against the natural, the present against the aeons. *Remains of Elmet* teaches accommodation, but not to the current human *status quo*. Its drive is towards acceptance of the natural rightnesses that inevitably mean the end of that. Our guide and exemplar in this movement towards accommodation is, in some poems, Hughes himself, appearing as one whose growth to maturity is also a growth away from the merely human. Poems in *River* and in the first section of *Moortown* also include Hughes, or another with the relevant skills, engaged in practical activities of an exemplary kind, giving another, complementary meaning to the phrase 'Shepherd of Being'. The quality of acceptance these poems advocate is neither a type of resignation nor a withdrawal from participation; it allows full play for sympathy, for indignation, for striving, and it encompasses and rests on all that Hughes has said previously about natural vitality.

Remains of Elmet is, like *River*, more directly personal than the third-period works, in which experience is transmuted into dramatic and symbolic form. But its chief reminiscences are confined to the years of childhood. An interesting piece in *Flowers and Insects* (1986) offers a personal, moralised memory from later in Hughes' life. 'Daffodils' begins with the quiet, flat statement of a memory of the purchase of some wild land. Commerce comes to stand for a self-deceiving, irreverent failure of attunement. Spring brings the surprise of a crop of daffodils, a recurrent bonus for the lucky purchaser, who also has the pleasure of being impelled into verse by them. To benefit to this extent and in this spirit is a sacrilege. The transaction has developed an imbalance, which Hughes at the time accepts: 'I was still a nomad. / My life was still a raid. The earth was booty.' This was an attitude not only to what surrounded him, but to himself too:

> I knew I'd live forever. I had not learned
> What a fleeting glance of the everlasting
> Daffodils are. Did not recognise
> The nuptial flight of the rarest ephemera –
> My own days!

Hardly more body than a hallucination!
A dream of gifts – opening their rustlings for me!

In *Flowers and Insects* the blooms, like animals in other collections, function as the representatives of the goddess. Metaphor in the present poem establishes them in this role, but here they are Hughes' own youth as well – a youth portrayed as falsely confident, exploitative and selfish. The last-quoted passage is followed by plain, simple confession: 'I thought they were a windfall. I picked them. I sold them.' We already know this will bring retribution. The description of the picking and preparing of the flowers for sale becomes almost that of a rape, then a murder, and is exaggerated and hypersensitive unless we understand the flowers as symbolic of more than themselves.

If commerce were a satisfactory way of dealing with the world, the successful sale would be the end of the matter, but the flowers haunt Hughes at night, fill his mind, force him into wakefulness and a closer, truer examination of his victims. He sees in them the glare of the holy sunlight which many poems in *Remains of Elmet* and *River* seek to capture for us:

> I learned
> That what had looked like a taffeta knot, undone
> And re-tied looser, crumpled,
> Was actually membrane of solid light.
>
> And that their metals were odourless,
> More a deep grave stoniness, a cleanness of stone,
> As if ice had a breath –
>
> They began to alarm me.

The religious diction which establishes their full worth as holy bearers of the light of the source also brings the notion of judgement and a final reckoning. Hughes' reaction is to drag himself free and 'flit', taking his burden of guilt with him, to be resolved later, perhaps in this poem.

Bibliography

Aeschylus, *Prometheus Bound, the Suppliants, Seven Against Thebes, the Persians*, tr. P. Vellacott (Harmondsworth, 1961).

Attar, Farid Ud-din, *The Conference of the Birds: Mantiq Ut-tair, a Philosophical Religious Poem in Prose*, tr. C. S. Nott (London, 1954).

Blake, W., *Complete Writings, with Variant Readings*, ed. G. Keynes, Oxford Standard Authors (London, 1966, corr. 1976).

Budge, E. A. W., *Egyptian Religion: Egyptian Ideas of the Future Life* (London, 1899).

Calderón de la Barca, Don P., *Life is a Dream: La Vida es Sueño*, tr. W. E. Colford (Woodbury, NY, 1958).

Camus, A., *The Outsider*, tr. J. Laredo (Harmondsworth, 1983).

Clark, R. T. R., *Myth and Symbol in Ancient Egypt*, pbk edn (London, 1978).

Crane, S., *The Complete Poems*, ed. J. Katz (Ithaca, NY, 1972).

Crossley-Holland, K., *The Norse Myths*, pbk edn (Harmondsworth, 1982).

Dickinson, E., *Complete Poems*, ed. T. H. Johnson, pbk edn (London, 1975).

Dutton, R., *Modern Tragicomedy and the British Tradition* (Brighton, 1986).

Dyer, D., *The Stories of Kleist: A Critical Study* (London, 1977).

Eliot, T. S., *The Complete Poems and Plays* (London, 1969).

Euripides, *The Bacchae and Other Plays*, tr. P. Vellacott (Harmondsworth, 1954).

Faas, E., *Ted Hughes: The Unaccommodated Universe, with Selected Critical Writings by Ted Hughes and Two Interviews* (Santa Barbara, Calif., 1980).

Fox, G., *et al.* (eds), *Writers, Critics, and Children* (London, 1976).

Frazer, J. G., *The Golden Bough: A Study in Magic and Religion*, abridged edn (London, 1922).

Frye, N., *Fearful Symmetry: A Study of William Blake*, pbk edn (Princeton, NJ, 1969).

Gifford, T., and Roberts, N., *Ted Hughes: A Critical Study* (London, 1981).

Girard, R., *Violence and the Sacred*, tr. P. Gregory (Baltimore, 1977).

Graves, R., *The Greek Myths*, 2nd edn, 2 vols (Harmondsworth, 1960).

——, *King Jesus*, pbk edn (London, 1983).

Haggard, H. R., *She: A History of Adventure*, pbk edn (New York, 1978).

Halifax, J., *Shamanic Voices: A Survey of Visionary Narratives*, pbk edn (Harmondsworth, 1980).

Hašek, J., *The Good Soldier Švejk and his Fortunes in the World War*, tr. C. Parrot, pbk edn (Harmondsworth, 1974).

Heidegger, M., *Being and Time*, tr. J. Macquarrie and E. Robinson (Oxford, 1962).

——, *Poetry, Language, Thought*, tr. A. Hofstadter (New York, 1975).

——, *The Question Concerning Technology*, tr. W. Lovitt (New York, 1977).

——, *What is Called Thinking?*, tr. J. G. Gray (New York, 1968).

Hopkins, G. M., *Poems and Prose*, ed. W. H. Gardner (Harmondsworth, 1953).

Jung, C. G., *Collected Works*, vol. 5: *Symbols of Transformation: An Analysis of the Prelude to a Case of Schizophrenia*, tr. R. F. C. Hull, 2nd edn (London, 1967, corr. 1970).

——, *Collected Works*, vol. 7: *Psychological Types*, tr. H. G. Baynes and R. F. C. Hull, 2nd edn (London, 1966).

——, *Collected Works*, vol. 8: *The Structure and Dynamics of the Psyche*, tr. R. F. C. Hull, 2nd edn (London, 1969).

——, *Collected Works*, vol. 9, pt I: *The Archetypes and the Collective Unconscious*, tr. R. F. C. Hull, 2nd edn (London, 1968).

——, *Collected Works*, vol. 11: *Psychology and Religion: West and East*, tr. R. F. C. Hull, 2nd edn (London, 1969).

——, *Collected Works*, vol. 12: *Psychology and Alchemy*, tr. R. F. C. Hull, 2nd edn (London, 1968).

——, *Collected Works*, vol. 13: *Alchemical Studies*, tr. R. F. C. Hull (London, 1968).

——, *Collected Works*, vol. 14: *Mysterium Coniunctionis: An Inquiry into the Separation and Synthesis of Psychic Opposites in Alchemy*, tr. R. F. C. Hull, 2nd edn (London, 1970).

——, *Collected Works*, vol. 16: *The Practice of Psychotherapy: Essays on the Psychology of the Transference and Other Subjects*, tr. R. F. C. Hull, 2nd edn (London, 1966).

Kafka, F., *The Trial*, tr. D. Scott and C. Waller (London, 1977).

Kerenyi, C., *Dionysos: Archetypal Image of Indestructible Life*, tr. R. Manheim, Archetypal Images in Greek Religion, no. 2 (London, 1976).

Kleist, H. von, *The Marquise of O– and Other Stories*, tr. D. Luke and N. Reeves (Harmondsworth, 1978).

Lawrence, D. H., *The Escaped Cock*, ed. G. M. Lacy (Los Angeles, 1973).

——, *Phoenix II: Uncollected, Unpublished and Other Prose Works*, ed. H. T. Moore (London, 1968).

——, *Selected Poems*, ed. K. Sagar (Harmondsworth, 1972).

——, *Women in Love*, pbk edn (Harmondsworth, 1960).

Leavis, F. R., *Thought, Words and Creativity: Art and Thought in Lawrence* (London, 1976).

Milton, J., *Poetical Works*, ed. D. Bush, Oxford Standard Authors (London, 1966).

Montgomery, J. W., *Cross and Crucible: Johann Valentin Andreae (1586–1654), Phoenix of the Theologians*, International Archives of the History of Ideas, no. 55, 2 vols (The Hague, 1973).

Neumann, E., *The Origins and History of Consciousness*, tr. R. F. C. Hull, Bollingen Series, no. 42 (Princeton, NJ, 1954, rev. 1969).

The Nibelungenlied, tr. A. T. Hatto (Harmondsworth, 1965, rev. 1969).

Pilinsky, J., *Selected Poems*, tr. T. Hughes and J. Csokits (Manchester, 1976).

Plato, *Collected Dialogues, Including the Letters*, ed. E. Hamilton and H. Cairns, Bollingen Series, no. 71 (Princeton, NJ, 1961, corr. 1963).

Popa, V., *Collected Poems 1943–1976*, tr. A. Pennington (Manchester, 1978).

Ransom, J. C., *Selected Poems*, 3rd edn (New York, 1969).

Roszak, T., *Where the Wasteland Ends: Politics and Transcendence in Post-industrial Society* (New York, 1972).

Sagar, K. (ed.), *The Achievement of Ted Hughes* (Manchester, 1983).

Scigaj, L. M., *The Poetry of Ted Hughes: Form and Imagination* (Iowa, 1986).

Shakespeare, W., *The Poems*, ed. F. T. Prince, New Arden Shakespeare (London, 1969).

Smith, A. C. H., *Orghast at Persepolis* (London, 1972).

Tennant, E. (ed.), *Saturday Night Reader* (London, 1979).

Weston, J., *From Ritual to Romance*, pbk edn (New York, 1957).

Whitman, W., *Complete Poetry and Selected Prose and Letters*, ed. E. Holloway (London, 1938).

Williamson, H., *Tarka the Otter: His Joyful Water-Life and Death in the Two Rivers*, pbk edn (Harmondsworth, 1949, rev. 1963).

——, *Salar the Salmon*, pbk edition (London 1972).

Wolfram von Eschenbach, *Parzival*, tr. H. M. Mustard and C. E. Passage (New York, 1961).

Index of Hughes' Works

Page numbers in **bold type** indicate major references.

General Index